THE MOTORWAY ACHIEVEMENT

Building the Network:
The North West of England

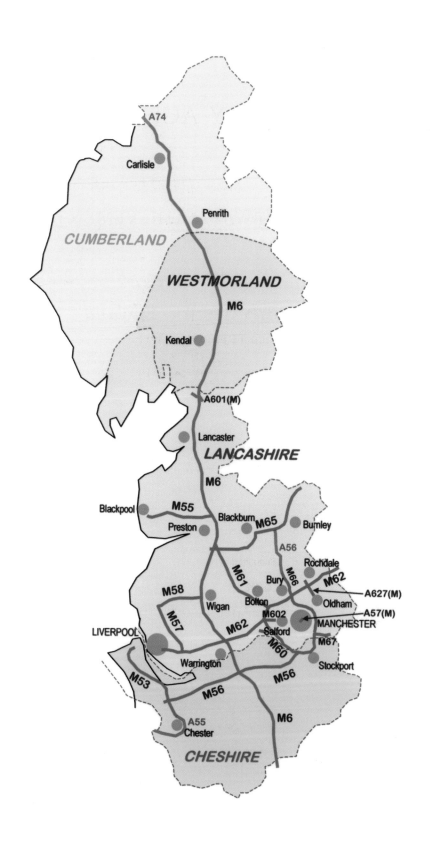

THE MOTORWAY ACHIEVEMENT

Building the Network:
The North West of England

HARRY L. YEADON
BscTech FREng FICE FIHT

FORMER COUNTY SURVEYOR AND BRIDGEMASTER OF LANCASHIRE

Supported by

Northwest
REGIONAL DEVELOPMENT AGENCY

Published for Motorway Archive Trust

PHILLIMORE

2005

Published for Motorway Archive Trust by
PHILLIMORE & CO. LTD
Shopwyke Manor Barn, Chichester, West Sussex, England

© Motorway Archive Trust, 2005

ISBN 1 86077 352 4

Printed and bound in Great Britain by
CAMBRIDGE PRINTING

Contents

Footnotes

The items referred to represent only part of the material available in the Regional Archive. The location given at the end of each note indicates the relevant County Record Office in which the documents are deposited (see also General Introduction).

Illustration Acknowledgements

In instances where photographs relate to Trunk Road Motorways, either the Department for Transport or the Highways Agency has given approval for use of the material. Other illustrations are reproduced courtesy of the following (all copyright reserved):

Alfred McAlpine plc, cover, pages 28 (bottom), 37 (top)
AMEC plc (photography by Winter & Kidson Multi-Media), pages 17 (right), 18, 26, 28 (top), 35, 37 (bottom), 68, 80, 92, 103
BAE Systems Heritage Group, page 105
Chris Barber, Manchester City Council, page 87
Ronald Bristow, page 94
N. Capelle, page 125 (top)
Cheshire County Council from the Authority's Collection, pages 32, 33 (right), 120, 128
Cumbria County Council from the Authority's Collection, pages 38, 40 (bottom), 47, 49
G. Dew & Co. Ltd, page 52
Halcrow Group Limited, page 116
Howard Humphreys (photography by Photographic Engineering Services), pages 141, 142
Lancashire County Council from the Authority's Collection, pages 6, 11, 20, 29, 70, 71, 75 (bottom), 76, 82, 85, 99, 138 (top)
Mills Media Ltd, page 135
Mouchel Parkman (photography by Photographic Engineering Services), pages 62, 64
Rendell Palmer & Tritton (photography by Photographic Engineering Services), page 24
Ian Shepherd, pages 133, 134, 136, 138 (bottom)
Simmons Aerofilms Ltd, cover, pages 28 (bottom), 33 (left), 34, 57, 60, 72, 75 (top), 76, 79, 90, 107, 112, 120, 127
Tarmac Construction Ltd (photography by Swan Photography), page 31
Tarmac Ltd & Bowmaker Ltd, page 17 (left)
Trafford Metropolitan Borough Council, page 53
Martin Welch, pages 40 (top), 125 (bottom)
Tony Williams, pages 43, 44, 45

'The building of a motorway is sculpture on an exciting grand scale, carving, moulding, forging and adapting the materials provided by nature – earth, rock and minerals – into a finished product, which must be both functional and pleasing to the eye, as well as economical and durable. But in trying to accomplish this, one must also be humanitarian and remember that all this affects people. The civil engineer on motorway projects, as on other public works, is the servant of the people, using his specialist knowledge on their behalf for the good of the whole community and, at the same time, mindful of the views and rights of the minority who are affected'

Sir James Drake

Preface

Sir James Drake, in his role as County Surveyor and Bridgemaster of Lancashire form 1945 to 1972, and through the County Surveyors' Society and the Institution of Highway Engineers, was a tireless advocate of the introduction to Britain of motorways on grounds of their economic benefit and their safety compared with all other kinds of public highway. When the Special Roads Act had been passed in 1949 and reconstruction of Britain's peace-time industries and her homes and schools after World War II had made enough progress, the money and the skills began in 1956 to be assembled for a first thousand miles of motorway to be built by the early 1970s. Drake himself was involved in design and construction of the first motorway to be opened, the Preston By-pass in 1958. It formed a small component in the Lancashire Roads Plan which Drake had persuaded Lancashire County Council to adopt in 1949 in order to sustain profound change which he foresaw in Lancashire's economy, with the decline of our textile and coal industries and huge new development of the aircraft, automobile, oil, chemical and nuclear power industries.

There followed the interlinking of Lancashire's towns and adjoining Counties by a uniquely close network of motorways, and the spreading of the benefit across the whole North West Region of Cheshire, Lancashire and Cumbria. A leading role in this task fell to the author of this book in his capacity as Sir James's successor as County Surveyor and Bridgemaster of Lancashire, Harry Yeadon. In what would be mistakenly called his retirement he has organised a team of former colleagues throughout the Region to endow the Motorway Archive Trust as an educational charity with a whole archive of the North West Region's motorways. On that archival foundation, built as it has been entirely by voluntary effort, this book presents their story – a story of my political lifetime and of a part of this country where it has been my privilege to play a part in representing its people and pursuing their interests.

I find pride in the achievement which Harry Yeadon relates, pride in the Region's people whom he has sought to serve, pride in his associates and pride in him, and I commend this book to all who are interested in how we can flourish by effort.

LYNDA CHALKER
Baroness Chalker of Wallasey

General Introduction

The Motorway Archive

At the initiative of Sir Peter Baldwin KCB, former Permanent Secretary of the Department of Transport, the Motorway Archive has been created to ensure the preservation and publication of a vast amount of material relating to the development of the motorway network within the UK. It has been collected by over 200 volunteers who, during their professional careers, were engaged in the preparation, design and construction of motorways. Many have contributed personal recollections and, together with associated documents, a substantial history of the various facets of the motorway network has been produced, thereby presenting the opportunity to pass on the body of knowledge acquired to an audience ranging from researchers, scholars, and academics, to school children and anyone else who may be interested. The material is deposited in establishments such as The National Archives, the Transport Research Laboratory, the professional institutions and certain of the county record offices.

The Motorway Archive Trust

The Motorway Archive Trust, which is responsible for managing the Archive, was registered as a Charity, Number 1078890, in January 2000, with Sir Peter Baldwin as its Chairman. In order to assist in achieving its object of making the contents of the Archive widely accessible it embarked, under the general heading of 'The Motorway Achievement', on the publication of three volumes:

  I. 'The British Motorway System: Visualisation, Policy and Administration'
 II. 'The Frontiers of Knowledge and Practice'
III. 'Building the Network', based on Executive Summaries covering the development in each of the Regions within the UK.

The Motorway Archive Website

The Trust's website, 'www.ukmotorwayarchive.org', includes brief summaries of the contents of Volumes I and II, and a comprehensive presentation of the conception, design and construction of all of the motorways built in the UK, a powerful search facility, a map of the motorway network, a list of sponsors, etc.

The North West of England Regional Archive

The counties within the Region, as referred to in the Archive, are the historic geographical counties of Cumberland, Westmorland, Lancashire and Cheshire.

The Regional Archive consists of a series of mini-archives each covering a major section of motorway, together with items of a general nature concerning motorways. Each mini-archive contains material such as:

(i)   copies of Reports, Opening Brochures and other documents,

(ii)   lists of relevant items held in establishments elsewhere, and

(iii)   papers prepared by personnel who were directly involved in the preparation, design and construction.

Depending on the geographical location of each section of motorway, the material relating to it is deposited in the most appropriate of the following County Record Offices:

- The Castle, Carlisle (Cumberland): M6 (part).
- The County Offices, Kendal (Westmorland): M6 (part).
- Bow Lane, Preston (Lancashire): M6 (part), A601(M), M60 (part), A6144(M), M61, A666(M), M62, A627(M), A57(M), M602, M57, M55, M66, M58, M67, M65.
- Duke Street, Chester (Cheshire): M6 (part), M60 (part), M53, M56.

'Building the Network: The North West of England'

Whereas the majority of the motorway projects within the Region were Trunk Road schemes and, therefore, the responsibility of the Secretary of State for Transport, a number were undertaken by the Local Highway Authorities, particularly in the urban areas.

The evolution of the various motorways within the Region, from their conception to completion, is outlined in Chapters 3 to 17 of the volume. They are listed broadly in the order in which the construction of the first section of each motorway began.

In each case, the text includes:

(i)   a brief history,

(ii)   the name of the organisation which undertook the preparation, design and supervision of construction, as listed in Appendix 1,

(iii)   the basic facts, e.g. the length of the motorway, number of bridges etc., and

(iv)   matters of particular significance in the design and construction.

The volume also identifies the major influences affecting the development of the network, and its resulting benefit to the Region.

The construction of the motorways was carried out by a large number of different firms of contractors and subcontractors. The Principal Main Contractors are listed in Appendix 2, and detailed information on the various contracts can be found in the Opening Brochures within the mini-archives.

In most instances, the tender figure for each of the main contracts is quoted in the relevant Opening Brochure. No attempt has been made to identify the final total cost of each section of motorway, which would include, not only the final payment to the contractors, but also ex-contract items such as the expenditure on land acquisition, compensation, design, supervision and the diversion of mains and services. Even if all this information was readily available, it would not be appropriate to make cost comparisons.

Appendix 3 lists the names of the senior personnel who were involved in the development of the network, a number of whom actively participated in the collection of artefacts for inclusion in the Archive, and in the preparation of written material.

The 'Principal Reference Documents' referred to in the footnotes, together with the Bibliography, represent only part of the mass of material in the Archive. It should, however, enable a researcher to obtain more detailed information from that provided in the text, as an initial stage in exploring the Archive.

The publication of the volume would not have been possible without the financial support of

Cheshire County Council,
Cumbria County Council,
Lancashire County Council,
Parkman Consultants Ltd,
Sir William Francis, and
Northwest Regional Development Agency.

The author and The Motorway Archive Trust acknowledge with thanks the assistance of all those who have participated in the development of the Regional Archive, in particular, Peter Hewitt for his work in the compilation of the draft of the volume.

1   Characteristics of the Region

1.1   Topography

The Region is an area of enormous variety. The plains of Cheshire and Lancashire are bounded by the Welsh hills and the Irish Sea to the west, and the foothills of the Pennines to the east. In the north, the Cumbrian mountains provide a massive barrier to any form of communication in that direction.

Several large rivers flow through the Region. The Dee, Mersey, Ribble and Lune discharge into the Irish Sea and the Eden into the Solway Firth at the Scottish Border. Bridging, at suitable crossing places, was the main reason for the development of the ancient cities and towns of Chester, Warrington, Preston, Lancaster and Carlisle, which became the focal points for early transport systems.

The Industrial Revolution had its roots in the Region. This mainly arose from the exploitation of the coalfields of Lancashire and the west coast of Cumberland, and the availability of ample supplies of water, resulting in major changes in economic activity within a substantial part of the area. A century or more of growth in textile manufacturing in the valleys of East Lancashire, in other industries such as engineering, and in the production of chemicals in North Cheshire arising from the huge deposits of salt, led to the expansion of many other towns and cities.

Of major significance, Manchester became a substantial commercial centre particularly for the textile trade, and the focus of a large conurbation. The Port of Liverpool had been recognised for many years as an essential element in the life of the Region and, although road and rail connections between the two cities already existed, the Manchester Ship Canal was constructed at the end of the 19th century. Historically, the industry located around the mouth of the Mersey had been mainly associated with shipping and ship building but, later, the Ship Canal provided access for tankers to North Cheshire and enabled the construction of oil refineries and the manufacture of petrochemicals.

The coal measures of Lancashire did not extend beyond the Calder Valley and, therefore, little heavy industry existed in the northern part of the Region apart from on the west coast of Cumberland. Agriculture, however, continued to be of considerable importance not only on the highly productive arable and dairy-farming land of Cheshire, West Lancashire and in the river valleys, but also from stock rearing on the hill farms.

At the end of the Second World War, with a population of over seven million living in a Region which was so complex both in physical, economic and social terms, there was general recognition that an adequate transportation system was of vital importance to its future prosperity. This was of special significance to an area suffering from the decline of mining, shipbuilding and textiles as new industries, such as those associated with aircraft manufacture and electronics, moved in. Their success is, to a large degree, dependent on the provision of improved links, particularly for those located in the less accessible areas, such as West Cumbria.

The growth in tourism has been of major economic benefit, arising from the increase in the number of visitors from outside the Region. The longstanding attraction of places such as the major seaside resort of Blackpool, and the Lake District have, for many years, had a great influence on traffic. It has been estimated that, in addition to the regular influx of day visitors to the Lake District National Park, the resident population may be exceeded threefold by those who stay for an extended period.

As in the rest of the country, the Region's road system, prior to the construction of the motorways, was predominantly the legacy of past centuries. Its development had been largely fortuitous and lacking in strategic purpose. The only exceptions were the provision of a number of local by-passes and the construction of the East Lancashire Road connecting Liverpool and Manchester, which was opened in 1934 – the only major new road in the Region since the turnpike era!

1.2 Geology

The proposals for the line of a north-south motorway through Cumberland and Westmorland were confined to a corridor lying to the east of the Lake District massif. A description of the geology of those counties is, therefore limited to that area.

The predominant Boulder Clay which exists in relatively shallow surface deposits and in drumlins has a wide range of moisture content, between 5% and 25%, and a varying silt, sand, gravel and boulder content.

In the Carlisle area there are deposits of sand and silt overlying Bunter Sandstone, and alluvium with sand lenses in the valleys of the Rivers Eden and Petteril.

North of Penrith, troughs of peat up to 20 feet in depth are found and in the area there is a volcanic intrusion known as the Cleveland-Armathwaite Dyke.

Further south the bed-rocks are closely jointed partially metamorphosed Silurian siltstones and mudstones and elsewhere the more recent Carboniferous deposits are encountered with the limestone containing numerous solution cavities.

In Lancashire, there are also Carboniferous rocks such as limestone, Millstone Grit and coal measures in the Pennines and in other high ground such as in the Forests of Bowland, Pendle and Rossendale.

The Carboniferous limestone outcrops in the area around Carnforth and, further south at Clitheroe, in the Ribble Valley. This relatively massive limestone can be seen in numerous quarries in both areas. Elsewhere, it is overlain by the strongly-bedded shales, sandstones and gritstones of the Millstone Grit series.

The coal measures, which overlie the Millstone Grit over a roughly triangular area to the south of the county centred on Wigan, Burnley and Oldham, are further sub-divided into 'lower', 'middle' and 'upper', with the quantity and quality of the coal tending to improve at greater depth. The seams occur in repeating sequences of mudstones, shales and sandstones, and old shallow workings have been frequently encountered.

Younger Permo-Triassic rocks cover the Carboniferous rocks on the low-lying Lancashire Plain, but there is generally a good cover of drift and there are few outcrops to be seen. The Sherwood/Bunter Sandstone and the Keuper Marl are relatively soft rocks, characterised by a red colour, and the underlying coal seams have been worked in some places by deep mining techniques.

The drift deposits are mainly glacial in origin and are thought to be the product of a glaciation between 2,000 and 12,000 years ago. The most extensive of these cover the Fylde, South-West Lancashire and the Mersey embayment as far inland as Manchester, and have been derived from Triassic rocks on the bed of the Irish Sea. Very stony till from the Lake District was deposited in the northern part of the county and some has intermingled with the Irish Sea drift, extending as far south as the Fylde. On the higher ground to the east, the local Pennine drift contains sandstone and shale fragments, sometimes indistinguishable from the meltwater derived head deposition on the steeper slopes.

In many places, there is a tripartite sequence of drift, with a heavily over-consolidated Boulder Clay overlying the bedrock. The over-consolidation pressure suggests thicknesses of glacial ice of the order of 800 feet. This Lower Boulder Clay is overlain by Middle Sands, glacial deposits of mainly fine to medium sand, with occasional inclusions of silt and clay, followed by Upper Boulder Clay.

The interglacial period responsible for the Middle Sands also produced locally important fluvio-glacial sand and gravel deposits in the vicinity of Carnforth, and to the north of Manchester in the Middleton/Heywood area. Several deep glacial channels have been recorded in the underlying bedrock, some extending well below present sea level. These channels are often associated with, but not always coincident with, today's rivers and are filled with relatively poorly-consolidated sand, clays and silts.

Lacustrine varved clays were deposited in ice-dammed glacial lakes in the Rossendale and Calder valleys. When the ice dams broke, the rapid draw-down of the water level destabilised the clay on the steeper slopes and landslips were a frequent occurrence. The slipped masses are often still recognisable from their upper scarp slopes and bulging toes, but are sometimes obscured by later deposits.

Post-glacial deposits include raised-beaches and blown sands resulting from the retreat of the ice and the sea, and also alluvium in river valleys and estuaries.

Peat deposits are of several basic types, extensive and sometimes deep basin peats, such as at Chat Moss, raised mosses on the poorly-drained till plains in the south and south-east of the county, and thin climatic peat on the plateau areas of the Forests of Rossendale, Bowland and Pendle.

In Cheshire, the western half of the county is generally flat and low-lying forming a plain which stretches from the River Dee to Congleton, where the ground rises to meet the Peak District and Pennines. The plain is broken by the Mid-Cheshire ridge, which extends south from Frodsham towards Malpas. The ridge is intermittent and continues north, though less pronounced, into the Wirral peninsula.

The majority of the solid rock on the plain is obscured by thick glacial deposits left after the advance and retreat of the (Irish Sea) ice sheet. Much of the obscured bedrock is of Triassic age with older Carboniferous rocks exposed to the east of the county around Macclesfield. Tectonic movements have folded the rocks into a basinal structure with generally shallow angles of dip.

To the east of the county the Red Rock Fault, extends south past Congleton and north towards Macclesfield and brings the weaker Triassic Bollin Mudstone formation formerly known as Lower Keuper Marl against the more resistant Carboniferous and marks the edge of the lowland plain. The Carboniferous rocks are of the Millstone Grit group and are present as shales and more resistant sandstones and gritstones. Coal measures outcrop only in the north-east of the county near Macclesfield.

The bedrock over the majority of the plain belongs to the Mercia Mudstone Group formerly known as Keuper Marl, a weak rock often eroded and weathered by the ice to form the characteristic red brown glacial till deposits which blanket much of the county. More resistant beds within the Triassic sequence are the Tarporley Siltstone formation formerly known as Keuper Waterstone and the Helsby Sandstone Formation formerly known as Keuper Sandstone which forms outcrops mainly on the ridges, around Peckforton, Beeston, and Delamere. These sandstones are of considerable thickness and are locally important aquifers.

The famous salt beds, the Keuper Saliferous beds now known as Northwich and Wilkesley Halite Formations, are present nearer the middle of the county, notably around Tatton, north east of Lymm, Middlewich,

Northwich and Winsford. The topography of the salt-bearing areas is marked with subsidence features often infilled with water to form flashes or lakes.

The retreat of the ice sheet left extensive sand and gravel deposits over the county as well as deeply cut channels where the melt waters broke through their temporary dams such as the Deva spillway just north of Chester. Some of the more extensive fluvioglacial sand and gravel deposits are located around Chelford, extending from Rudheath to Gawsworth and as far north as Knutsford and south to Sandbach; and from Sandiway south to Little Budworth. Some of the sands are thought to represent multiple glacial advances and were formerly described with the glacial clays as the tripartite sequence formed of the Lower Boulder Clay, Middle Sands and Upper Boulder Clay. These Middle Sands are present around Congleton where they are quarried. Current thinking is that the glacial deposits represent only the final glacial episode with perhaps relics of previous glacial events surviving only in hollows, and that the complexity of the deposits is caused by progressive melt-out, pockets of stagnant ice, ponding of water and complex drainage relationships.

The main rivers draining the county today comprise the Mersey, Dane, Weaver, Gowy and Dee. They are associated with alluvial deposits and often terraces formed of gravels. The largest are the Dee and the Mersey, both set in extensive alluvial flood plains, which have meandering form. The Dee flows almost due north close to the western edge of the county and through Chester, before feeding into a straightened channel within the salt marshes of its estuary. Also of importance is the Gowy, which rises on the mid-Cheshire ridge and drains north-west towards Frodsham Marsh and Ellesmere Port before discharging into the Mersey Estuary. Although a relatively small river, it is associated with considerable thicknesses of peat, which lie between Bridge Trafford and Thornton le Moors.

The Region, with its very strong association with the Industrial Revolution has, as would be expected, many areas which have been extensively modified as a consequence, and contains colliery, quarry and chemical waste heaps, as well as household waste disposal sites adjacent to the urban concentrations.

2 The Origins of the Motorways of the Region

2.1 The Early Years

Although not the first consideration given to the possibility of constructing motorways in Britain, in 1936 the Institution of Highway Engineers published a plan for a network of such roads.

A few years earlier, the Lancashire County Council had reached conclusions on proposals for improving the A6/A49 existing north-south route through the county. It was the intention to provide a high-standard all-purpose road of dual carriageways, cycle tracks and footpaths within an overall width of 120 feet.

However, in 1937, the County Council had become 'seriously perturbed' by the number of accidents on the Liverpool-East Lancashire Road which had been opened by King George V only as recently as July 1934. As an all-purpose road with an overall width of 120 feet, it had a single carriageway 40 feet wide and a very large number of surface level access points, which was the main reason for the high accident rate. Roundabouts had been provided at several of the more important road junctions, but frequent requests were being received for some form of control to be installed at all the various crossings. It was felt, however, that this would tend to reduce the efficiency of the road and would ultimately defeat the object for which it had been constructed.

The County Council expressed the view,[*] therefore, that with regard to the earlier proposals for the north-south route, 'these evils' should 'not be perpetuated'. Taking this factor into account, and the extensive property demolition which would have been involved in improving the existing A6/A49 route, it was decided that an entirely new route, with controlled access, was required. Further, that it should be restricted to the use of motor traffic, i.e. a 'motorway', and in that respect the proposal was in conformity with the plan of the Institution of Highway Engineers.

The most significant factor, however, in generating widespread interest in motorways during that period was undoubtedly the development of the German *autobahnen*. Also in 1937, a Group known as the German Roads Delegation, numbering 224 members, including Members of Parliament,

Motorways proposed by the institution of Highway Engineers in 1936

* 'North and South Route', Report of the Highways and Bridges Committee, March 1937, Lancashire County Council (Preston Record Office).

representatives of Highway Authorities, Highway Engineers and others involved in vehicle operation, took part in a tour of inspection of the system. There were no representatives of the Ministry of Transport.

James Drake, the newly appointed Surveyor of Blackpool, was a member of the Group and he was so impressed with what he saw that he later recommended that a 'ring road', which had been proposed for the busy seaside resort, should be constructed as a 'motorway'.

National plan for motorways: County Surveyors' Society 1938

The report of the Group's visit was considered by the County Surveyors' Society and in May 1938 published its own plan for approximately 1,000 miles of motorway linking the main industrial centres in the Country. In July, it was forwarded to the Ministry of Transport by the County Councils' Association on behalf of the Society.

The Society gave the proposals the widest possible publicity, which led to representatives attending a meeting of the Roads Group of the House of Lords and the House of Commons.

Although only drawn to a small scale, both of those pre-War plans included a proposed motorway from London to Carlisle, passing through Cheshire, Lancashire, Westmorland and Cumberland. In South Lancashire, however, the 1936 plan showed an alignment through the Manchester area whereas the route in the later plan, as proposed by the then County Surveyor and Bridgemaster, was sited further to the west, near Warrington.

Meanwhile, the Minister of Transport at that time, the Rt Hon. Leslie Burgin MP, had also visited the *autobahnen* and recommended that, as an experiment, approval should be given to a scheme put forward by Lancashire County Council for the construction of a motorway 62 miles long, passing through the county from Warrington to Carnforth. Wigan was to be by-passed on the western side, and Preston and Lancaster to the east. However, after correspondence with the Chancellor, he agreed that in view of the national financial situation, he would not pursue the proposal, but the County Council continued with some preliminary survey work.

In May 1939, a statement was issued by the Minister in regard to the *autobahnen*, in which the geographic and economic differences between Britain and Germany were referred to. It was considered, therefore, that whatever might be decided in the future as to the economic value of motorways, the policy of reconstructing and improving the existing main roads would continue.

The outbreak of war, in September 1939, precluded any further action at that time, but in July 1941, at the behest of the Prime Minister, the Rt Hon. Winston Churchill MP, the Cabinet commissioned, through its Post-

War Reconstruction Committee, proposals in which motorways would play a major role. In 1942, Sir Frederick Cook, the recently retired Chief Highway Engineer of the Ministry of War Transport, prepared a brief for the War Cabinet and encouraged the County Surveyors' Society to work-up proposals in which the Institution of Civil Engineers and the Institution of Municipal and County Engineers played a crucial role.

Apart from the early work undertaken for a proposed north-south motorway through Lancashire, the County Surveyors elsewhere in the Region were also actively involved. In 1942, the County Surveyor and Bridgemaster of Cheshire produced an estimate for the cost of the construction of the section through his county amounting to £2.01 million. Land was valued at £60 per acre, roadworks at £40,000 per mile, and bridges at £11,500 to £20,000 each. He was also involved in discussions with the Ministry of Transport on the proposed standards of layout.

The origin of the scheme in Westmorland and Cumberland stemmed from the endemic traffic congestion in Kendal, Penrith and Carlisle, and the need to provide an all-weather route avoiding Shap Fell, where the A6 was frequently blocked during the winter. In 1943, Geoffrey Lockwood, the County Surveyor of Cumberland, published a 'Report on Highway Development in the Immediate Post-War Years' within his county.* Not only did it include the section of a proposed north-south motorway by-passing Carlisle on the west side, but also a 'Regional Motorway' between Carlisle and Egremont, in order to make West Cumberland more accessible. The local Member of Parliament, at that time, was the Rt Hon. Hugh Dalton who, as President of the Board of Trade, was a member of the Cabinet, where the subject was raised – believed to be the first occasion on which a specific motorway proposal was considered at such a level of government. In the event, it was decided that, for a number of reasons, the proposed north-south motorway should pass to the east of the city and that a 'motorway' route to Egremont could not be justified.

In late 1944, the Chief Engineer of the Ministry of War Transport, recommended a National Motorway Plan and it was decided subsequently that initial survey work should be carried out on those motorways considered to be of the first priority. The drafting of a Bill to provide the necessary legislation for the construction of motorways began in 1945. While defining the basic principles underlying the provision of such roads, e.g. restricted access and a dual carriageway layout, design standards were proposed by Major H.E. Aldington, then Chief Engineer in the Ministry, which included the following:

* Report on Highway Development in Immediate Post-War Years, booklet discussing proposed motorway in Cumberland, June 1943 Cumberland County Council (Carlisle Record Office).

Design speed	75mph
Formation width	For dual two-lane carriageways: 93 ft For dual three-lane carriageways: 109 ft
Marginal strip	1 ft wide at each side of the carriageway, flush with it and of a contrasting colour
Carriageways	Dual two-lane: each 22ft wide, excluding the marginal strips. Dual three-lane: each 30ft wide, excluding the marginal strips.
Verges	Normally 15ft wide and clear of obstructions, but some planting of small trees and shrubs to be permitted. The width may be reduced to 5ft at bridges.
Central Reservation	Not less than 15ft, with the width to be maintained at bridges.
Curves	Radius not less than 3000ft
Gradients	Normal maximum 1 in 30, but up to 1 in 20 to be permitted in some hilly country
Lay-bys	To be provided at intervals, to enable drivers to draw off the carriageway to rest or make minor repairs.
Roadside Facilities	No frontage access allowed, but areas to be provided for the supply of petrol, refreshment, and for Police purposes. Parking places to be provided off the highway, particularly at view-points.
Bridges	Modern designs with the forms of construction, and the materials, to be appropriate to the circumstances.
Pavement design and surfacing	Attention to foundations essential. All road surfaces should, as far as practicable, be non-skid.

2.2 Planning for the Future in the Post-War Period

Since the end of the Second World War, the road network of the Region has seen changes incomparably greater in scale and impact than any which has gone before – beside these developments, even the Roman roads and the turnpikes seem modest. As elsewhere in the Country, the motorway network, and the huge growth in private and commercial traffic which is inextricably linked with it, have been the subject of much debate.

In 1945, Drake was appointed County Surveyor and Bridgemaster of Lancashire, a post he was to hold for 27 years. At that time, the emphasis was on planning for the future and, in 1947, the County Council accepted his suggestion that a 'road plan' should be prepared.

The principal types of traffic movement were carefully analysed, i.e. that passing through the county on long-distance journeys; cross-border movements to and from points within the county; and traffic movements within Lancashire itself. The results showed that, despite some improvements undertaken in the 1930s, the existing road network was quite unable to cope effectively with all these movements. It was also clear that the situation would deteriorate further, as the volume of traffic increased.

In order that the future road network should be as safe as possible, a major pioneering research programme was undertaken. By analysing the accidents which had occurred, a new understanding was obtained of how different layouts, traffic controls and other features affected the number and types of accident. Using this information, it was possible to forecast the accident savings which could be achieved, as an element in establishing the economic justification for any proposed scheme.

The Trunk, Class I and Class II roads had to bear the brunt of heavy through-traffic and it was felt that their importance warranted a fairer system of funding than hitherto. Lancashire, with its heavy industries and popular holiday resorts, had to cater for a weight of traffic quite out of proportion to the mileage of its main road system. It was, therefore, contended that resources should be allocated according to population as well as road mileage.

A great deal of traffic data was collected from which projections of future traffic flows and road capacities were made. This enabled the future network to be defined on a basis of three categories of traffic route of which the 1st Group comprised 12 'express routes' with dual carriageways, totalling 217 miles in length; 94 miles were to be of motorway standard and all these routes were chosen to attract the highest volumes of traffic.

They included a north-south motorway and a Liverpool-Manchester-Yorkshire route, both of which had been included in a 10-year construction programme of national routes announced by the Minister of Transport, in 1946. The latter route was to incorporate the existing Liverpool-East Lancashire Road, as far as Worsley, and then be a motorway following a line through the northern part of the Manchester Conurbation to the Yorkshire boundary.

Also within this category, it was proposed that the western section of a Manchester Outer Ring Road, crossing the Manchester Ship Canal by a high-level bridge, should be constructed as a motorway.

The function of the 2nd Group was defined as connecting large towns to a 1st Group route or to each other, and serving as important links. It was proposed that links from the proposed north-south route to Blackpool and to Morecambe should also be constructed as motorways.

In 1949, the 'Road Plan for Lancashire' was approved by the County Council* and the various proposals were included in the County Development Plan, which enabled future land use to be controlled. This allowed 'corridors of interest' for the proposed new roads, including the motorways, to be protected against development, thereby making it much easier to achieve rapid progress in carrying out the necessary statutory procedures when schemes were eventually programmed.

* 'Road Plan for Lancashire', 1949, Lancashire County Council (Preston Record Office).

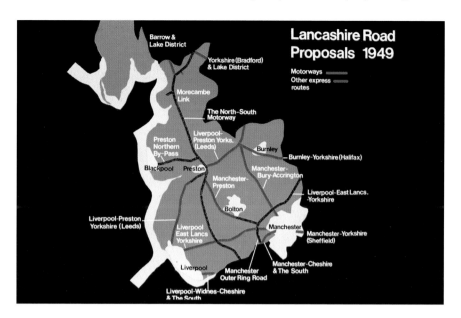

Road Plan for
Lancashire 1949.

In due course, the Development Plan was accepted by the Government of the day and therefore, in effect, the Road Plan received the general approval of the Ministry of Transport. However, because of the large financial commitment involved, the Ministry, not unexpectedly, did not endorse it in its entirety but the Plan proved to be of considerable importance. Not only did it form the basis of highway strategies within a major part of the Region for more than thirty years, but many of the processes which were developed in its preparation were subsequently adopted nationally.

The original Plan was, however, subject to continual review to take account of traffic growth and demographic changes, leading to the introduction of further motorway projects. By the end of the 20th century, out of a total of 18 separately numbered motorways in the Region, there were 16 within the geographical county of Lancashire.

In Cheshire, there was serious traffic congestion in places such as Chester, Frodsham, Stockton Heath, Tarporley and Knutsford. The River Mersey is the traditional boundary with Lancashire and together with the Manchester Ship Canal they have formed major transport barriers. The Ship Canal needed 75 feet clear headroom for ocean-going vessels and the main road crossings were swing bridges which took at least 10 minutes for each opening. The county has a strategic location lying astride all north-south routes west of the Pennines. With industry in the northern part of the county, good east-west communications linking Merseyside and the Manchester Conurbation on the south side of the Canal have always been recognised as essential. However, road planning was not undertaken in isolation but was linked with plans for the surrounding counties and conurbations, notably, Lancashire, Staffordshire, Merseyside, Greater Manchester and Clwyd.

Its Development Plan of 1958 included a number of major road proposals. A road plan was prepared for internal use but, unlike the 1949 Road Plan for Lancashire, it was not published. However, in addition to the early design work for the M6 carried out by the County Council, several major studies were undertaken which were of major significance in the further development of the motorway network.

In January 1965 'The Blue Report'* established the case for the North Cheshire Motorway M56. Later, in 1968, a Report was prepared on the 'Proposed Major Road Network for the Chester Area', which referred to the urgent need to extend

(i)   the M56 west of Hapsford,
(ii)   the M53 south of Hooton passing to the east of Chester and
(iii)   joining the Southern Ring Road, and
(iv)   the Ellesmere Port Motorway M531

Elsewhere in the Region, Manchester City Council had published a 'City Plan' in 1945, which included a range of major projects for new roads. Subsequently, all the Local Authorities in South East Lancashire and North East Cheshire (SELNEC) became involved in a major traffic survey, which resulted in the publication of a SELNEC Highway Plan, in 1962. It envisaged a large motorway and dual carriageway network, including a ring road of the city and various radial routes. However, apart from those motorways which had already been proposed by the Lancashire and Cheshire County Councils in their own plans, only a few of the others were to be constructed (for example, the Mancunian Way) and the completion of the Outer Ring Road.

In Merseyside, a similar traffic survey was carried out, leading to the preparation of a 20-Year Plan for new roads, which was published in 1965. In due course, however, proposals for an inner ring motorway in Liverpool, with radial motorways, connecting to the national system, were to be abandoned. In consequence, the development of the motorway network in the area was to be confined to the construction of the Liverpool Outer Ring Road, M57, and the northern section of the Mid-Wirral Motorway, M53, connecting with the 2nd Mersey Tunnel.

In the late 1960s major transportation studies were undertaken in the two Conurbations, namely the 'SELNEC Transportation Study' and the 'Merseyside Area Land Use/Transportation Study' (MALTS). In the event, however, the subsequent decisions taken by those Authorities concerned did not materially influence the planned development of the motorway network.

The preparation, design and construction of each section of motorway within the Region is outlined in the following chapters.

* North Cheshire East-West Motorway, Report (The Blue Report), January 1965, Cheshire County Council (Chester Record Office).

3   The North-South Motorway M6

3.1   Preston By-pass

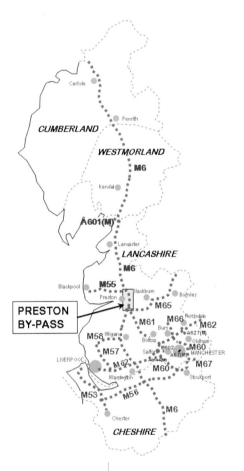

In the mid-1940s, Drake had obtained the approval of Lancashire County Council to proceed with the preparation and preliminary design work for a north-south motorway through the county. It was found that the basic alignment, as envisaged in 1937, was still appropriate and only comparatively minor adjustments had to be made. It was realised, however, that economic factors made it impracticable to embark on the construction of the whole of the motorway as a single project. In 1952, therefore, consideration was given to the possibility of constructing those sections of the motorway by-passing Lancaster and Preston,[*] in order to relieve the serious traffic congestion and reduce the number of accidents within those conurbations.

Encouraged by the preparatory work carried out by the County Council the Minister of Transport announced, in 1953, that the construction of the 8¼-mile long Preston By-pass was to be included in his expanded road programme to commence in the 1956-57 financial year and that a start was to be made on the statutory procedures.

At the time, the Minister described the By-pass as a 'guinea pig' – in other words, as an experiment for all other British motorways. In view of its significance and the lessons which were learned in carrying it out, this particular project is referred to in much more detail than any other section of motorway.

The County Council was appointed the Minister's Agent Authority for the design and resolved to carry out the widest possible public consultations. Drake suggested that, rather than relying solely on drawings to illustrate the proposals, a large model should be constructed and, in order that the design programme should not be delayed, members of the staff keen to see the project proceeding, agreed to build the model in their own time. At subsequent public meetings which were held throughout the area, it proved to be of enormous value in explaining the scheme.

The route of the By-pass followed a line very close to the eastern edge of the built-up areas of Fulwood, Preston, Walton-le-Dale and Bamber

* 'North-South Motorway', Proposed By-passing of Lancaster and Preston, Report to the Highways and Bridges Committee, November 1952, County Surveyor and Bridgemaster (Preston Record Office).

13

Bridge, with only one farmhouse and three other dwellings directly affected. For many years, a corridor to provide for the future construction of the motorway had been 'protected' and, in several instances, post-war housing development within the urban areas had not been allowed to extend beyond its western boundary. Apart from terminal roundabout connections to the A6 at each end, there was to be only a single interchange junction with the A59 at Samlesbury, approximately halfway along its length.

Following the advertising of the proposals, only a few formal objections were received and these were resolved by agreement. The Minister was therefore able to complete the statutory procedures without a Public Inquiry. This was quite remarkable, in the light of the vociferous opposition to similar proposals which was generated elsewhere in the Country as motorway schemes became the subject of formalised and lengthy Public Inquiries, often disrupted by objectors not directly affected. Part of the explanation lies in the fact that there was close personal involvement of both the members of the County Council and the County Surveyor, in the consultation process. As a result, those affected had full confidence that their interests would be properly considered, both in the detailed design of the works and during construction.

It could be argued that, as there had been no previous experience of motorway construction in Britain, members of the public could not appreciate the full impact of the construction and the use of a road of such magnitude. If this had been so, those likely to be affected when other sections of the motorway came to be considered might have been inclined to raise strong objections. In the event, however, by adopting a similar approach, all the statutory procedures for the whole of the 62 miles of the M6 through the county were completed without difficulty.

Based on the experience of motorway construction and operation in Italy, Germany and the United States, various design principles had been established for use in Britain, with several significant changes from those proposed in 1945, by the Chief Engineer in the Ministry of War Transport. The design speed was to be 70mph, although there was to be no 'speed limit' when the motorway was opened to traffic. Instead of lay-bys, hard shoulders eight feet wide were to be provided adjacent to the carriageways except at bridges, where the risk of a vehicle breaking down and blocking a traffic lane was considered to be minimal. With a verge only four feet wide at such locations, a considerable saving was achieved in the cost of the structures. The overall width was to be 112 feet with the two-lane carriageways each 24 feet wide and a central reservation of 32 feet, in which a hedge was to be planted as a screen against the effect of opposing headlights. The limiting gradient was to be 1 in 25.

Drake had recommended two important design features but the Ministry, which was financing the whole of the cost as a 'trunk road' scheme, was not prepared to accept their introduction.

The proposal to provide a 'positive' drainage system using conventional gullies and pipes was not accepted and instead, it was decided that surface water run-off would be collected in stone-filled trenches, known as 'french drains', located either in the central reservation or behind the hard shoulders. This followed the practice adopted for the drainage of runways in the construction of airfields during the Second World War.

On the basis of his own traffic predictions, Drake had argued that the carriageways should be constructed with three traffic lanes rather than with two lanes, which the Ministry considered to be adequate. However, a compromise was accepted whereby the overall width of the By-pass was to be increased, the bridges designed accordingly, and the central reservation made sufficiently wide to allow for the addition of a third lane to each carriageway at a later date. In due course, therefore, the carrying capacity could be increased with minimal disruption to traffic and without the need for structural alterations to bridges.

Lancashire had two main sources of materials for road construction. In the south of the county there were massive deposits of Burnt Red Shale, which had been accumulated during many years of coal mining, while in the Clitheroe and Carnforth areas existing quarries produced high quality limestone aggregates, properly screened and graded to meet any specification. The form of carriageway construction was to be such that the maximum possible use would be made of mechanical plant and several pilot projects had been carried out on County roads in which a pre-mixed waterbound limestone macadam, to be known as 'wet mix', was developed as a material for the base.

At that time, it was common practice in the construction of new roads, particularly where major earthworks were involved, to defer the laying of the final surface until the carriageways had been subjected to traffic use. It was considered, therefore, that only a temporary surface should be laid, so that any early deformation could be remedied before completion, thereby ensuring a high standard of running surface over an extended period.

Taking all these factors into account, it was decided that the carriageway construction should consist of a sub-base of Burnt Red Shale, varying in thickness from 12 to 36 inches depending on ground conditions, followed by a 9-inch-thick layer of 'wet mix' and a surface of a 2½-inch-thick tarmacadam base course with a ¾-inch thick temporary wearing course of fine cold asphalt. The form of construction of the hard shoulders was to be little more than that of a hardened verge.

Twenty-two bridges were required and great care was taken to ensure that each type was aesthetically suitable for the particular site. Designers were allowed a fairly free hand and there was a great deal of innovation with a preference for concrete construction employing differing prestressing systems. The use of concrete was also in recognition of the anticipated difficulties of providing access on a 'live' motorway for the future maintenance painting of steel structures.

The design loading for highway bridges was set out in Memorandum 577 which required all bridges, with the exception of accommodation bridges, to be capable of carrying a specified uniformly distributed load, plus a knife-edge load representing the excess of the heavy axles over the other axles in the 'Standard Loading Train'. In addition, bridges carrying motorways were required to be designed to carry 45 units of Abnormal Load which was simplified into two knife-edge loads of 15,000 lbs per foot, 10 feet long and 25 feet apart, with modifications for transverse members. For this loading, a permissible overstress of 25 per cent was allowed.

In general, for spans up to about 50 feet, a desirable shallow construction depth was to be achieved using pretensioned prestressed beams placed side by side and infilled with concrete, but the Ministry required such decks to be transversely prestressed. There were no standard beam sections available, and as the beams were to be cast and stressed using the long-line system, much experimental design work was carried out.

In order to reduce the tunnel effect in instances where the motorway crossed a minor road, such that the span of the bridge was very much less than its width, light wells were to be provided within the central reservation.

For one particular single span bridge over the motorway, the deck was designed with beams 99 feet long to be cast on site and post-tensioned using the 'Magnel-Blaton' system.

Another over-bridge was required to carry 30-inch and 24-inch water mains in the footways, and the depth of construction required to accommodate them determined a single span arrangement. Steel plate girders with the deck constructed in two halves enabled the mains to be temporarily diverted in turn, in order to maintain full water supply to Preston, and avoid undue restrictions to traffic.

Two major bridges were required to carry the By-pass over the River Ribble and the A59 at Samlesbury, and across the valley of the River Darwen. In both cases, steel was the preferred form of construction for the superstructure.

At Samlesbury, various arrangements of spans were investigated, i.e. two, three, four and five spans. Following discussions with the Chief Bridge Engineer of the Ministry, a three-span continuous steel box girder structure with curved soffits was chosen. At that time, this form of construction was comparatively new. Three-inch-long sections of rolled steel channel welded to the top of the eight girders as shear connectors to the reinforced concrete deck slab ensured composite action. The 420-feet-long deck was to be supported on mass concrete abutments with wing walls and two mass concrete piers contained within permanent sheet pile cofferdams. A steel interlocking toothed expansion joint at the southern end of the deck was to be concreted into the deck and the curtain wall of the abutment.

The six-span 474-feet-long Higher Walton Bridge was designed with a superstructure of welded steel plate girders and reinforced concrete deck, carried on reinforced concrete trestle piers.

Hot-rolled asphalt was specified as the carriageway surfacing on the bridges and it was assumed that this would be impervious. However, a waterproof membrane was to be provided under the side verges and the central reservation.

It was decided that a separate contract should be entered into for each of the two major bridges. The principal contract, however, was for all the roadworks and 19 other bridges. Tenders were invited by the County Council, early in 1956, and approval was given, by the Ministry, to the acceptance of the lowest bids, which enabled construction to commence in June of that year. Drake was appointed as Engineer for all the three Contracts.* The provision of a bridge carrying the Preston-Longridge Line over the motorway was to be undertaken by British Rail.

The two-year period for completion was based on the presumption that the weather would approximate to that of average summers and

Preston By-pass
inauguration

North Escarpment

winters in Lancashire but, in the event, almost continuous rain fell from the start of the work.

In order to deal with the massive earth-moving programme, the principal Contractor had assembled a fleet of heavy plant which included tractors, scrapers, large capacity excavators and rear-dump trucks. However, the rains in autumn 1956 made it virtually impossible to work the sandy clay sub-soil and the major earthworks were postponed until the following spring. Due to the exceptional circumstances, the contractor was granted a five months' extension of time.

Following a brief spell of fine weather early in the following year, there was a similar period of very heavy rain, which was repeated in 1958. This caused the 'loss' of large quantities of excavated material which,

* 'Preston By-pass', Inauguration Ceremony Brochure, 2 June 1956, Ministry of Transport and Civil Aviation/Lancashire County Council (Preston Record Office).

in normal weather conditions, would have been used for embankment construction. As a result, it had to be taken to tip and replaced by imported material.

The adverse weather did not materially affect the bridgeworks' programmes. However, several issues of an unexpected nature arose during the period of construction.

The Contractors sought approval to the use of ready-mixed concrete from a plant which had been established recently some 15 miles from the site. At that time, the use of material provided in this way was a new development in the area. Understandably, concern was expressed at the extent to which it would be possible to control the mixes, particularly, in regard to the water/cement ratio of the high strength concrete for use in prestressed elements of structures. Arrangements were made, therefore, for members of the supervisory staff to visit the plant when critical mixes were to be delivered. Not only were the materials inspected, but the moisture content of the aggregates was tested in order to ensure that the amount of added water was appropriate for the mix.

The conventional practice in the painting of steel bridges was to use a neutral colour, such as grey. Drake expressed the view that a variety of brighter colours should be introduced, for two reasons. Firstly, to enhance the appearance of the bridges and secondly, and perhaps more important, as a safety measure to ensure that drivers did not suffer from boredom while driving on the motorway.

In the early stages of painting Samlesbury Bridge, and before the surfacing had been laid on the deck, it was found that, in one localised area, the paint had been stripped from the face of one of the outside girders. Tests showed that rainwater seeping through a minor defective area of the deck concrete had become highly alkaline with a PH value approaching that of caustic soda. Repairs were carried out and the painting was completed satisfactorily.

Samlesbury Bridge

An examination of concrete used elsewhere in the project indicated that this was a common phenomenon. Enquiries directed at the cement suppliers established that the cause was due to inadequate 'burning' during the manufacturing process, which arose from the high demand within the construction industry at that time. The problem was well-known in other countries, such as Denmark, where there was experience of corrosion of the steel in reinforced concrete structures. The advice which was received, was to the effect that, in most instances, the PH value of the leachate would reduce rapidly and further testing showed this to be the case.

The inner surfaces of the steel box girders of Samlesbury Bridge were to be painted, but it was considered that some means should be provided for measuring the humidity of the interior. A tap was, therefore, fitted on each of the access manhole covers to enable air samples to be extracted. It was found, however, that during periods of changeable weather the expansion and contraction of the air within, was so great that the girders could be heard to 'breathe'. Meanwhile, consideration was being given to controlling the humidity by placing silica gel within the girders in order to reduce the frequency of maintenance painting. This form of treatment was found to be successful, by completely sealing the boxes by the fitting of air-tight gaskets to the covers and the removal of the taps.

In view of the innovative nature of the design of many of the bridges, arrangements were made for the Ministry to carry out the test-loading of several of the completed structures prior to the opening of the By-pass. The results were used in the development of future design standards.

Extensive landscaping was carried out, not only within the limits of the motorway but also on adjoining land acquired after negotiations with the owners, and in the areas where unsuitable excavated material had been tipped. This was followed by an extensive tree planting scheme and the provision of hedges along the boundaries and within the central reservation.

It had been decided that lighting was only needed at the Samlesbury Interchange and at the terminal roundabouts. Lighting schemes were designed in accordance with the appropriate standards in use at the time. However, towards the end of the construction period, when most of the lighting columns in the Interchange had been erected, the Minister visited the site. On viewing the Interchange from the south escarpment of the Ribble Valley, he expressed concern at the effect on the surroundings of the large number of columns in such a small area and immediately ordered their removal – a further indication, even in those days, of the interest in minimising any adverse effect on the environment of the area.

On 5 December 1958 the Preston By-pass, Britain's first motorway, was opened to traffic.* In view of the national importance of the event the ceremony was performed by the Prime Minister, the Rt Hon. Harold Macmillan MP, and a granite plinth marking the occasion was erected at the Samlesbury Interchange.

In January 1959, however, a small amount of frost damage affecting the carriageways occurred as a result of an exceptionally rapid thaw, when the temperature rose from 8°F to 43°F within a period of 36 hours. This situation had arisen primarily because of the exceptionally wet weather during construction, which meant that there was still a high water table in the formation below the carriageways. As the hard shoulders were

* 'Preston By-pass', Official Opening Brochure, 5 December 1958, Ministry of Transport and Civil Aviation/Lancashire County Council (Preston Record Office).

Preston By-pass at opening.

not paved and, therefore, were permeable, surface water run-off was able to drain directly into the formation, thereby exacerbating the problem. Furthermore, the Burnt Red Shale used in the sub-base had not been screened or graded and, where it contained an excess of fine material, capillary action took place, drawing ground water to the surface. In the circumstances, the thin temporary surface of the carriageways proved to be inadequate for resisting the effect of the freeze/thaw cycle when subjected to heavy traffic.

In view of the fact that there was no speed limit, it was decided, for safety reasons, that the motorway should be closed temporarily to enable repair work to be carried out. This led to much criticism, which failed to recognise that, under a financial regime requiring the maximum economy in design and construction for a type of road new to Britain, it was probably inevitable that problems would arise.

Because of the importance of food production, at that time, it was necessary to restrict the acquisition of agricultural land to the absolute minimum. Based on the original site investigation, it was considered that the cuttings could be formed with slopes as steep as 1 in 1½ but, due to the nature of the material, surface slips occurred both during construction and after the motorway had been opened to traffic. The remedial work was both costly and disruptive.

Many other important lessons had been learned and it was considered vital that the experience gained in the preparation, design, construction and operation of this first section of motorway should be taken into account in carrying out future schemes. It was clear that attention needed to be given to a number of aspects, particularly in respect of the following:

(i)   The extensive public consultation carried out throughout the whole process, had not only assisted in the smooth passage of the statutory procedures but also in dealing with complaints during the period of construction.

(ii)   In order to ensure that as much suitable excavated material as possible is used in the construction of embankments, the responsibilities of the Contractor in carrying out the earthworks should be more clearly defined in both the Specification and the Bill of Quantities. In that respect, it is incumbent on the Contractor to employ appropriate types of plant, having regard to the ground and weather conditions.

(iii)   Great care should be taken in the design of the slopes of cuttings and embankments, having regard to the characteristics of the materials involved.

(iv)   The carriageway sub-base material should be of properly screened and graded material complying with a clearly defined specification.

(v)   The surface-water drainage system had proved to be unsatisfactory.

(vi)   The principle of laying a temporary surface on the carriageways of motorways should not be perpetuated.

(vii)   It soon became evident that continuous hard shoulders would have been a valuable asset, (a) as a means of access for emergency vehicles when a breakdown or accident occurred which brought traffic to a halt, and (b) for use as additional traffic lanes when it was necessary to close the normal running lanes for maintenance purposes.

(viii)   The form of construction of the hard shoulders was inadequate, as it was not unknown in jacking-up a heavy vehicle, for the jack to be driven into the surface instead of lifting the vehicle.

(ix)   The explosive growth of traffic, which occurred within a short period after opening, demonstrated the need for all future motorways to be constructed with dual three-lane carriageways at the outset, unless there were very strong reasons to the contrary.

(x)   Irrespective of the type or surfacing, bridge decks should be fully waterproofed.

(xi)   Hedges are unsuitable for use as any form of barrier in the central reservation, particularly due to the effect on growth arising from winter gritting operations. In view of the liabilities of the Highway Authority for the maintenance of the motorway boundary 'fencing', doubts were expressed at the suitability of hedges for this purpose.

(xii)   Light-wells in the central reservation of underbridges are a potential hazard.

(xiii)   There was a favourable reaction to the use of different colours in the painting of steel bridges.

Following the frost damage to the carriageways, local repairs were carried out and immediate steps were taken to improve the drainage system. The final four-inch-thick hot-rolled asphalt surface was laid within 12 months and much earlier than originally intended. In 1963, the hard shoulders were reconstructed and paved, with their distinctive red surface giving a contrasting colour as an aid to drivers.

A safety barrier was erected in the central reservation in replacement of the hedge and to prevent out-of-control vehicles crossing from the opposing carriageway.

Within eight years, traffic flows had increased to such an extent that, as provided for in the original design, it became necessary to add a third lane to each carriageway by reducing the width of the central reservation.

Following several failures during the construction of box girder bridges in Britain, and abroad, in the late 1960s, national concern was expressed at the adequacy of this type of design. Temporary lane closures were, therefore, applied to all such bridges until an independent check had been carried out. It is pleasing to note that Samlesbury Bridge was one of the few which did not require any strengthening.

Despite its problems, the construction of the By-pass undoubtedly gave good value for money compared with later motorways designed and constructed to higher standards.

The Road Plan had included a proposal for a northern by-pass of Preston, to connect with the M6 at Broughton and continue westwards as a motorway to Blackpool and the Fylde Coast. In the early 1960s, representations were made to the Ministry of Transport for an early start to be made on its construction, and preliminary preparation and design work was carried out by the County Council. However, as a result of the general increase in traffic, particularly on the M6, and with the prospect of further increases arising from the development of the Central Lancashire New Town, it was decided to undertake a Study of the need for improved east/west communications throughout the whole of the Preston area.

The Study Report, published in September 1969, concluded that, on the basis of predicted traffic flows, a full network of by-passes, to be known as the 'Preston Box', would be required by 1980. In addition to the Northern By-pass, which merited the highest priority, it was considered that both Southern and Western By-passes were necessary.

The preparation, design and construction of the Northern By-pass, subsequently numbered M55, is referred to elsewhere. The crossing of the River Ribble by a Western By-pass subsequently became more viable by the closure of Preston Dock to large merchant vessels. By the early 1990s considerable progress, in terms of design and public consultation, had been made in respect of both the Southern and Western By-passes, which had become the responsibility of the Department of Transport (DTp). Meanwhile, a Study carried out in 1984-86 drew attention to the need for the widening and improvement of the Preston By-pass Section of M6 between the junctions with the M61 (J30) and the M55 (J32).

In 1987 following several multiple fatal accidents, the DTp included the project in the Trunk Road programme contained in the White Paper 'Policy for Roads in England'. The firm of Rendel Palmer and Tritton (RPT) was commissioned to appraise the situation, prepare an appropriate scheme and process it through to completion by acting as the Engineer for the Contract.

Although the whole length of the original Preston By-pass between Bamber Bridge (J29) and Broughton (J32) had been widened to three lanes, the hard shoulders had remained discontinuous at all the bridges. The number of lanes available, therefore, during maintenance operations, or when dealing with accidents, was inadequate to cope with the volume of traffic which had increased to a maximum of 140,000 vehicles a day.

The section between J30 and J32 is a common link for both east-west traffic (M61-M55) and north-south traffic (M6) and was particularly overloaded when tourist traffic to and from the Lake District and Blackpool coincided.

The DTp considered 'speed' to be of the essence in preparing and carrying out the scheme, with initial target dates which proposed a start on site in 1991-92, but it was agreed that even an accelerated programme would take somewhat longer. In the event the following dates were achieved:

- 1989 – Public Consultation and Exhibition,
- 1991 – Public Inquiry, and
- March 1993 – Main Contract let.

In July 1993, the Minister announced that further work on the Southern and Western By-passes would be deferred until traffic conditions on the widened section of the M6 could be assessed. However, it was decided that the route of the By-passes 'should be protected for planning purposes'.

The approved scheme widened the M6 between J30 and J32 to a dual four-lane motorway and added extra lanes to both M6 and M61 at J30.* Lighting, gantry signs and signals, CCTV and upgraded motorway communications were provided throughout. Consideration was given, in the traffic studies, to the contiguous scheme for the Blackburn Southern By-pass Section of the M65, joining south of J29, and the possible extension of it via the proposed Southern and Western By-passes.

It was decided that, although dual four-lane carriageways might not, in later years, be always free from congestion, the recommendation of anything greater than this could not be justified. The original DTp requirement was to maintain three lanes in one direction and two in the

* M6 Widening & Improvements between Junctions 30 & 32 Explanatory leaflet, March 1993, Department of Transport/Rendel, Palmer and Tritton (Preston Record Office).

other, during construction. This was later increased to three in each direction and greatly influenced the design.

The options for widening a live motorway are,

(a)   'Symmetrical' – where width is added on both sides

(b)   'Asymmetrical' – where width is added on one side only, and

(c)   'Parallel' – where a new section of road is constructed off-line.

The approved scheme was a combination of all three options. From the M61 overbridge at J30, the widening was all to the west (Asymmetrical). The alignment came back to cross Samlesbury Bridge 'on-line' and then the widening swung across to the east (Asymmetrical), with a section of new carriageway 'off-line' (Parallel) under Longridge Road before rejoining the existing alignment at J32.

Samlesbury Interchange under re-construction.

The scheme required the demolition of all 11 overbridges, their replacement by eight new structures, and one underbridge. The four remaining underbridges were widened and strengthened.

During the design process the Commission for New Towns appointed RPT to examine the possibility of providing a new junction (J31a), between J31 and J32 to give access to their proposed Preston East Employment Area. A half junction was eventually approved with south facing slip roads only, and the underbridge and stub slip roads were constructed as part of the M6 widening Contract. The junction was completed and opened to traffic in 1995.

Ground conditions proved more difficult than expected and earthworks were suspended over one winter. This meant that the Contractor's accelerated programme would not be achieved, but the dual four-lane carriageways came fully into use in August 1995. Two bridges with discontinuous hard shoulders remain south of J30. These could be widened using M65 and M6 for traffic diversions.

The difficulties in carrying out the work were considerable. The Engineer, the Contractor and the Police exercised great skill in dealing with the traffic during the progress of the work but it was inevitable that serious disruption would occur, from time to time. This was reflected in the very high cost of the project and reinforces the view expressed at the outset that it would have been preferable, and more economic overall, to have embarked on the construction of the Southern and Western By-passes first, before carrying out the M6 widening.

3.2   Lancaster By-pass and Carnforth Link Road A601(M)

The construction of the 11½-mile Lancaster By-pass Section of the M6, the County Council's second priority, had followed a year after the work on Preston By-pass had started. In many respects, it was similar; for example, it would also have dual two-lane carriageways with a wide central reservation for the future addition of third lanes.*

Following the appointment of the County Council as the Minister's Agent Authority, there had been extensive Public Consultation but the statutory procedures were completed without difficulty. It had been considered to be necessary, however, to move a section of the line at the southern end from that originally proposed in order to avoid a major objection, as it passed through land designated for the building of the future University of Lancaster. The effect was to take it through a wooded area which no doubt in later years would have brought vociferous protests from environmentalists.

By-passing the City of Lancaster on its eastern side, with connection to the A6 at each end, it was not the intention to provide an intermediate interchange as part of the project. However, the Road Plan for Lancashire had included a future proposal for a motorway link road to Morecambe and the Port of Heysham, to connect with the By-pass by means of a two-level interchange at Halton, on the north side of the River Lune. It was accepted that this was unlikely to be constructed for many years and, therefore, serious concern was expressed at the difficulties likely to be experienced by the emergency services in gaining access to the By-pass.

The only road of any importance crossed by the By-pass is the A683, leading from Lancaster north-eastwards along the south side of the River Lune. The emergency services were based in the city and it was decided that a connection should be provided for their sole use, with the County Council agreeing to pay 25 per cent of the cost. The design standards of this junction were lower than those of a normal interchange, with the carriageways of the slip roads separated only by double white lines. Subsequently, however, local representations were made for the junction to be opened for general use and this was eventually agreed. The result is a unique sub-standard interchange on a British motorway.

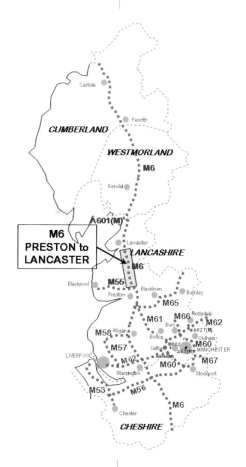

* 'Lancaster By-pass', Inauguration Ceremony Brochure, 5 July 1957, Department of Transport and Civil Aviation/ Lancashire County Council (Preston Record Office).

Lune Bridge under construction (above) and completed (left).

A total of 27 bridges was required. The major obstacle along the line of the By-pass was, however, the River Lune. The design chosen for the 400-feet-long bridge at Halton incorporated a reinforced concrete open spandrel fixed arch with a clear span of 230 feet and a rise of 44 feet. Because of their width, bridges carrying motorways are normally designed as two structures separated by a narrow gap. In casting such a large arch, massive support is necessary and the Contractor built a temporary timber gantry across the river to carry the scaffold and shuttering for the first half. On completion, this was lowered slightly, winched sideways as a complete unit on to a second gantry, raised to the correct level and used to form the second arch. Users of the motorway are, unfortunately, unaware of this impressive bridge in such an attractive setting.

Work on the construction of the By-pass was well advanced before the problems experienced on Preston By-pass became apparent. In view of the close proximity of major limestone quarries in the Carnforth area at the northern end of the By-pass, a sub-base of this material had already been specified, but it was only possible, at that late stage, to introduce a few of the other desirable design changes.

A 'positive' drainage system was installed and the carriageway construction included the laying of a 4½-inch thickness of hot-rolled asphalt, as the permanent surface. Following the paving of the hard shoulders on

Page 27:

* 'Lancaster By-pass', Official Opening Brochure, 11 April 1960, Ministry of Transport/Lancashire County Council (Preston Record Office).

† Birmingham-Preston Motorway. Lancashire Section (Preston-Warrington), Inauguration Ceremony Brochure, 24 February 1961, Ministry of Transport/Lancashire County Council (Preston Record Office).

Preston By-pass in 1963, a similar operation was undertaken on Lancaster By-pass in the following year.

With difficult ground conditions similar to those experienced at Preston, and the bad weather during the same period, delays and disruption were inevitable, but the By-pass was opened to traffic in April 1960.[*]

At the northern end of the By-pass, at Carnforth, a one-mile-long link road provided the connection to the A6, and was subject to the motorway traffic regulations. In due course, when the M6 was extended northwards a grade-separated roundabout Interchange was constructed and the link road was designated A601(M). On the east side of the M6, large quarries had been worked for many years. The main access was via the B6254 which ran from the centre of Carnforth and crossed the M6 immediately south of the Interchange.

In the late 1980s, a short single carriageway link road was built to connect the B6254 to the Interchange roundabout, and this was also designated A601(M). Quarry traffic was, therefore, provided with direct access to the M6, thus giving considerable relief to the Town.

3.3   Warrington–Preston Section

In June 1958, while the Preston and Lancaster By-passes were under construction, the route of the 27 miles of motorway between Thelwall and Preston, bypassing Warrington on the east and Wigan on the west, was confirmed, with the County Council acting as the Minister's Agent Authority.[†]

Two major bridges were required – the 4,414-feet-long 36-span Thelwall Bridge (commonly known as the Thelwall Viaduct), rising to a height of 93 feet above the Manchester Ship Canal and the River Mersey, and the 800-feet-long six-span Gathurst Viaduct across the Douglas valley west of Wigan. Because of their size and complexity an early start on their construction was vital and work began in September 1959. This was one of the earliest examples of the system of 'advance works' in motorway construction, a practice which became generally accepted as a means of dealing with particularly difficult obstacles.

Thelwall Viaduct was of sufficient width to accommodate dual three-lane carriageways and a central reservation but, in order to reduce the cost of the structure, hard shoulders were not provided. This proved to be the cause of accidents when vehicular breakdowns blocked the running lanes and a source of serious traffic problems when lanes were closed during maintenance operations.

M6
WARRINGTON
TO PRESTON

Thelwall Viaduct

M6/A580 Interchange
at Haydock

Ground conditions were particularly difficult, with soft alluvial deposits over the whole of the site. The land between the Canal and the River had been used for the disposal of Canal dredgings and was overlaid by a layer of silt some 45 feet deep. In consequence, the reinforced concrete piers, which varied in height from 30 to 80 feet, had to be carried on piles up to 130 feet in length, to provide a satisfactory foundation. The superstructure consists of steel plate girders supporting a reinforced concrete deck. The erection of the girders in the 336-foot main span across the Canal had to be undertaken without affecting shipping, which included ocean-going vessels of up to 12,000 tons and the Contractor completed this difficult operation by cantilevering the girders from each side of the crossing.

Of the further 79 bridges included in the main Contract,* which commenced in February 1961, the most significant was that required to carry the motorway over the junction with the Liverpool-East Lancashire Road A580. Instead of two separate structures, with an embankment on the roundabout in-between, it was decided to construct a viaduct 565 feet long in eight spans. The 'boat-shaped' piers were designed to provide adequate sight-lines for traffic using the junction. In due course, it was named 'The James Drake Bridge' in recognition of his major contribution to the development of the motorway network.

Early site investigations had identified a wide variety of soil conditions, with clays of varying plasticity, soft and hard grey shales, dry and very wet sands, peat, sandstone and even coal, all of which required different forms of treatment.

For 13 miles, the motorway passed through mining areas and in several places the seams were exposed during construction. Some 13,000 tons of good quality coal were excavated and handed over to the National Coal Board, which had rights of ownership. Unrecorded shallow mine-workings were also found and, depending on their depth, were either back-filled or protected by reinforced concrete slabs, as were many old mine shafts, some up to 900 feet deep.

Gathurst Viaduct

Future subsidence was expected over a length of almost ten miles and the carriageways, drainage systems and eight bridges were designed to cater for up to 13 feet of settlement.

A feature of the southern part of this section of motorway was the presence of Bunter Sandstone. In many of the cuttings it was encountered during excavation and, not only did it provide an excellent formation, but the material taken out was used both in the construction of embankments and as a sub-base for the carriageways. Additional material of this type was obtained by the Contractor from a major borrow pit alongside the motorway, thereby reducing the amount of construction traffic on the local road network if other sources had been used.

In contrast to the Preston and Lancaster By-passes, a stronger form of carriageway construction was adopted with, in general, a base of 6½ inches of cement-bound granular material overlaid with 3½ inches of dense bituminous macadam. However, in the areas likely to be affected by subsidence, the bituminous material was used for the full depth, to give greater flexibility.

Apart from the Interchanges at the ends of this Section, i.e. immediately north of Thelwall Viaduct and at Bamber Bridge south of Preston, there are seven other junctions with the existing road system of which three required the construction of substantial link roads. Whereas the all-purpose Winwick Link joined the A49 to serve the northern part of Warrington, the motorway-standard South Link and a new section of road

Page 28

* Birmingham-Preston Motorway. Lancashire Section (Preston-Warrington), Progress Reports, August 1962, Ministry of Transport/ Lancashire County Council (Preston Record Office).

at Shevington, north of the town, provided Wigan with full access to the motorway.

The first motorway Service Area in the North West was developed at Charnock Richard between Wigan and Preston. From the experience gained in the operation of Service Areas elsewhere in the country, improved facilities within a better planned layout were introduced.

Whereas progress on both the Preston and Lancaster By-passes had been seriously affected by long periods of heavy rainfall, the memorable freeze-up early in 1963 brought work to a halt for a period of eight weeks. However, due to the considerable efforts of the Contractors, this section of motorway was completed by the summer.

The motorway was already under construction through Cheshire and, in order to ensure that the traffic problems of Warrington would be relieved as soon as possible, arrangements had been made for the early completion of a 1½-mile-long length from the A50 at Lymm to the southern end of the Thelwall Viaduct. The whole length between the A50 and Preston was, therefore, opened to traffic in July 1963[*] with Thelwall Viaduct the longest motorway bridge in use in Britain at that time.

By the early 1980s, a serious situation had developed along the six miles of the M6 between the junction of the M56 and the M62. This heavily trafficked section of motorway had to cater for not only north/south movement between the West Midlands, the North West, and Scotland, but also for east/west traffic between the Merseyside and Manchester Conurbations, wishing to cross the Manchester Ship Canal. With traffic flows regularly up to 140,000 vehicles per day, the dual three-lane carriageways were frequently subject to queues and delays. The comparatively steep approaches to Thelwall Viaduct, and the absence of hard shoulders on the structure, added to the capacity problem. Furthermore, inspections of the Viaduct showed that the deck was suffering from severe chloride contamination brought about by the effects of de-icing salt.

Pell Frischmann Consultants Ltd were appointed by the Department of Transport to carry out a feasibility study into the options for increasing capacity on the section between the two junctions, and to consider the form of treatment necessary to renovate the deck of the Viaduct.

Both on-line and off-line widenings to the east and west of the existing motorway, were investigated. The scheme, which provided for upgrading to dual four-lane carriageways, including the construction of a new viaduct on the east side of the existing, was the subject of a Public Inquiry held in May 1990 and the statutory procedures were completed in August of that year. Following detailed design, tenders were invited and work on the construction of the second viaduct began in January 1993.

The new viaduct, the centrepiece of the widening scheme, accounted for almost half the scheme's cost. The structure, designed to complement its 30-year-old neighbour, was commended by the Royal Fine Arts Com-

* Birmingham-Preston Motorway. Lancashire Section (Preston-Warrington), Official Opening Brochure, 29 July 1963, Ministry of Transport/Lancashire County Council (Preston Record Office).

The new viaduct

mission for embracing advances made in bridge design and construction technology since the early 1960s. The new structure has integral cross-heads and a totally continuous welded plate girder deck which, at 4,500 feet in length, is the longest such structure in the world. The majority of the 26 170-feet-long spans are 1½ times the length of those in the original structure, yet the deck girders are only marginally greater in depth. The piers consist of pairs of seven-feet diameter columns, except at the canal span where solid leaf piers provide the fixity for the deck. All the foundations are piled, the piles being an average 80 feet in length providing a mixture of end bearing into gravels and skin friction into clay. The deck is fixed to the pier nearest its centre point and each end can move by up to 24 inches due to expansion and contraction between temperature extremes. This movement was a major consideration in the design, requiring particular attention during construction, when movement of up to four inches per day had to be accommodated.

In recognising the importance of future maintenance, the design included the provision of an access walkway beneath the full length of the viaduct, with transverse walkways at the mid-point of each span. The spans over water were to be decked out completely.

Traffic management was paramount to the project's overall planning and design. The programme required the construction of the new viaduct, with conventional widening of the existing section of motorway to dual four-lane standards. The new viaduct would temporarily carry all the motorway traffic, whilst the original viaduct was being renovated under a separate contract. In April 1995 the first lane of traffic used the new viaduct and, in the following month it became fully operational, by carrying three lanes in each direction.

The renovation Contract included the complete demolition and reconstruction of the concrete deck; work on the substructures; modifications to the steelwork to reduce the number of expansion joints; the replacement of all bearings; and the installation of maintenance access facilities. The Contractor made the important decision at the outset that all the structural steelwork would remain in place, and that the renovation would be carried out 'half at a time', to enable longitudinal access to be available at deck level, at all times.

Apart from the work on the viaducts, the project entailed the demolition of 14 bridges, sign gantries and retaining walls, and the construction of five over-bridges and five under-bridges, together with other major works.

The renovated viaduct was opened to traffic in December 1996,[*] thereby enabling dual four-lane carriageways, with hard shoulders, to be brought into use throughout the whole of the section between the two junctions.

* 'Thelwall New Viaduct', Official Opening Brochure, 25 July 1995, Highways Agency/ Pell Frischmann Consultants Ltd (Preston Record Office).

3.4   The M6 in Cheshire

In 1955, it was reported that the County Surveyor had carried out some preliminary work on the design of the motorway within Cheshire. Further investigations were undertaken and, in May 1957, representations were made to the Ministry of Transport for the County Council to be appointed as Agents for the whole of the length between the adjoining county boundaries.

The terrain through which the motorway would pass is rolling open countryside, containing many high-quality dairy farms. There were no serious difficulties in producing a free-flowing alignment with long sight-lines, to conform with the highest standards applicable at that time. Farm severance was minimised, and only a few cottages would be directly affected.

The Ministry was minded to employ Consulting Engineers and, in view of the resources which were considered to be necessary in order to meet the programme for construction, it was agreed that the work would be divided into two distinct sections. The Southern Section, between the Barthomley Interchange at the Staffordshire County Boundary and the proposed junction with the A54 at Holmes Chapel, was allocated to the firm of Scott, Wilson, Kirkpatrick & Partners. The County Council was to be responsible for the Northern Section as far as the southern end of the proposed Thelwall Viaduct. The Consulting Engineers were also commissioned to design the bridges on the Northern Section, thereby ensuring that all the bridges in Cheshire were of a similar 'pedigree'.

However, on the basis of the earlier work carried out by the County Surveyor, the preferred route and vertical profile of the whole of the proposed 25-mile length of the dual three-lane motorway were established to the extent that the statutory procedures were then undertaken, and these were completed without undue difficulty.

On the nine-mile Southern Section, only one intermediate interchange was required. At the junction with the A534, it would serve the small but ancient market town of Sandbach, one mile to the west of the motorway. For many years, the town had been a popular stopping place for drivers using the A533, the A534 and the North/South Trunk Road A50. In the design of the motorway, provision was made for a service area to be constructed at a later date.

The Northern Section intersected three major traffic routes along its 15-mile length. Interchanges were to be constructed, therefore, at the

Radway Green Lane Bridge

junctions with the A54 at Holmes Chapel, the A556 near Knutsford, and the A50 near Lymm. There was to be a service area at Knutsford.

The soil surveys indicated clays varying in plasticity, poorly graded sands with some of uniform particle size, silts, peat and rock. As a result of the high water table over much of the area, many of the sands were saturated and the clays were generally soft.

M6/A556 Interchange at Tabley (left) and Dane Viaduct (below)

As a result of these investigations, a major amendment was made to the profile in the vicinity of the valley of the River Dane. This was done in order to reduce, as far as possible, the constructional and subsequent maintenance problems which would have arisen from a deep cutting through saturated sands overlying highly compressible clays.

A total of 61 bridges was required along the 25-mile route, of which two carrying railways over the motorway were the responsibility of British Rail. It was considered to be advantageous to categorise bridges so that within each group they conformed, in principle, to a single design, although, on account of differences in skew and width, variations in detail inevitably arose. Such grouping attracts the consequential advantage of speed of construction and economy. At the same time, it was recognised that it might produce a monotonous uniformity.

Certain bridges, however, required individual treatment. There were 10, of which the largest is a viaduct, 270 feet in length, carrying the motorway over the River Dane. 45 bridges carrying local roads over the motorway, and linking farms severed by it, were grouped into four types.

The foundations of the bridges varied according to the ground conditions, as ascertained from boreholes and, in general, either strip footings, driven piles, or cylinders, were used.

With the exception of the two railway bridges, concrete was used as the principal material of construction. The choice as to whether mass, reinforced, prestressed, pretensioned, post-tensioned, precast or cast in-situ design should be adopted was made after careful consideration, bearing in mind suitability, economy and aesthetics.

Separate Contracts were awarded for the two Sections and work began in June 1961 with a period for completion of 27 months. However, provision was made in the Northern Contract for the early completion, within 24 months, of the 1½-mile section between the A50, at Lymm, and the Thelwall Viaduct. This was to enable the crossing of the Manchester Ship Canal and the River Mersey to be brought into use as soon as the construction of the motorway between Warrington and Preston had been completed.

Lymm Interchange

As expected, the varied geology caused difficulty in carrying out the major part of the earthworks during 1962. The saturated sands could only be handled following extensive dewatering schemes. In the north, the Keuper Marls, which were classified as rock, required blasting techniques in order to carry out bulk as well as trench excavations, particularly in the construction of the Lymm Interchange.

The weather played a major part in the programming of the works when the whole of the site was brought to a standstill during the 'big freeze' in the winter of 1962/63. In order to enable the roadworks to continue, a procedure known as 'Winter Working' was devised by the Contractor and the Resident Engineer, whereby only short lengths of formation, of the order of 50 to 100 feet, were exposed each day. These were covered by plastic sheeting, a three-inch-thick layer of sand, and a layer of sub-base as frost protection. Work was able to continue, albeit slowly.

North of Lymm, the motorway was opened to traffic in July 1963.* A Contract for the construction of 9½ miles of the motorway in North Staffordshire had commenced earlier and the works were completed at the same time as those within Cheshire. The Joint Opening in November 1963 meant that there was then a continuous length of 87 miles of the M6 in use between Birmingham and Preston.

* Birmingham to Preston Motorway (M6), Hanchurch to Lymm Section M6, North Cheshire/South Cheshire/North Staffordshire, Official Opening Brochure, 15 November 1963, Ministry of Transport/ Cheshire & Staffordshire County Councils/Scott, Wilson, Kirkpatrick & Partners (Chester Record Office).

3.5 Preston–Lancaster

The sections of the M6 through Lancashire, which had been completed earlier, provided by-passes of major centres of population. Between Preston and Lancaster, however, the motorway was to have the effect of superseding a substantial length of the A6. Due to its unsatisfactory alignment, and the large number of junctions serving local traffic, congestion and the number of serious accidents had increased to an alarming extent. Completion of this section by the County Council would close the gap in the M6 between Stafford and the northern end of Lancaster By-pass and increase its continuous length to 111 miles. With no intermediate interchanges along its 13½-mile length through an area which is rural in character it was, at that time, to be the longest stretch between junctions on a British motorway.

In order to minimise the extent of farm severance, the selected route was on the eastern side and immediately adjacent to the West Coast Main Line over a length of several miles. This had the effect of requiring an exceptional number of occupation bridges, over the proposed motorway, to connect directly with those which had been provided when the railway was constructed in the 19th century.

Historically, all the north-south modes of transportation through this part of the country had followed a line on the eastern edge of the low-lying coastal plain close to the rising ground of the Pennine foothills. In consequence, therefore, within a corridor of less than half a mile in width south of Garstang there had been a Roman road; the Preston-Lancaster Canal still in use; traces of a turnpike road; more recently, the West Coast Main Line; the A6 by-pass of the town constructed in the 1930s; and in the 1960s there was to be the 'motorway'.

The southern Interchange, at the northern end of Preston By-pass, had to cater for the future M55 serving the Fylde Coast. A conventional two-level layout with a roundabout would not have allowed continuous flow between the two motorways and so a three-level Interchange was designed. It was the first of its kind in Britain and included the impressive 11-span Fylde Junction

Fylde Junction Higher Bridge

Higher Bridge, 1,300 feet in length. The main steel spine girder of box section 14 feet wide by eight feet deep was welded in-situ. Cantilever arms supported a reinforced concrete deck slab 44 feet wide between parapets.

The connection with the southern end of the Lancaster By-pass was to be a 'Trumpet' type of interchange providing full free-flowing movement through to the roundabout junction on A6.

Tenders were invited for three different types of carriageway construction, namely flexible, semi-flexible and rigid. The lowest, which was accepted, provided for 12 miles of the length to have the dual three-lane carriageways constructed in concrete. Concern had been expressed, however, about the performance of concrete roads in Britain both in terms of the design standards which were in use and the adequacy of the available plant. Arrangements were made, therefore, for a visit to be made to the USA by the County Surveyor, as Engineer to the Contract, the Resident Engineer, and representatives of both the Contractor and the cement industry, to examine current practice.

A number of recommendations were made to the Ministry of Transport for approval to be given for changes to be made in the design and specification, one of the most significant being the means of catering for the expansion of the concrete slabs which were to be laid mechanically. It had been found in the USA that, with closer spacing of the contraction joints, it was possible to eliminate expansion joints, which are notoriously difficult to form and maintain. However, the Ministry was not prepared to agree to such a major change but accepted a compromise that the spacing of the expansion joints could be increased to a maximum of 480 feet with contraction joints 40 feet apart.

A semi-flexible pavement construction was to be used at the approaches to the underbridges in order to reduce the effect of any differential settlement, on the slip road carriageways at the interchanges, and in the hard shoulders. The Contract commenced in September 1962 and was scheduled for completion in April 1965.

It was estimated from the soil survey that a considerable proportion of the 3¼-million cubic yards of bulk excavation in the Boulder Clay, sand, silt, peat, shale and gritstone would be unsuitable for use in the construction of embankments. Provision was made, therefore, in the Contract, for importing suitable filling, with a requirement that it should be used in forming shallow embankments, and also in a two-feet-thick layer at the top of all other embankments. The effect was to ensure a more stable and consistent formation below the carriageway construction, than might otherwise have been the case.

The Contractor was able to obtain planning permission to open a borrow pit in a gravel deposit adjacent to the motorway, from which other materials such as selected filling to drain trenches were obtained. Subse-

Concreting train (above) and Snow Hill Lane Bridge (below)

* Preston-Lancaster Motorway M6, Official Opening Brochure, 29 January 1965, Ministry of Transport/Lancashire County Council (Preston Record Office).

† 'M6 in Lancashire' Brochure to mark the completion, January 1965, Lancashire County Council (Preston Record Office).

quently, a landscaped lake was formed, which provided an attractive environmental feature.

It was somewhat ironic that, whereas progress on other contracts in progress during the early months of 1963 was seriously affected by severe frost, these conditions facilitated the excavation and removal of large quantities of unsuitable material, which otherwise would have been very difficult in normal circumstances.

Laid on a sub-base of crusher-run limestone, the 10½-inches thick reinforced concrete carriageway slab was to have a lower layer 7½ inches thick using limestone aggregate and a top layer with a granite aggregate to give a high skid resistance.

The Contractor adopted various methods unique to Britain by employing items of specially imported equipment to form a 'concreting train'. In order that it should operate as efficiently as possible, it was essential that it should be able to move forward at a steady rate. The earthworks, drainage, carriageway base and the majority of the 44 bridges had therefore to be completed by the spring of 1964, to enable the concreting to be carried out during the summer. The concreting train could lay, in a single operation, the full 36-feet width of the slab for one of the carriageways. The maximum length laid in a 12-hour working day was 2,520 feet, a European record at that time.

In January 1965, this section of M6, including the Service Area at Forton, was opened to traffic* and the Snow Hill Lane Bridge carrying a minor road over the motorway at Scorton, received a Civic Trust Award. Apart from a short length of three miles north of Carnforth, the M6 in Lancashire was then complete.† The design and supervision of the construction of the whole of the 62 miles of motorway with interchanges, 174 bridges and 12 miles of link and slip road had been undertaken by the County Council as the Agent Authority for the Minister of Transport.

3.6   Penrith By-pass

The market town of Penrith and the city of Carlisle had long been in need of relief from traffic congestion. Apart from the effect of local traffic movement, they both lay at the junction of major traffic routes. The most important factor, however, was the influence of the London-Carlisle-Glasgow-Inverness Trunk Road A6, passing through the centre of the two urban areas.

In particular, Penrith suffered from the effect of what was known as 'Arnison's narrows', a single lane section of the A6 controlled by traffic lights. A similar constriction existed in the village of Eamont Bridge.

A report was prepared as long ago as 1930 on behalf of the Cumberland and Westmorland County Councils, and the Penrith Urban District Council, which considered eight proposals for by-passing Penrith. However, it was not until July 1962, when through traffic volumes had reached 25,000 vehicles per day, that the Ministry of Transport invited Cumberland County Council, as the Agent Authority, to carry out surveys and prepare a scheme for a by-pass to be designed to dual three-lane carriageway motorway standard. Fourteen different possible lines were considered before the chosen route was finally selected.

The southern starting point of the By-pass at Hackthorpe, where a temporary junction with the A6 was to be built, was determined by the Ministry in conjunction with Scott & Wilson Kirkpatrick & Partners, who had been appointed for the design of a section of the proposed motorway through Westmorland. The topography did not favour a route to the east of the town and it was considered that a western by-pass would provide better opportunities for east-west connections.

Approximately halfway along the eight-mile length of the by-pass, and close to the town, it was proposed that a two-level interchange should be constructed connecting with the A66 Trunk Road. From the interchange, major works were to be carried out on the A66, involving the construction of two miles of new dual two-lane carriageway in each direction, westwards towards Keswick and

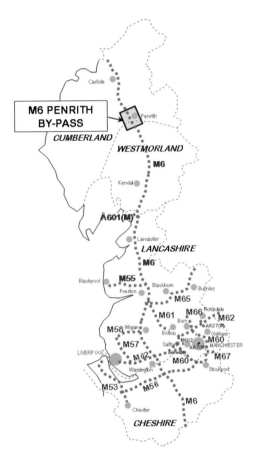

Penrith Interchange

Workington, and eastwards towards Scotch Corner and Middlesbrough.

At Catterlen, a further two-level interchange was to be provided as a northern terminal of the By-pass, with link road connections eastwards to the A6, and westwards to the B5305, the route to Wigton. In due course, the motorway was to be extended northwards from this interchange.

At public meetings, where the proposals were described, the benefits to the town centre which the motorway would bring were recognised. More detailed discussions took place with major landowners which proved to be particularly fruitful. The Lonsdale Estate was affected over the major part of the route and was prepared to consider modifying farm boundaries in such a way that there would be a reduction in the extent to which tenancies would be split by the motorway, thereby reducing the number of accommodation bridges.

In the design, a great deal of care was taken to ensure that the effect on the environment was reduced to the minimum, by ensuring that the horizontal and vertical alignments were coordinated to avoid optical kinks, earthworks were rounded and landscaped by making use of surplus materials, deep cuttings were taken out on a curve to avoid interference with the skyline, and a visibility envelope was prepared to examine the effect of the motorway on the adjoining land, and vice versa.

The statutory procedures were completed without significant problems and the Contract for the construction of the motorway was awarded by Cumberland County Council with a starting date of 1 November 1966 and a period for completion of 27 months.

From the site investigations which had been carried out it was found that Boulder Clay was the predominant soil type. Full-scale trials had been undertaken before the award of the Contract, the information having been made available to all tenderers. Because of its silt content, the clay was very moisture-susceptible but the materials with the higher moisture content were easily distinguished as unsuitable for use in embankment construction,

Because of the possibility of an increase in moisture content, Bunter Sandstone filling 12 inches thick was placed on the top of all embankments immediately below sub-base level to overcome loss of strength, and in cuttings, because of the frost susceptibility of the formation; an early example of the use of what came to be known as a 'capping layer', a practice adopted elsewhere in the construction of other lengths of motorway.

In all, 22 bridges were required. Three were designed by British Rail to carry the West Coast Main Line over the motorway and the new westerly section of the A66. The superstructures were of post-tensioned in-situ concrete, each built alongside the railway track and traversed into position using closed circuit television as a means of controlling the operation.

A variety of differing types of design was used for the other bridges, the most unusual being the Lowther Bridge. The substructure consists

Penrith By-pass
– railway bridge under
construction (left)
and Lowther Bridge
(below)

of four reinforced concrete skew arch ribs springing from bearings on thrust blocks founded on rock. A cast in-situ reinforced concrete slab deck is carried on two spans of Preflex beams.

In general, piled foundations were not necessary. In recognition of the location of the By-pass, on the fringe of the Lake District, masonry facing was used on 13 of the bridges, with the majority in natural stone.

Earthworks started early in February 1967, and although the bulk of the operation was carried out before the end of September, a wet October prevented its completion as programmed. Abnormal weather conditions were experienced in March 1968, which caused further delay, and highlighted the need for additional river protection at bridge sites.

The works were completed three months ahead of schedule and the By-pass was opened to traffic on 7 November 1968.*

* Birmingham-Preston-Penrith-Carlisle Motorway M6, Penrith By-pass Section, Official Opening Brochure, 7 November 1968, Ministry of Transport/Cumberland County Council (Carlisle Record Office).

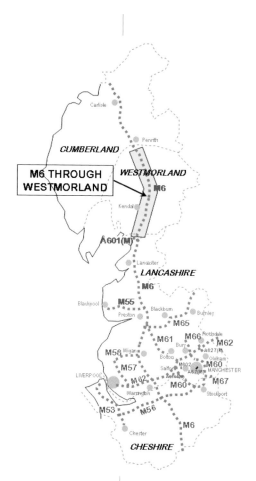

3.7   The M6 through Westmorland

The various small-scale plans proposed during the 1930s for a network of motorways showed a line for a north-south route through Westmorland. It was, however, diagrammatic in that no detailed investigations had been carried out at that time.

The perennial difficulties of communications between Scotland and England because of the weather problems of the existing A6 route over Shap Saddle (approximately 1,390 ft), and keenly felt during the Second World War, led to the concept of an alternative route via Tebay and the Lune Valley. After the war this was taken up by the Ministry of Transport, and the route was surveyed and set out on the ground.

In 1959 a local resident called a meeting in Kirkby Lonsdale to protest at the route on environmental grounds. The unanimous conclusion of the meeting to condemn the route through the Lune Valley was conveyed to the Ministry, who called in Consulting Engineers Scott, Wilson, Kirkpatrick & Partners, 'to consider all possible and practical alternative routes between the end of the Lancaster By-pass and Penrith, and recommend the one to adopt'.

Any route had to deal with an east-west mountain barrier at mid-point that was only relieved by a glaciated valley to the east epitomised by a length near Tebay known as the Lune Gorge. Either use had to be made of this valley or a more direct route had to be found using tunnels and/ or high viaducts. In addition to the use of the Lune Gorge, tunnel routes making use of the Long Sleddale Valley plus the Lowther or Hawerswater Valleys, or along the line of the existing A6 to Shap village were identified: a viaduct route on the line of the A6 was also identified. Numerous alternatives were found south of the mountain barrier, which could be combined with these, resulting in some 30 possibilities to consider. These combinations were discussed in an Interim Report submitted in mid-August 1960.

A number of special studies were undertaken. Aerial photographs viewed stereoscopically reduced the choice of routes to a few in number. Newly established techniques enabled maps to be drawn of probable depths of rock and the extent of various soil formations. An Origin and Destination survey was carried out so that traffic could be assigned to alternative networks.

Traffic on the A6 was frequently brought to a halt by wintry conditions with bad visibility a particular problem. For the first time on a motorway project, a meteorological study was, therefore, undertaken to judge the effects of wind, low temperature, snow and reduced visibility on traffic using the alternative routes.

The Final Report, in two volumes, was submitted by the Consultants in March 1962.* In addition to the matters described above, the Report analysed the results of the various surveys and studies, and how they led to three alternatives for final comparison viz:

- Direct Route
- Killington Route
- Lune Valley Route

They were described in detail, and the effects of the following factors were assessed:

- Weather
- Land Use and Landscaping
- Capital and Maintenance Costs
- Traffic Operating Costs

As a first stage, the Killington Route was compared in detail with the Lune Valley Route, and the conclusion was drawn that the Lune Valley Route was to be ruled out and that, if the chosen route was to pass through the Lune Gorge, then it should be the Killington Route.

The Killington Route was then similarly compared with the Direct Route. The choice here was less clear-cut. The Direct Route was shorter, but its capital cost was greater, due to the use of tunnels. A short single three-lane carriageway in an unventilated tunnel under Hucks Brow was to carry the climbing north-bound carriageway. Further north at the head of Crookdale, twin ventilated two-lane tunnels 6,800 feet long were proposed, one for each two-lane carriageway; a third two-lane tunnel between these was to be added when justified by traffic growth. This central tunnel could then be bi-directional, used only for climbing traffic, or tidal flow.

Emergency crossing places within and outside the tunnels were proposed. However, the total recurrent costs, comprising traffic operating costs, road maintenance costs, and, in the case of the Direct Route, tunnel operating costs, were shown to be less for the Direct Route even after the construction of the third tunnel.

A cost-benefit analysis showed a return of almost nine per cent on the additional cost of the Direct Route. Provided the extra capital was available, the Direct Route was recommended as the best route from long term and strategic points of view.

However,

(a) it was not possible to rank these returns with those from other road schemes for which the additional funds might be used,

(b) the Direct Route was less effective from a weather viewpoint, and

(c) the tunnels placed restrictions on the movement of dangerous goods. For these reasons the Killington Route was selected.

* Lancaster-Penrith Motorway Report on Alternative Routes, Vol.1, March 1962, Ministry of Transport/ Scott, Wilson, Kirkpatrick & Partners (Kendal Record Office).

Separated carriageways

Apart from the terminal interchanges, it was only necessary to provide four junctions with existing roads along the 36 miles of the route.

In carrying out the design, great care was taken to fit the motorway to the landscape, and the designers found that the motorway alignment standards were particularly suited to the terrain, which meant that north-bound traffic would encounter long climbs along certain lengths and desirable constant gradients were achieved in all of these. The reduction of earthworks achieved by stepping carriageways in steep side-long ground was utilised for 2½ miles south of Killington, and for 3½ miles in the Lune Gorge. In the latter case the vertical separation reached 30 feet.*

North of Tebay the carriageways are separated over a distance of 4½ miles, the maximum separation being 800 feet. North of Shap Interchange separation of carriageways occurs over a length of 2½ miles. It was concluded that sheep farming could continue between the carriageways, and sheep 'creeps' were designed along established sheep 'corridors' to facilitate this. Protection from drifting snow for the vulnerable lengths north of Tebay was generally achieved by designing embankments with a minimum height of two feet and cuttings with side slopes flatter than 1 in 6.5.

It was decided to separate surface water and sub-soil drainage, the former being effected by a specially designed channel section, with an in-line graded approach with slotted steel covers to gullies. The latter were buried and comprised standard porous pipes together with filter material designed to prevent clogging from the surrounding soil. In one area north of Dillicar Knott larger, deep intercepting sub-soil drains connected to the motorway drainage system were designed to prevent slips in the steep Boulder Clay slopes.

In order to make use of wet material, and as a result of experience gained from a full-scale trial embankment constructed on the line of the motorway, embankments were designed to be laid in 8½-feet-thick layers separated from one another by drainage layers. In one area of steep sidelong ground deep intercepting sub-soil drains were used above the motorway for additional protection. In pre-determined areas excavation to a vertical face in cuttings was specified to minimise 'suitable' material becoming 'unsuitable', after periods of rain.

Extensive use was made of computer programs in the calculation of horizontal alignment, intersection and merging geometry, and the setting out of horizontal control lines from setting out beacons. For the first time in this country, actual computer print-out was incorporated into contract drawings.

* Design of Lancaster-Penrith Section of M6 Motorway, Paper by Halls/Knowles/McNee, 1969, Scott, Wilson, Kirkpatrick & Partners (Kendal Record Office).

There are 160 structures on this section of the motorway of which 77 are bridges or underpasses. Cost studies led to open abutments being selected generally, so that for standard situations overbridges have three or four spans, but most underbridges have single spans. In one case an overbridge carrying a minor road was designed with three spans rather than four, so as to frame a magnificent early view of the approach to the Lune Gorge for north-bound travellers.

Borrowbeck Bridge

Within a length of 2½ miles in the gorge, eight underbridges were required to carry the motorway, and three to carry the diverted A685. The 73-feet-high Borrowbeck Bridge is close to and 10 feet higher than the stone arch railway viaduct carrying the West Coast Main Line to Glasgow. The central span of the curved motorway viaduct was designed to frame the railway viaduct when viewed from the realigned A685, itself carried on a new curved bridge over Borrow Beck.

The railway line had to be crossed in three places. These were all skew crossings, one having an extreme skew of 70°. Precast reinforced concrete beams square to the tracks were used to minimise temporary works over the railway. For the smaller skews, the free edges followed the skew and a trapezium of reinforced concrete lapped with the precast beams to form a portal construction. For the extreme skew the bridge has beams square to the track throughout, with sections protruding on either side of the motorway construction above.

The location of Service Areas was treated as an environmental as well as an amenity matter. Connecting overbridges were avoided, and sites were selected alternately for north- and south-bound traffic with the two southernmost ones, Burton and Killington, being some distance apart. However, where the carriageways are separated north of Tebay, the Service Areas are opposite one another. All are designed to provide views away from the motorway, and at Killington the Service Area overlooks the Reservoir and is well screened from the motorway by ground contours.

Construction was to be carried out under five separate Contracts. Contract periods allowing for two full winters of earthwork construction were considered essential. The Contract for the section through the Lune Gorge, because of its major structures and large quantities of rock excavation, was given a lead time of 10 months over the other Contracts when tenders for it were invited in October 1966. Construction commenced in October 1967.

Rock face at Jeffrey's Mount

Jeffrey's Mount provided a 'planning' challenge for the Contractor. The A685 was on the line of the M6, and had to be diverted up-hill to the west as an initial task prior to the construction of the motorway itself. Both A685 and M6 had to be excavated to form ledges in the steep rock with the West Coast Main Line immediately below the latter. Pre-splitting techniques were suggested to tenderers as a suitable technique for avoiding overbreak, and to maintain the stability of up-hill slopes or construction. This technique was used extensively and successfully in this location.

In the event, the condition of the exposed rock proved more difficult than could have been anticipated from visual examination of exposed surfaces, and drill-hole results. The adopted solution was to use rock bolting, previously a little known technique. It was used extensively to good effect.

Where the motorway runs close to and above the railway on steep sidelong ground near Dillicar Knott, a safety fence comprising anti-submarine netting fixed to steel rails concreted into the ground was erected prior to commencing the earthworks. It was tested successfully by using a 'runaway' D6 crawler tractor.

Also in the Lune Gorge, site access was very difficult, and a pre-constructed continuous haul road off the motorway alignment was considered to be imperative. Imported rock from a disused quarry was used to supplement the rock excavations through Jeffrey's Mount and around Dillicar Knott at the entrance to the Gorge. The former provided a continuous source of input to a crusher sited nearby. Material from the haul road was subsequently re-excavated to provide material for drainage layers elsewhere.

Bailey and Callendar Hamilton temporary bridges capable of taking 35-ton loads were used where the haul road crossed the River Lune. The 8,300-feet realignment of the A685 was a first priority, and intricate programming was involved in completing this section.

Lune Gorge

The motorway was opened in October 1970[*] with a maximum eleva-
tion of 1,036 feet compared with that of the A6 it replaced, of 1,390 feet.
It received a Civic Trust Award and the following wording appears on a
plaque in a lay-by off the A685 overlooking the Lune Gorge: 'This award
for an outstanding contribution to the appearance of the Westmorland
landscape relates to the 36 miles of M6 Motorway between the Lancaster
and Penrith by-passes.'

From the Interchange at the junction with the A65, it was the
intention to provide a new high-standard dual-carriageway road running
in a north-westerly direction as an improved means of access to South
Lakeland. To be known as the Kendal Link, it was to be an 'all-purpose'
road and not a 'motorway'. In accordance with Ministry policy, the future
maintenance of the boundary fence would, therefore, be the responsibility
of the adjoining landowners.

The road was to pass through a deer park and special deer-proof fences
would be required. Initially, the landowner raised no objection in principle
to the road, but was not prepared to accept responsibility for the fences
which were to be erected as accommodation works, with the cost met by
the Ministry. He, therefore, formally objected at the various stages of the
statutory procedures, which led to other objections by interested parties.
This resulted in the need for a Public Inquiry and, although the objections
were over-ruled in the Minister's decision, it was to be several years before
the Link was opened to traffic.

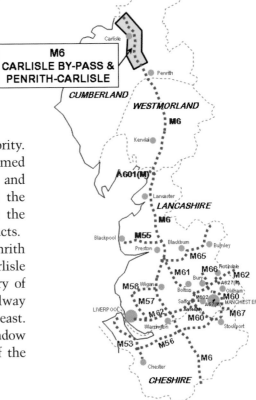

* M6 Motorway
Lancaster By-pass to
Penrith By-pass, Official
Opening Brochure,
23 October 1970,
NWRCU/ Scott, Wilson,
Kirkpatrick & Partners
(Kendal Record Office).

3.8   Carlisle By-pass and Penrith–Carlisle

As these two sections of the M6 were constructed within
the same timescale, they are considered together. The initial survey, preparation and design was undertaken by the
Cumberland County Council as the Minister's Agent Authority.
The North Western Road Construction Unit (NWRCU) was formed
on 1 April 1967. Unlike the County Councils of Cheshire and
Lancashire, Cumberland did not participate and completed the
design and undertook the supervision of construction, with the
County Surveyor acting as Engineer under the various Contracts.

From the two-level interchange at the northern end of Penrith
By-Pass at Catterlen, the selected route for the Penrith to Carlisle
Section was along the valley of the River Petteril, a tributary of
the River Eden. To the west of the West Coast Main Line railway
it was also within the same corridor as the A6 lying to the east.
Passing through an agricultural belt of pasture, arable, meadow
and woodland, the 12-mile route provided excellent vistas of the
Pennine range.

It was proposed that a Service Area would be provided near to the village of Southwaite.

Alternative routes for Carlisle By-Pass were examined both to the east and west of the city, having regard to the alignment of both the A69 to Newcastle, and the A595 linking West Cumberland. However, the existing urban development suggested an eastern route as being preferable, in order to avoid major disruption, although this meant the postponement of improvements to the western approaches to the city.

From a two-level interchange connecting with the A6 at the Golden Fleece, the proposed seven-mile route was to pass through a series of cuttings, and under the A69 where a further two-level interchange was to be provided at Rose Hill. Emerging into the Eden valley, with a down-grade to the river flood plain, distant views of the Scottish Lowlands could be seen. After crossing the river and the line of Hadrian's Wall, the motorway was to terminate north of the city at the Greymoorhill Interchange close to the junction of the Carlisle-Edinburgh Trunk Road A7 with the Carlisle-Glasgow Trunk Road A74.

From this point, it was proposed that the existing A74 should be reconstructed over a length of 4½ miles in order to provide a high standard dual carriageway all-purpose road extending as far as the crossing of the River Esk, approximately one mile south of the Scottish Border. The new 604-feet-long Esk Bridge was to be the latest replacement for the iron structure originally built by Telford and for a more recently constructed reinforced concrete bridge which, each in turn, had proved to be inadequate for the increased traffic needs. Eight other bridges were required in the reconstruction.

There were similar consultation meetings with members of the public and major landowners to those undertaken for Penrith By-pass. Again, the statutory procedures for the motorway were completed without undue difficulty. The only Public Inquiry to be held was in respect of the Southwaite Service Area, when fears were expressed at the possibility of intrusion by way of noise and lighting.

A number of advance works contracts were undertaken, the most significant being the Low Hurst Railway Bridge designed by British Rail to carry the West Coast Main Line over the motorway at the northern end of the Penrith to Carlisle Section. East of the City, two other bridges were constructed in advance, to carry the motorway over the Skipton-Carlisle and the Newcastle-Carlisle Lines. Other advance works involved drainage and earthworks, including a surcharged embankment built on the alluvium of the Eden flood plain.

Carlisle By-pass.
Rosehill Interchange.

With a population of 75,000 in the City, priority was given to the construction of the Carlisle By-pass Section, in order to provide early traffic relief. Work on the main Contract began in December 1968.

Tenders had been invited for alternative forms of construction for the dual three-lane carriageways, namely 'flexible', 'composite' and 'rigid'. The lowest tender, which was accepted, allowed for composite construction but, in the event, the Contractor offered to provide a flexible pavement at no extra cost which resulted in the whole of the M6 through Cumberland having this type of carriageway.

The designed profile had aimed at a balance of cut and fill in carrying out the earthworks, having regard to the disposal of unsuitable material. In a similar manner to the practice adopted in the construction of Penrith By-pass, a 12-inch-thick 'capping layer' of Bunter Sandstone was to be provided below the sub-base.

Apart from those constructed in advance, a further 19 bridges were required, the most significant being the eight-span 720-feet-long structure carrying the motorway over the River Eden. Preflex beams composite with a reinforced concrete deck permitted rapid construction.

Where suitable clays and sandstones were encountered at economic depths, the structures were supported on strip footings, otherwise foundations were piled. Wide use was made of Universal beams composite with reinforced concrete decks of up to five spans, carried on piers, bank seats and, in some cases, sloped abutments. The By-pass was opened to traffic in December 1970.[*]

A separate Contract was awarded for the A74 Reconstruction and work had started in September 1969 with provision for completion of the Greymoorhill Interchange by the same date as the opening of the By-pass.

Meanwhile, in March 1969, work had begun on the main Contract for the 12-mile-long Penrith to Carlisle Section which was to be constructed to similar standards.

The Boulder Clay was found to have a high silt content, thereby making it more susceptible to the adverse effect of wet conditions. The higher pore water pressures made it necessary to make extensive use of Bunter Sandstone as imported fill, together with the provision of additional drainage. A volcanic intrusion known as the Cleveland-Armathwaite Dyke was encountered, as expected, but caused no particular difficulty as the rock was largely fragmented.

In addition to the advance railway bridge at Low Hurst, 19 other bridges were required. Apart from the use of precast concrete pre-tensioned beams, many of the bridges are of trapezoidal steel box construction. During the design and construction period, considerable development and changes in the design 'rules' took place, most notably leading to modifications to the steel box structures, following the Merrison Report. This

* M6 Motorway Carlisle By-pass, Official Opening Brochure, 15 December 1970, Department of the Environment/ Cumberland County Council (Carlisle Record Office).

Monks Lane Bridge,
south of Carlisle

* M6 Motorway
Penrith-Carlisle Section
and Trunk Road A74
Reconstruction, Official
Opening Brochure,
1 July 1971, Department
of the Environment/
Cumberland County
Council (Carlisle Record
Office).

resulted in additional diaphragms and stiffeners being inserted in to some of the bridges at a late stage of construction.

The opening of the Penrith to Carlisle Section in July 1971 marked the completion of the M6 through the North West Region. Together with the dualling of 4½ miles of the A74 north of Carlisle, the route stretched from the Staffordshire boundary to the Scottish Border, a length of 155 miles.*

4   The Manchester Outer Ring Road M60

4.1   The Stretford–Eccles By-pass (M62/M63) and Carrington Spur A6144(M)

Although the completion of the M6 was a priority, the Lancashire County Council had given early attention to the needs of the other parts of the County where there were serious traffic problems. The 1949 Road Plan had identified the western sector of a proposed Manchester Outer Ring Road as one of the Express Routes to be constructed as a motorway, to bypass Stretford/Eccles, and to serve the large Trafford Park industrial area.

It would also relieve the Barton Swing-Bridge which carried the busy A575 across the Manchester Ship Canal and where serious traffic delays occurred when the bridge was closed to allow shipping movements. Therefore, the main feature was to be a high-level bridge carrying the motorway over the Canal.

As the A575 was a Principal Road, for which the County Council was the Highway Authority, the By-pass was eligible for a 75 per cent Government grant and, in 1953, it was included in the programme of grant-aided schemes.

In the same year a nearby steelworks was having difficulty in finding a disposal site for its slag and the County Council, therefore, made arrangements for this to be tipped and compacted on the site of the south approach embankment of the proposed bridge. A Public Inquiry into the proposal had been held, but the work was actually carried out in advance of the Minister's decision. In that a favourable decision might not have been forthcoming, the County Council undoubtedly took a risk in proceeding with this work at such an early stage. It would, however, have been economic to re-excavate the embankment and move the material to another site, instead of paying the cost of importing from other sources. The not unreasonable County Council's view was that the Minister was certain to give his assent and, by using some 400,000 tons of 'free' material, a substantial saving was achieved. This embankment, which was completed at insignificant cost, was the first physical step in the construction of a motorway anywhere in Britain – even in advance of Preston By-pass!

With four intermediate interchanges, giving an average spacing of only 1¼ miles, this was probably the first urban motorway in the country.

Standards for such roads had not yet been determined but, as some sections of the route passed through residential areas, the need to reduce land acquisition to a minimum was recognised in the designs which were adopted.

The County Surveyor's traffic forecasts indicated that dual three-lane carriageways were needed, but the Ministry would only countenance the issue of a grant for a dual two-lane scheme. The County Council, therefore, had no alternative but to proceed accordingly.

The construction of the five-mile long By-pass, which included a total of 22 bridges, started in April 1957 when work began on the first of several contracts.*

Although shorter than Thelwall Viaduct, the 2,425-feet-long, 18-span High Level Bridge was similar in many respects. With a maximum gradient on the approaches of 1 in 25 and rising to a height of some 100 feet above the level of the Canal, the piers varied in height from 30 to 80 feet above ground level.

The superstructure consisted of eight steel plate girders of riveted construction carrying a reinforced concrete deck. The major part of the splicing of the girders was carried out prior to lifting them into position.

The length of the main span crossing the Canal was 310 feet comprising two cantilevers each of 77 feet 6 inches carrying a simply supported 155-feet-long centre suspended span. The anchor arm spans were 175 feet long.

On the south side of the Canal, sections of the anchor arm and cantilever girders were lifted individually and supported on temporary trestles. Regrettably, the trestles formed of tubular steel scaffolding collapsed under the load and several lives were lost. Military trestling was used in subsequent operations.

A different method was employed on the north side in that each anchor arm and cantilever girder was spliced on the ground and lifted into position on the main pier. The steelwork sub-Contractor had been experiencing serious difficulties due to the demands of a militant group of his steel erectors, to the extent that he was forced into liquidation. Four of the girders had been erected and jacks were in position to enable fine adjustments to be made in line and level, in order that bracings could be fitted.

The main Contractor appointed a replacement sub-Contractor but, unfortunately, the arrangements for the 'hand-over' proved to have been unsatisfactory. A jacking operation was undertaken which caused the girders to fall over and several fatalities occurred.

The Inquest which followed not only examined the cause of death but also considered the responsibilities of the various parties involved in the Contract. In that respect, it was a 'test case' and led to some of the early Health and Safety legislation affecting the construction industry.

* Manchester Outer Ring Road Stretford-Eccles Motorway By-pass, incorporating Barton High Level Bridge, Inauguration Ceremony Brochure, 10 April 1957, Lancashire County Council (Preston Record Office).

Neither the County Council as the Employer, nor the County Surveyor as the Engineer under the Contract, were held to be in any way responsible for the accidents.

Whereas in the case of the Thelwall Viaduct, the suspended span girders were lifted into position using a crane on the tip of the cantilevers, at Barton a Bailey bridge launching nose was used.

Barton High Level Bridge. Launching suspended span.

The accidents caused a delay in the completion of the By-pass. In one respect the delay was fortuitous. Steelworks slag from a different source to that used on the south approach to the Bridge had been utilised in the construction of embankments for the northern section of the By-pass. Prior to the final surfacing being carried out, it was found that the carriageway formation had 'heaved' and investigations showed that this was due to the ingress of water causing the particular slag to swell. During the period of delay, the effect dissipated and a stable formation was achieved before the surfacing was completed. Also along this section, mining subsidence of up to twelve feet was expected and provision was therefore made for the decks of the bridges carrying the motorway over the Bridgewater Canal to be capable of being jacked-up to maintain the required headroom.

Barton High Level Bridge

At the Public Inquiry objections had been made to the northern terminal roundabout at Worsley, because of the perceived detrimental effect on the surroundings. On completion of the work, however, the County Council received a Civic Trust Award for the design and landscape treatment. When the By-pass, at that time numbered M62, was opened in October 1960* it represented another 'first' for Lancashire – the first 'County motorway' in Britain, in that the County Council was the Highway Authority, not the Minister of Transport.

In the 1970s, the Ring Road south of the Eccles Interchange was redesignated M63, with this interchange numbered as Junction 1.

The Carrington Industrial Complex lies to the west of the motorway, and on the south side of the Ship Canal. For many years, serious concern had been expressed at the movement of heavy goods vehicles, some

* Manchester Outer Ring Road Stretford-Eccles Motorway By-pass, incorporating Barton High Level Bridge, Official Opening Brochure, 21 March 1961, Lancashire County Council (Preston Record Office).

Carrington Spur

carrying hazardous substances, on residential roads in Ashton-on-Mersey, Flixton, Davyhulme and West Sale.

It was, however, February 1986 before work began on a Contract for the construction of a 1½-mile length of motorway, known as the Carrington Spur.

In order to provide a connection to the M63, it was necessary to construct an interchange, which included Hallam Farm Bridge crossing over the heavily-trafficked live motorway. The 100-feet-long single-span precast prestressed concrete beam and slab bridge was to be supported on a reinforced concrete substructure on piled foundations.

Designated as the new 'Junction 6' of the M63, the works also included a link road running parallel to it on each side. The provision of additional lanes north of this junction was the first stage in the upgrading to dual three-lane carriageway standard.

Ground conditions along the line of the Spur were poor and nearly 50,000 cubic yards of peat was removed and replaced with selected fill. Elsewhere vertical drains were installed under a two-feet-thick drainage blanket to accelerate consolidation of the alluvium flood plain.

Special measures were taken to protect and monitor the movement of a high pressure processed-fuel pipeline which crossed the site at five locations. This collected refined petroleum products from refineries at Milford Haven and Fawley for distribution throughout the Midlands and the Manchester area.

A two-span continuous composite steel and concrete bridge crossing the River Mersey, a footbridge and an underpass, together with steel sign gantries, were also required.

The design was undertaken by the Greater Manchester County Council, and the supervision of the works by the Major Highways Consortium on behalf of Trafford Borough Council and the Department of Transport.

The Spur was opened to traffic as the A6144(M) in October 1987,[*] 10 months ahead of schedule. Although a single carriageway motorway, with two-way traffic, it was intended that, in due course, it would be extended to the south and west and upgraded to meet the requirements of future development.

The second stage in the upgrading of the M63 involved the widening and improvement of the section between Junctions 1 and 3. This included the Barton High Level Bridge which, by the early '80s, was carrying traffic flows of 75,000 vehicles per day, some 50 per cent in excess of the road's design capacity. Hold-ups at peak times were common due, in part, to the restraint imposed on heavy vehicles by the relatively steep approaches.

[*] Carrington Spur A6144(M) – M63 Improvement Stage 3, Opening Brochure, 18 October 1987, Trafford Metropolitan Borough Council/ Department of Transport (Preston Record Office).

In 1967 the Ring Road had been designated a 'Trunk Road' and the Department of Transport appointed Mott Hay and Anderson, Consulting Engineers, to undertake the design and the supervision of the widening of the Bridge.

In order to provide dual three-lane carriageways and hard shoulders, an additional welded steel plate girder was to be erected on each side of the existing deck. These were to be supported on new rectangular hollow reinforced concrete piers carried on large diameter bored piles.

The original nine-inch-thick reinforced concrete deck was to be totally replaced and be continuous across the full width of the bridge. Additional cross bracing was to be installed between the existing central girders to provide continuity.

The design and supervision of work on the other bridges in the Interchange at Peel Green (Junction 2) was undertaken by Ward Ashcroft and Parkman. This firm of Consulting Engineers was also responsible for the road works.

The reconstruction of Barton Old Hall Railway Bridge, carrying the Manchester–Liverpool Line over the M63, was also necessary, and this was carried out by British Rail Engineering.

The High Level Bridge is a major crossing of the Ship Canal and there are few suitable alternative routes available. The Contract, which was awarded in March 1986, included a series of detailed traffic management schemes. These were aimed at maximising the use of the motorway during the construction, whilst at the same time allowing the Contractor the necessary possession and lane closures to carry out the very complex and difficult work, which was completed in December 1988.

The next stage in the upgrading of the motorway was the widening and improvement between Junctions 3 and 5, for which the design and supervision of construction was undertaken by Parkman Consulting Engineers.[*]

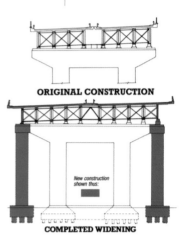

ORIGINAL CONSTRUCTION

New construction shown thus:

COMPLETED WIDENING

Barton High Level Bridge – widening

* Barton High Level Bridge M63 Improvement: Junction 1-3, Formal Opening Brochure, 20 December 1988, Department of Transport/Mott Hay and Anderson/Ward Ashcroft and Parkman (Preston Record Office).

4.2 Sale Eastern and Northenden By-pass (M63) and Sharston By-pass (M56/M63)

The construction of the section of the M62 Lancashire-Yorkshire Motorway between Worsley and Whitefield had formed, in effect, part of the proposed

Manchester Outer Ring Road, as a north-easterly extension of the Stretford Eccles By-pass. Progress around the southern and eastern parts of the periphery of the conurbation was, however, much slower, with programming largely influenced by financial restraints. The principle of constructing a series of local by-passes to form elements of the Ring Road was, therefore, adopted. Sale Eastern and Northenden By-pass, together with Sharston By-pass, were such schemes.

Prior to 1967, the design of the Sale Eastern and Northenden By-pass was the responsibility of the three Highway Authorities through whose areas the road would pass, namely the Lancashire and Cheshire County Councils, together with Manchester City Council, which appointed G. Maunsell and Partners as Consulting Engineers.

When the Ring Road became a Trunk Road, responsibility was transferred to the North Western Road Construction Unit of the Department of the Environment, with the design of the four miles of the route from Stretford to north of the Glazebrook–Godley Line in Gatley shared by the Lancashire and Cheshire Sub-Units and by G. Maunsell & Partners.

The obvious route for the By-pass was through the mainly undeveloped corridor of the River Mersey Valley. Several possible alternatives were investigated before the decision was taken to adopt an alignment along the southern edge of the Valley, skirting the residential development. This route was found to be the most economic and one which kept to the minimum the disturbance both to property and to the recreational areas in the Valley, consistent with the need for a standard of design appropriate to a motorway.

From the end of the Stretford-Eccles By-pass, the motorway would cross over Chester Road A56, the River Mersey, the Bridgewater Canal and the Manchester–Altrincham Line. Continuing in a south-eastwards direction, it would be generally on embankment through to the crossing of Princess Parkway, a major radial route which had been built to near urban motorway standards, and to serve the City of Manchester.

The main engineering problem in deciding to build a motorway through the Mersey Valley – partly across the actual flood plain of the river – was the need to keep above the flood level. In order to achieve this, the motorway had to be built mainly on high embankment with only short lengths in cutting.

The flood plain itself is made up of post-glacial materials such as normally consolidated alluvium and terrace gravels. Below the recent deposits, the 'solid' rocks of the Triassic system were found at depths of from less than 20 feet to more than 60 feet. The measures necessary to deal with these recent deposits were important features of the project: on the one hand how to use them as a source of fill and, on the other, how to construct an embankment up to 40 feet high without causing failure either to the embankment or to the very weak alluvium below.

In addition there was the problem of finding some two million cubic yards of material which would need to be imported. If it was brought in from sources outside the site, it would result in large numbers of heavy lorries transporting material along already congested local roads. It was proposed, therefore, that material for the embankments should be excavated from an area between the motorway and the River Mersey known as the Sale Ees, and the use of this material led to substantial savings in cost. The excavation was to be permanently filled with water from the river, with the intention that the Greater Manchester Metropolitan County Council and Trafford Borough Council would develop it for recreational purposes. It would also provide the Mersey and Weaver River Unit with increased flood storage capacity.

On Sale Ees, large scale laboratory tests showed that a skeletal system of vertical sand drains would accelerate settlement of the motorway embankment and reduce both the amount of temporary overfilling and the period for which it would be required. An advance contract was carried out:

(i)   to provide this 'skeleton' and install the system of piezometers necessary to measure the pressure of the groundwater in the soil beneath the embankment, and

(ii) to control the rate of its construction so that there was no risk of a slip occurring in the soil beneath.

Another technical problem inherent in planning a motorway through the valley was the need for repeated crossings of the river. The route chosen on the south side involved fewer points of crossing than any alternative but, even so, it crossed the course of the river five times. However, by diverting a loop of the river near Didsbury Golf Course, clear of the motorway, the need for two of these crossings was removed with a considerable saving in cost. This diversion was carried out in advance of the motorway construction by the Mersey and Weaver River Authority.

Three interchanges were required, at Chester Road (A56) in Stretford, at the Hardy Lane Extension in Sale, and at Princess Parkway (A5103). The By-pass required the construction of 35 bridges, various culverts, retaining walls and a piled raft. The principal bridges forming the Princess Parkway Interchange were of either single or double spine box post-tensioned structures. The requirement that there should be no bridge piers in the central reserve of Princess Parkway, resulted in the main spans of the crossing being of the order of 115 feet.

The Palatine Road Viaduct has eight and nine spans carrying the west- and east-bound carriageways of the motorway over Palatine Road and the River Mersey.

Princess Parkway
Interchange

The first major contract, undertaken in advance, included the construction of two slip roads and a fly-over bridge in the Chester Road Interchange, and bridges over the Mersey Overflow Channel. Work began in May 1971 and this was followed by the main Contract, in February 1972.

Meanwhile advance works for the construction of Sharston By-pass had also begun. This scheme, designed by Howard Humphreys & Sons, Consulting Engineers, was primarily designed to relieve Sharston by removing traffic from several major traffic routes passing through the area. It was, however, an important element in the further development of the M63.

The first of the two main Contracts began in January 1972. The most significant feature was the construction of the major Kingsway Interchange which provides a junction between M63, M56 and the A34 (Kingsway), a main radial route between central Manchester and the South.

To the west of the Interchange a half-mile section of motorway completed the Sale Eastern and Northenden By-pass and, to the east, the M63 was extended for a length of over a mile to a junction with the A560.

The major part of Sharston By-pass, however, connecting with the Bowdon-Wythenshawe Section of the M56, formed the eastern end of that motorway. The western half of this two-mile length of the By-pass was constructed under a further Contract extending from a two-level interchange at the junction with Sharston Road. Works in this contract began some 12 months later to enable the re-siting of various business premises, mostly shops.

Extensive bridge engineering was involved, much of it concentrated at the Kingsway Interchange. The majority of the 27 bridges required, had to be designed as 'one-off' structures because of the restricted nature of the site, with little scope for standardisation.

A major bridge was needed to carry the dual-carriageway Kingsway, widened by slip roads, over the M63. It had to be constructed on the line of Kingsway with as little disruption as possible to the heavy commuter traffic. This was achieved by designing and constructing the four-span bridge in separate 75-feet and 40-feet widths. The decks are continuous in-situ reinforced concrete slabs, carried on precast reinforced concrete columns which were, in turn, placed in five-feet diameter cased holes on top of piles. The abutments are formed by concrete faced contiguous reinforced concrete bored piles. This method of construction obviated the need to complete the full depths of general excavation before completion of the structure, with consequent considerable temporary support works.

A 10-span viaduct was designed to carry the south-east slip road over the motorway, the west-south and west-north slip roads, and Kingsway. It is a continuous trapezoidal spine box girder composite with an RC deck slab which cantilevers each side of the box. The bridge is on a horizontal curve of a radius of 500 feet, and the deck is supported on single rectangular reinforced concrete cantilever columns with flared heads, enlarged below ground and supported on spread footings. The end supports are three-leg reinforced concrete skeletal abutments with cantilevered reinforced concrete return wing walls.

The bridge carrying the M56 over the Cheadle Link Line, and the M63 over the Glazebrook-Godley Line and the eastbound carriageway of the M56, both have a skew of 61°. The decks are of reinforced concrete, composite with steel Universal Beams spanning square between the abutments and pier in the centre, and steel box girders in the triangular edge areas.

The bridge carrying the Styal Line over the motorway was designed by British Rail and constructed under their supervision. This is a three-span continuous prestressed concrete through girder bridge with eight-feet-deep edge beams. The complete deck was built alongside the track and launched sideways into position in a single track possession, the excavation under the bridge taking place subsequently.

The Merrison Committee's Interim Report on box girder bridges was published after the bridge designs had been completed and the Contract was about to go out to tender. This required a complete reappraisal of the steel box girder bridges resulting in some design modifications which were completed by the contract starting date.

The high motorway embankments adjacent to the bridge carrying the M63 over the Glazebrook-Godley Line are situated in the flood plain, where a layer of alluvium was found in the initial soil survey at depths varying from five to 15 feet. Preliminary studies indicated that the placing of embankments over 20 feet in height would require extra care. Piezometers to control the rate of construction were installed under the embankments and provision was made for varying rates of placement fill. The fill material used in the embankment up to flood level, about 10 feet in height, was free draining and, above that, pulverised fuel ash (PFA) was used as a lightweight filling. Approximately 750,000 cubic yards of material was excavated and placed in embankments, and some 550,000 cubic yards of material was imported as filling.

The Sale Eastern and Northenden By-pass was opened to traffic in September 1974. The M63 section of Sharston By-pass, together with the Kingsway Interchange, was, however, completed in January 1974 and the remainder in May 1975.[*]

* Sale Eastern and Northenden By-pass and Interchange with Sharston By-pass M56/M63, Opening Brochure, March/September 1974, NWRCU/G Maunsell & Partners/ Howard Humphreys (Chester Record Office).

4.3   Stockport East–West By-pass (M63)

By September 1974, the completion of Sale Eastern and Northenden By-pass, together with Sharston By-pass, had extended the M63 as far as Cheadle Heath. The need for its continuation, therefore, by the early construction of the 2½-mile-long Stockport East-West By-pass, became increasingly important, not only as part of the Manchester Outer Ring Road but also as a means of relieving the A560 within the town.

L.G. Mouchel and Partners, Consulting Engineers, were appointed by the Department of Transport to undertake its design and the subsequent supervision of construction.

From Cheadle Road, the proposed By-pass was to pass under the slip road connecting it to the A560, and continue alongside a sewage disposal works, before passing under a railway line and over the River Mersey. It then ran close to the Glazebrook-Godley Railway Line, and through disused sidings to a two-level interchange at Travis Brow, with connections to the A6.

Continuing under two of the arches of the viaduct which carries the Manchester-Crewe Main Line, and the A6, it was to pass through the site of a former railway station before crossing the River Tame.

The By-pass was to terminate at a two-level interchange at the junction of Tiviot Way, the A560, and Brinnington Road, Portwood.

A total of 13 bridges and three pedestrian subways was required. The bridge carrying the Cheadle Exchange Railway Line over the By-pass was to be a four-span reinforced concrete structure designed, and the construction supervised, by British Rail. The River Mersey Bridge was designed with spans of 50 feet, 100 feet and 50 feet, and a continuous post-tensioned prestressed concrete superstructure, at a 45° skew.

The route of the By-pass occupied part of the bed of the River Mersey, which it was necessary to divert between retaining walls. On the north side, the wall was to be 200 feet long and 40 feet high and on the south side, 500 feet long and 25 feet high.

The scheme for the dual three-lane carriageway By-pass was the subject of a Public Inquiry in 1977. A favourable decision enabled work to start in June 1979 on the first of two Contracts, followed by the second in February 1980.

Large areas of land required for the By-pass had been cleared by Stockport Borough Council under slum-clearance provisions. The works involved the demolition of over 100 houses and shops, 18 industrial premises, five public houses, a petrol station and three car showrooms.

The construction of the By-pass through the urban area entailed a number of unusual features.

Some 35,000 cubic yards of sewage sludge from the works at Cheadle Heath had to be removed to a site at Altrincham.

Passing under the railway viaduct, with Travis Brow Interchange in the background

St Mary's Church and School are immediately north and about 80 feet above the level of the By-pass, which is in a deep cutting at that point. The lower 50 feet is in sandstone rock and the soft ground above it is retained by a contiguous piled brick-faced wall held by ground anchors.

East of Lancashire Hill and in order to minimise the land-take, the By-pass is contained within reinforced-earth retaining walls, with precast concrete facings.

The Main Line Railway Viaduct is a dominant feature within the centre of the town. Designed by George Watson Buck, it was completed in 1840 and is reputed to be the largest brick-built viaduct in the country. As the By-pass was designed to pass through two of the spans in shallow cutting, it was necessary to underpin the foundations of one of the piers in order to ensure adequate support.

Major service diversions were required, and much of this work had a considerable influence on the construction sequence. A6 is a main traffic artery and its importance was recognised by a requirement in the relevant Contract, that it must be kept open at all times. It was necessary for the existing Wellington Road Bridge, carrying the A6, to be replaced and a temporary bridge was constructed, which was also used for diverted services.

The carriageway construction in the western of the two Contracts is a continuous reinforced concrete pavement, except over the River Mersey Bridge. Elsewhere, the carriageways are of conventional flexible construction with a wearing course of hot-rolled asphalt.

The By-pass was completed and opened to traffic in July 1982.*

* Stockport East-West By-pass, Opening Brochure, 30 July 1982, Department of Transport/ L.G. Mouchel and Partners (Chester Record Office).

4.4   Portwood to Denton (M63/M66)

The four-mile Portwood to Denton Section of the Manchester Outer Ring Road was the penultimate length to be constructed.

The firm of Parkman Consulting Engineers was appointed by the Department of Transport to undertake the design and subsequent supervision of the construction.

Public Consultation into the proposals was held in February 1977. The only alternative put forward had been assessed previously, when it had been found that it did not have many of the advantages of the scheme under consideration.

A Public Inquiry was held in July 1982 and modifications, some of which were introduced to overcome objections, were considered at a further Public Inquiry in October 1985. The Scheme involved the extension of the M63 from Portwood to Brinnington, the construction of a section of the M66 from Brinnington to Denton, and a by-pass of part of the A560. At the time, that part of the Outer Ring Road on the eastern side of the Conurbation was numbered M66, as a southern extension of the Bury Easterly By-pass.

Following a favourable decision, a Contract was awarded in 1986 and work commenced between Brinnington and Denton in September 1986 and, on the other length, in January 1987.

Apart from the completion of the Interchange at Portwood and the building of bridges for the Denton Interchange, the Contract required the construction of Brinnington Interchange. This was to connect with not only the A6017, Ashton Road, but also the A560 by-pass. In addition it was designed to allow for the future connection of the proposed A6(M), Stockport North-South By-pass.

A total of 16 bridges and two subways was required. The most significant, and spectacular, is the new Brinnington Railway Bridge which was designed, and the construction supervised, by British Rail. It was constructed alongside the track and moved into position during a weekend closure of the line. The Warren-girder steel bridge is the largest single-span structure carrying full British Rail traffic to be built by this method. Close by, a four-span bridge was to be provided to carry the Lingard Lane/Brinnington Road over the motorway.

Over 3½ million cubic yards of ex-cavation was carried out in cuttings, of which less than one third was used in the building of embankments, the major-ity of the remainder being utilised in landscaping treatment.

A section of the River Tame was diverted to a new alignment, and a large three-span bridge was constructed to carry the motorway over the river.

In the crossing of the Goyt valley, the river was diverted to the south, in order to improve the appearance of the area and simplify construction. The former course of the river was back-filled.

Brinnington Interchange and Brinnington Railway Bridge

The linked subways accommodated a diverted public footpath under the M63 and the A560 By-pass. It provided a main pedestrian route between the recreational areas within the two valleys.

Major drainage works were required, including the construction of a 78-inch-diameter culvert discharging into the diverted River Goyt, and tunnelling under Welkin Road. A twin 30-inch-diameter inverted syphon carries a watercourse under the M66.

The complex nature of the project involved the construction of a combination of 2½-mile lengths of both dual three-lane and dual two-lane carriageways of the motorway. In addition, two miles of all-purpose road and some four miles of link road were also required.

The section of motorway was opened to traffic in April 1989.*

* Manchester Outer Ring Road M63/M66, Portwood to Denton, Opening Brochure, 28 April 1989, Department of Transport/Parkman Consulting Engineers (Chester Record Office).

4.5 Denton–Middleton

In 1976 the firm of L.G. Mouchel & Partners, Consulting Engineers, was appointed to design the scheme for the long-awaited final section of the Manchester Outer Ring Road. Between December 1978 and August 1980 a Public Consultation exercise was carried out. Although a line had been protected by the Local Authorities in the area since the 1960s, several local variations were also submitted for consideration.

A Public Inquiry was held during 1986-87 and the line was finally determined in 1988. Following a further Public Inquiry in 1991-92 into the Side Road and Compulsory Purchase Orders, the statutory procedures were completed in 1993.

The 10-mile section of motorway extends from the M67/M60/A57 Interchange at Denton to the M60/A576 Interchange at Middleton. The route passes through a wide variety of landscapes, much of it urban in character. There were to be four interchanges with the A635 west of Ashton, A62 at Hollinwood, A663 Broadway and a partial junction with the A664 Rochdale Road. The existing Interchanges at Denton and Middleton were to be converted to full movement operation.

After considering various options, it was decided to separate the work into four major roadworks Contracts and several large advance works contracts.

The southern section of the route passes through one of three reservoirs at Audenshaw. To replace the water storage capacity lost to North West Water, a 20-mile-long water main was laid in advance, from the Goyt valley in Derbyshire to feed the remaining two reservoirs.

Another significant water supply to the Manchester area is provided by a pipeline from Haweswater in the Lake District. The route of the Ring Road crosses this pipeline at several locations in the Moston/Blackley/Audenshaw area. Realigning the road to avoid it would have required the demolition of additional residential properties. It was decided, therefore, to divert the pipeline.

The route crosses four railway lines radiating from Manchester. One of these required an overbridge in the Ashton Moss area, remote from public roads. It was possible to arrange access to the site for a separate contract to be completed before the roadworks Contract started.

Two major drainage outfalls were laid in advance, the most significant being two miles in length, discharged into the River Medlock. The topography of the area and the profile of the motorway, in deep cutting, required a tunnel over half a mile long.

In June 1993 work on the first major Contract began. This involved the widening of the dual two-lane Middleton Link M66, which had been constructed in 1970/71, at the same time as the Lancashire-Yorkshire Motorway M62.

The junction of this one-mile length of M66 with the M62 was designed as a three-level interchange. The M62 was to be at the top level, the M66 at the bottom level, and a roundabout with connecting slip roads at the mid level.

At the southern end of the Link, the junction with Middleton Road, A576, a large roundabout had been constructed. Provision had been made for the M66 ultimately to be taken under it and extended to the south, as the first part of the north-east quadrant of the Ring Road.

The 'upgrading' Contract included the substantial reconstruction of the Link, widening to provide dual four-lane carriageways, and a new bridge over the River Irk.

The Contract was completed in February 1996.

Meanwhile, in April 1995, work on the largest of the Contracts had begun. It involved the construction of a four-mile length of motorway with dual three- and four-lane carriageways between the Denton Interchange and the River Medlock, within a contract period of three years.

The most unusual feature was the construction of a 1,200-yard length of earth dam across the Audenshaw Reservoir to replace that section to be breached by the motorway. The site investigation had shown that there would be an adequate quantity of excavated clay available, to form the dense clay core of the dam. This was not forthcoming and severe delays occurred until suitable material was found beneath the 'floor' of the redundant part of the reservoir.

Major lengths of permanent road diversion, link roads, and the construction of seven bridges was necessary, including a 400-feet-long bridge over the Manchester-Leeds Canal and another of 360 feet over the Ashton Canal.

Also in 1995, a further Contract was awarded for various works on the remaining length of the project. In effect, an 'advanced contract', in that it involved the diversion and bridging of major radial road and rail routes serving Manchester. The task was further complicated by the need to maintain all traffic flows on these important commuting routes.

Audenshaw Reservoir dam.

It included a number of structures, for example, a bridge carrying the Manchester-Oldham Line over the motorway, where the deck was placed during a 72-hour possession of the track. Close by, a new entrance had to be constructed, and platforms moved at Hollinwood Station. It was also necessary to divert a length of the Rochdale Canal.

Before awarding the final Contract, to complete the motorway, the Highways Agency, acting on behalf of the Department of Transport, gave careful consideration to the Form of Contract. Concern had been expressed that, in carrying out the first three Contracts, final costs and completion dates were overrunning. Among the various reasons for such a situation was criticism of the '5th Edition' of the ICE Conditions of Contract, which had been used. It was decided, therefore, that a 'Design and Build' Form of Contract should be adopted, with 'quality assessment' of tenders.

As the successful tenderer, Balfour Beatty Major Projects became responsible for the design, supervision and construction of the works, within a set of agreed constraints. The firm appointed Gifford and Partners as their Designer, and Mouchel Consulting Ltd was appointed Employer's Agent, by the Highways Agency.

The Contract, which began in May 1998, included the construction of five miles of dual two-, three- and four-lane carriageways of the motorway between the River Medlock and the Middleton Interchange, and the provision of eight bridges and 14 retaining walls.

In the crossing of a 1½-mile section of peat, at Blackley, a concrete piled raft was constructed. Piles were driven through the peat to a depth of 40 feet into the stiff clay below.

In early 1998, the whole of the Manchester Outer Ring Road, including the M63, sections of the M62, and the Middleton Link, M66, was renumbered M60. There are 27 junctions at an average spacing of 1.3 miles. A major programme of re-signing began in the spring of that year, which included 'Compass Point' signing for the various sectors. As well as strategic destinations, over 35 local destinations are signed at exits from the motorway.

The Denton-Middleton Section was opened to traffic in October 2000.[*] This was 40 years after the completion, in 1960, of the first section, Stretford-Eccles By-pass.

In comparison, the first 2½-mile length of M25, the London Orbital Road, was opened in 1975 and the final section 11 years later in October 1986.

The M25 is 117 miles long compared with the 35 miles of the M60. Why should it have taken so long to complete the latter? Was it an example of the so-called 'North-South divide', in the allocation of financial resources?

* 'The Final Link in the M60 Manchester Outer Ring Road' Denton-Middleton Section, Opening Brochure, 30 October 2000, Highways Agency/ L.G. Mouchel and Partners (Preston Record Office).

5 The Manchester–Preston Motorway M61

5.1 Horwich Link to Preston By-pass M6

The 1949 Road Plan had proposed an Express Route between Manchester and Preston, to be achieved by improving sections of the A6 and constructing several town and village by-passes. However, by the early 1960s it became evident that there was a strong case for building a motorway, linking the proposed M62 at Worsley with the M6 near Preston.

In 1963, Lancashire County Council was appointed as the Minister's Agent Authority for the preparation and design of the motorway and the statutory procedures were completed for three separate sections.

The route of the motorway north of Chorley crossed the south end of the Preston-Lancaster Canal at three points. As the canal was already disused and rapidly deteriorating, it was agreed by the Ministry of Transport and British Waterways Board that the expense of bridging it was not justified. The Board therefore promoted a Bill in Parliament to denavigate the canal between Town Lane, Whittle-le-Woods and Walton Summit, a length of three miles. A scheme was then prepared by the Board to fill in the canal with a view to returning the land to agriculture, where possible, and the Ministry agreed to meet the cost of providing unsuitable material from the motorway cuttings.

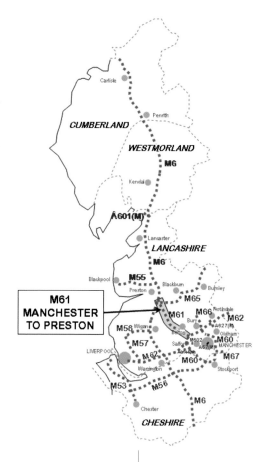

The 13-mile length between Horwich and Preston embraced the two northerly sections. The by-passing of Adlington, Chorley and Whittle-le-Woods was to be achieved by the connection with the M6, and the provision of link roads to the A6 from two-level interchanges, constructed at the southern end and at a point immediately north of Chorley.

At the proposed southern interchange, a new length of dual carriageway all-purpose road 1.1 miles long, and to be known as the Horwich Link, was to be constructed to connect with the A673 and provide a northerly access to Bolton.

Major earthworks were necessary and 42 bridges were required. It was considered, therefore, to be essential to carry out advance works to deal with a number of difficult problems, likely to cause major interference with the programming of construction in the two main contracts which were to be awarded.

A watercourse known as Pearl Brook passed under Crown Lane on the centre line of the motorway and lay within the motorway land-take for a distance of approximately 350 yards. The motorway at this point was to be on embankment with a maximum height of 35 feet and, due to the poor nature of the ground, it was considered necessary for the embankment to be constructed early to allow any settlement to take place. The Pearl Brook Diversion consisted of the construction of two reinforced concrete box culverts connected by an open concrete paved channel of a total length of 550 yards.

The diversion of the aqueduct carrying the main water supply from Rivington Lakes to Liverpool passed under the line of the motorway consisted of the laying of twin 42-inch-diameter steel pipes surrounded with concrete and with chambers at each end.

The connection of M61 with the Preston By-pass Section of M6 at Bamber Bridge involved the construction of Blacow Bridge to carry the north-bound carriageway of M61 over M6.

The Thirlmere Aqueduct which carried over 40 million gallons of water daily to the Manchester area also passed under the line of the motorway. The diversions consisted of the laying of twin 72-inch-diameter steel pipes surrounded with concrete.

The first of the advance works contracts awarded by the County Council began early in 1967. However, a major change took place on 1 April of that year when the first Road Construction Unit (RCU) covering the North West of England came into being, with Drake appointed as its Director, on secondment from the County Council. In accordance with the terms of the partnership agreement between the Minister and the County Council, the Lancashire Sub-Unit of the NWRCU was established by the allocation of appropriate members of the staff of the County Surveyor's Department. This ensured continuity in the preparation and design of the project, and in the supervision of construction.

Alternative tenders were invited for three different types of carriage-way construction. For both Contracts, flexible construction with a base of eight inches of dense bituminous macadam proved to be the cheapest with the same Contractor successful in each case.

Work began on the southerly of the two Contracts on 1 January 1968 followed by a start on the other Contract five months later. Both were scheduled for completion in November 1969.

A prominent feature along the line of the motorway was the 100-year-old Botany Railway Viaduct, which had carried the Chorley-Cherry Tree Line over the Leeds and Liverpool Canal at Chorley. This viaduct had an overall length of 385 feet and the width between spandril walls was 28 feet 6 inches. It consisted of nine masonry faced semi-circular arches each of

33 feet clear span carried on 4 feet 6 inches-wide masonry piers, and was demolished on 10 November 1968 by means of explosives.

A total of 51 houses had to be demolished, of which 44 in the Botany Brow area of Chorley were due for clearance by 1970 under a re-development scheme. Arrangements were made with the Housing Authorities concerned for the re-housing of tenants where required.

Soils encountered along the route consisted of Boulder Clay of varying plasticities, sand, silt, peat, shale and gritstone. Over a length of 800 yards immediately north of Red Moss Railway Bridge, a deposit of peat with an average depth of 13 feet was dug out and replaced with granular materials, before the motorway embankment could be formed.

At Gale Moss a deposit of water-logged peat, reaching a maximum depth of 42 feet, was encountered, and was dealt with by a combination of excavation and displacement techniques to replace the peat with granular material. Test bores were taken through this granular material to prove that the removal of the peat below the formation was complete.

At Whittle-le-Woods, the route of the motorway passes through a valley between hills, from which gritstone had been quarried. During site investigation, this valley was found to be an old glacial channel and, although rock appears on

Hill Top Bridge

both faces of the motorway cutting, peat, silt and other soft materials were found at motorway formation level. These conditions, combined with a water table which was virtually at existing ground level, made excavation extremely difficult.

Shallow mine workings were found in the cutting near Nick Hilton Lane and, where the top of the 'seam' was within 17 feet of finished motorway level, all material was excavated out to the bottom of the 'seam', and back-filled with granular material. Where the depth was greater, an eight-inches-thick double reinforced concrete raft was provided extending four feet beyond the outer edges of each carriageway.

Eight old mine shafts were exposed and these were proved for the depth of fill. The shafts were then covered either with a substantially reinforced concrete slab at rockhead level, or with a thick concrete plug. One of these shafts proved very difficult to locate due to dredgings from the canal which overlaid it to a depth of approximately 30 feet.

Approximately six million tons of material were excavated and more than five million tons of fill were imported to make up the deficiency of suitable material required to form the embankments and backfill the peat excavations.

The imported material was mainly obtained from four sources, the most important being Healey Nab lying adjacent to the line of the motorway. By excavating the top of this hill to a depth of 30 feet some 2½ million tons of rock was obtained with the advantage that direct access to the line of the motorway could be obtained without haulage vehicles having to use existing roads. This was an important factor in enabling the Contractor to obtain planning permission and, with strict conditions concerning reinstatement, the resulting appearance of the hillside was very little different from the original.

Another source of material was an old tip at Blackrod from where some 300,000 tons of Burnt Red Shale was obtained. A further example of the construction of a motorway improving the environment, by using waste materials.

Whereas 20 of the bridges had to be constructed to carry the motorway over roads, railways, a canal, rivers, footpaths and streams, 16 carry other roads and four carry footpaths over the motorway.

The bridges carrying the motorway are generally of one or three spans, whilst those over the motorway are mainly four-span, the elevations being necessarily asymmetric in a few instances. The unusual elevations add interest to the appearance of the motorway.

Piled foundations were necessary for 21 of the bridges. To suit the differing design requirements, prestressed concrete, reinforced concrete, steel girders and preflexed girders were used to form the decks. For most prestressed and steel deck bridges, standard I-section beams were used.

The Horwich to Preston Section of the motorway was opened to traffic in November 1969* and, in the early 1970s, a Service Area was constructed and brought into use at Anderton.

* Manchester-Preston Motorway M61, Horwich Link-Preston By-pass, Opening Brochure, 28 November 1969, NWRCU/Lancashire Sub-Unit/Lancashire County Council (Preston Record Office).

5.2 Worsley Braided Interchange to Horwich Link and Kearsley Spur A666(M)

The outstanding feature of the 6½-mile section of the motorway south from Horwich was the construction of the Worsley Braided Interchange, connecting the M61 with the M62, the A580 (East Lancashire Road) and the A666(M) Kearsley Spur.

The first stages in the construction of the M62 between Worsley and Whitefield had begun in August 1966.

The purpose of the Kearsley Spur, which was to be constructed as part of the Interchange, was to provide a connection to the A666 Farnworth-Kearsley By-pass, an all-purpose Principal Road built to motorway-standard by Lancashire County Council. Opened to traffic in December 1967, it was later to be extended northwards by the eastern limb of the Bolton Inner Relief Road, built by the County Borough Council to a similar standard. The Spur was, therefore, of considerable importance in linking Bolton, and the other towns served by the A666, directly to the national motorway system.

In a heavily built-up area, such as exists in this part of the Region, the location of an interchange of this magnitude was governed by the availability of land free from development. The presence of extensive peat deposits up to 20 feet in depth on the Linnyshaw, Kearsley, Clifton and Wardley Mosses had restricted development in the past and, therefore, provided such a site.

Following detailed investigations carried out in the area, it was found that it would be possible to drain the Interchange below the lowest level of the peat by means of an outfall half a mile in length. This was a critical factor in determining the vertical profile of several of the routes in order to produce the most economic design. For example, an early proposal for one particular section would have required a bridge over a mineral railway, the excavation of a substantial depth of peat and its replacement with suitable filling material. As a result of being able to lower the profile, an estimated saving of over £2 million was achieved.

In controlling movement between various routes, the design was based on the principle that traffic leaving the main route does so in advance of traffic joining it.

Heavily skewed crossings of link and slip roads were necessary in order to form a relatively compact free-flowing design. One of the bridges was required to carry a two-lane slip road over a dual four-lane section of motorway at a skew of 70°. The initial design envisaged through

M61. Worsley Braided Interchange. Riders Farm Bridges.

girders and a considerable depth of construction but, in order to achieve the correct sight lines, a substantial increase in width would have been required. The alternative was a change in the design speed and/or a reduction in the skew angle, neither of which was acceptable.

The solution to the problem was to make the bridge span 'square' to the line of the motorway with longer structures over each carriageway. The tunnel effect was reduced by an arrangement of columns supporting the deck.

A similar design was used for two other smaller, but heavily skewed bridges within the interchange. It was estimated that the saving in the cost of the three bridges would be £1 million, and on the earthworks and drainage £¾ million.

In the event, the design of the Interchange necessitated the excavation of 1½ million cubic yards of peat. In order to avoid the movement of vehicles carrying this material on the existing road system an additional 96 acres of moss land alongside the Interchange was acquired to provide tipping space. After settlement had taken place, it was the intention that the land would be made available for agricultural use.

The first advance works contract was awarded by the County Council and began in February 1967, prior to the formation of the NWRCU. It involved the construction of a 42-inch-diameter outfall to Unity Brook for the purpose of not only draining the peat area, but also the M61 itself from as far as the junction with A58 at Westhoughton, 5½ miles to the north.

One year later, a further advance works contract was awarded by the NWRCU. Over two miles of channels, 80 feet in width, were formed involving the excavation of 325,000 cubic yards of peat and other unsuitable material. The haul roads, which were formed in the channels, were incorporated in the permanent motorway construction. 1½ miles of motorway drains, up to 48 inches in diameter, were laid.

The main NWRCU Contract, which included not only the construction of a substantial part of the Worsley Braided Interchange, but two other two-level interchanges and a total of 26 bridges and several large retaining walls, began in January 1969.

Within the total excavation of 4½ million cubic yards of material, a heap of approximately 160,000 cubic yards of highly caustic chemical waste presented a major disposal problem in the Interchange. Deposited on Kearsley Moss over the past 90 years, the material, which gave off a very pungent odour, had polluted the surrounding ground and water courses, including the River Irwell. The River Authority stipulated that, wherever the material was tipped, measures must be taken to prevent any further nuisance. In consequence, the Contract required that this material be incorporated as a core to a motorway

Chemical waste,
Kearsley Moss

embankment about 30 feet high and, in order to seal the material and prevent any further pollution, it was clad with clay, 10 feet thick on the sides, and 15 feet thick on the top.

Shallow mineworkings and old mine shafts were encountered and these were treated in accordance with the methods used on earlier sections of motorway. Where the Kearsley Spur passes under A666, grouting techniques were adopted. The area was drilled on a 10 feet square grid and each borehole was injected with a pulverised fuel ash (PFA)/ cement grout. Some 90 tons of cement and 1,500 tons of PFA was used in over 1,000 boreholes.

Approximately 3½ million tons of fill was imported to make up for the deficiency of suitable material and in backfilling the peat excavation below carriageway formation level. Of this, almost one million tons of unburnt colliery waste was extracted from unsightly tips in the area.

The comparatively high cost of construction in this particular area was considered to be fully justified by the improvement to the environment resulting from the use of land which would not otherwise be developed, and by the utilisation of waste materials.

In view of the complex traffic movements involved, lighting was provided throughout the whole of the Interchange. On the dual carriageway sections, a system of longitudinal catenary lighting was installed over a length of seven miles. Similar lanterns were mounted conventionally on 19 miles of single carriageway link roads.

The opening of this Section of motorway in December 1970 marked the completion of the M61.*

Worsley Braided Interchange

* M61-M62 Motorway and the Worsley Braided Interchange, Official Opening Brochure, 17 December 1970, NWRCU/Lancashire Sub-Unit/Lancashire County Council (Preston Record Office).

6 The Lancashire–Yorkshire Motorway M62

6.1 Eccles to the County Boundary

During the 1930s the need for a fast road route across the Pennines had been the subject of much discussion between the Highway Authorities in Lancashire and Yorkshire. It was eventually agreed that it would be

an extension of the East Lancashire Road, but little positive action was taken before the Second World War, except for the reservation of land for the future construction of an all-purpose road, then known as the Yorkshire Branch Road.

Although the proposal was included in the 1949 Road Plan for Lancashire, it was not until 1961 that the Ministry of Transport invited the County Councils of Lancashire and the West Riding to survey and recommend a route for the motorway.[*] Reconnaissance on foot was followed by an aerial survey of the whole area and extensive traffic surveys were carried out on both sides of the Pennines. Meteorological data was also examined to identify the alignment which would be least affected by fog, snow and high winds.

The section within Lancashire presented the design engineers with two principal and contrasting problems. Firstly, there was the task of finding a route through urban areas in the west and north of the Manchester conurbation with its residential property and old industrial workings, and a network of roads, railways, canals and rivers to be crossed. The second problem was the long and steep climb up to the county boundary, where the obstacles were not existing roads but rather the lack of them. In the event, the route which was selected reached an altitude of 1,220 feet and, when completed, it became the highest motorway in Britain.

A study of existing records showed that the geology of the route was divided into two sections. The lowland section from Eccles to Milnrow lies on the fringe of the Lancashire Plain. Almost the whole of this area is covered by a blanket of glacial deposits and several peat mosses. West of the River Irwell, coal measures had been extensively worked and further subsidence seemed unlikely, but to the east of the river the coalfield was still being exploited. Significant subsidence could therefore be expected, both during construction of the motorway and after it was opened to traffic. In the foothills east of Milnrow there were mudstones, shales, coal seams

* Lancashire-Yorkshire Motorway M62, Route location and Preliminary Design. Personal memories (A.C. Henry), Lancashire County Council (Preston Record Office).

and sandstone which was fissured, weathered and steeply bedded. Millstone Grit formed the Pennine massif and, except for rocky outcrops, the whole of the moorland was covered by a layer of peat up to six feet thick.

Traffic forecasts indicated that dual three-lane carriageways would be necessary. The widths of the strips of land which had been reserved since the 1930s in urban areas such as Prestwich were, therefore, quite inadequate and unfortunately more than 100 houses had to be demolished and the residents rehoused.

Prior to the formation of the Road Construction Unit, all the contracts for the construction of the motorway were awarded by the County Council. These included several advance works contracts, the first of which began in March 1966. The principal aim was the building of bridges at key locations in order to provide access for construction traffic along the line of motorway, thereby avoiding the use of existing roads, particularly in the urban areas.

The East Lancashire Road, A580, was lowered up to a maximum depth of 50 feet and involved the driving of a 54-inch-diameter segmented tunnel outfall 310 yards in length to provide drainage. This work was necessary in order to allow for the construction of Wardley Hall Bridge carrying the motorway over the A580 at the optimum vertical profile. A major structure of eight 120-feet-long spans, it was designed to cope with the possibility of future settlement arising from the existence of old mine workings in close proximity to the site.

The bridge over the River Irwell has a single skew span of 200 feet. Ground conditions revealed the existence of an active geological fault – The Pendleton Fault – and underlying shallow coal measures. Although it was founded on rock and it was not anticipated that there would be any major problems, old tunnels were encountered. These had been dug by Brindley to dewater early collieries which had functioned at the turn of the 18th century. Steel box girders supporting a reinforced concrete slab provided a stiff lightweight deck capable of speedy and safe erection and be able to withstand the predicted ground movements.

The most significant bridge constructed in advance of the main works was, however, the spectacular six-span 840-feet-long Rakewood Viaduct crossing the Longden End Brook 140 feet above the valley floor. Its early completion was essential to enable the haulage of excavated rock for use in embankments further to the west. Due to the height of the bridge, and the very exposed site subject to severe weather conditions, it was desirable that the superstructure should be capable of erection without temporary falsework and with a minimum of site work. The continuous steel plate girders were launched from one end, braced in pairs.

In May 1968 work began on a series of main Contracts. They were all awarded by the Road Construction Unit, with the exception of that for the section between Worsley Court House and the A580. As a one-

Rakewood Viaduct
(top); Windy Hill
Cutting at the County
Boundary (above)

mile extension of the Stretford-Eccles By-pass, the scheme was undertaken by the County Council and financed with a 100 per cent grant from the Ministry as a 'potential Trunk Road motorway'.

The excavation in cuttings, and the construction of embankments, along the whole of the 19 miles of the motorway between Eccles and the County Boundary was a massive operation requiring the movement along the line of the motorway of almost 16½ million cubic yards of material, including 10 million cubic yards of rock.

The strata dipped steeply into the north face of the rock cuttings near the summit, which in places were 120 feet deep. This resulted in sizeable landslips, which necessitated the removal of additional material and the provision of terracing to stabilise the slope. At these locations a wide concrete-lined ditch was provided behind the hard shoulder of the motorway to serve not only as a drainage channel, but also as a 'rock catcher' to prevent any loose rock from rolling on to the hard shoulder and carriageway.

Apart from the many crossings of existing roads and private accesses, a considerable number of interchanges with major roads had to be constructed. Connections to other elements of the motorway system were provided at Worsley Braided Interchange (M61); at Simister, with the Middleton Link (M66); and at Thornham, with the Rochdale-Oldham Motorway A627(M). Elsewhere, the A572 and the A575 were connected to the M62 at Worsley Court House; the A666 at Clifton; the A56 at Whitefield; the A6046 at Heywood; and the A640 at Milnrow. Due to the different circumstances at each location, a wide variety in their design characteristics had to be adopted.

Of the 67 structures, there were seven viaducts and 49 over- and under-bridges. Two bridges, designed by British Rail, carry railways over the motorway, the largest being at Besses o' th' Barn. This bridge forms the upper level of a three-level crossing comprising a railway, an all-purpose road and the motorway. The Manchester-Bury Line is carried at a considerable skew on a three-span prestressed concrete structure and is articulated to cater for anticipated severe subsidence due to coal mining.

A56 Interchange at Whitefield (Besses o' th' Barn) with the Railway Bridge shown right

The motorway was opened in stages* and at a later date a Service Area was provided at Birch, near Middleton. Concurrently, further sections of the motorway were completed within Yorkshire. The historic significance of linking the two counties by this engineering feat of our age was recognised in October 1971, when the 27-mile section between Eccles and Outlane near Huddersfield was formally inaugurated by Her Majesty the Queen.

The Trunk Roads Act of 1936 had transferred to the Minister the responsibility for the major national routes. With a few exceptions, none of the roads within the County Boroughs were designated as Trunk Roads.

The original concept of a ring road around the Manchester Conurbation was, therefore, considered by the Ministry to be the responsibility of the Local Authorities. Later, however, it was accepted that the proposed Outer Ring Road would have 'Trunk Road status', with the Stretford-Eccles By-pass, the section of the M62 between Eccles and the Simister Interchange, and the Middleton Link, as its first elements.

* 'Motorway across the Pennines', The Lancashire-Yorkshire Motorway M62 and Scammondem Dam, Brochure of Inaugural visit by HM The Queen, 14 October 1971, Department of the Environment/Lancashire and West Riding County Councils County Borough of Huddersfield (Preston Record Office).

6.2 The South Lancashire Section: Queens Drive (Liverpool) to Eccles

The 1949 Road Plan for Lancashire included the following highway proposals in South Lancashire:

- The dualling of the East Lancashire Road, A580, with provision for the grade separation of junctions
- A by-pass of Huyton between Roby and Rainhill Stoops
- A by-pass of Cadishead and Irlam, together with the upgrading of the A57 between Warrington and the proposed North-South motorway (M6)

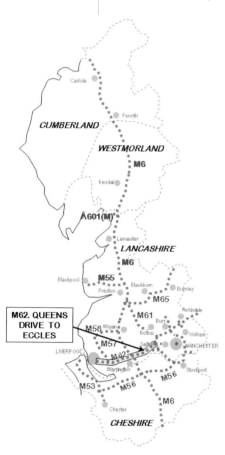

On the completion of the M6 through Cheshire, it was envisaged that traffic moving between Liverpool and the south would use the Runcorn-Widnes Bridge and the A533/A530/A54 route to connect with the M6 at Holmes Chapel Interchange (Junction 18). By the early 1960s, it became apparent that these proposals would be inadequate, as there was an urgent need to connect the Port of Liverpool directly into the motorway network, and reduce the number of traffic accidents in the Merseyside/South Lancashire area.

In 1962, Drake visited the USA where he saw, at first hand, the development of the Interstate system of expressways and returned with the strongly held view that there was a case for a completely new section of motorway from Liverpool across South Lancashire to connect with the M6. It was an imaginative proposal, initially referred to as the Merseyside Expressway, but after further consideration, and preliminary traffic studies, it was concluded that it should be extended eastwards to connect with Stretford-Eccles By-pass section of the Manchester Outer Ring Road. It would, therefore, link with the future motorway, which was to supersede the proposed Yorkshire Branch Road, thereby resulting in a continuous length of motorway from Liverpool through to the Yorkshire boundary.

Initially it did not gain the support of the Ministry of Transport as it was considered that, as the East Lancashire Road had been designed to a comparatively high standard, and could be upgraded, its duplication was not justified.

Following further representations, the scheme was added to the Road Programme in 1963.[*] Investigations into possible routes and the preliminary design work began in 1965, within the County Surveyor's Department. On the formation of the North West Road Construction Unit, in April 1967, the design team became part of the Lancashire Sub-Unit.

* M62 South Lancashire Motorway Liverpool to Manchester Route Location and Design (S Coleman), October 1998, Lancashire County Council/NWRCU/ Lancashire Sub-Unit (Preston Record Office).

In an area such as South Lancashire, much of it with a history of industrial development, a great deal of consultation had to be carried out with the many interested parties, particularly the utilities and statutory undertakers. These included British Rail whose lines would be affected at six major crossings, together with the Canal, River and National Gas Pipeline Authorities. It became evident that a major ICI ethylene pipeline, and the Haweswater and Vyrnwy Aqueducts, would be crossed by the motorway.

Extensive discussions were held with the National Coal Board in regard to past and future subsidence. There were three active collieries operating in the area, and coal seams which were to be worked. This significantly influenced the choice of route.

It had been the intention for the motorway to penetrate into Liverpool, as an element of the road network proposed for the central area of the city. Later, however, the City Council abandoned the proposals, due to the extensive property demolition which would have been involved. It was decided, therefore, that the western terminal of the motorway would have to be at an interchange with Queens Drive, a ring road which had been constructed in the 1920s.

The proposed route of the Huyton By-pass had allowed for connection to the A5080, one of the city's main radial routes, and this determined the location of the interchange. The initial problem involved the identification of a line through the urban area of Bowring Park, which would have the minimum impact on properties, whilst still allowing access to those not directly affected.

The existing Roby Road had a variable vertical profile, was fronted by high grade development, and was not suitable for upgrading to motorway standard, which would have introduced unacceptable environmental intrusion. It was clear, therefore, that the 'springing point' for the route, as it left the urban area, should be the open land to the south, partly occupied by the Bowring Park Golf Course.

Further to the east, it became evident that subsidence from mining at Cronton Colliery would be a major factor in route location when it was found, in checking an Ordnance bench mark, that settlement of 12 feet had occurred. After discussions with the National Coal Board, the proposed alignment was diverted through an area where settlement was complete.

Beyond this point, the proposed route passed through mainly Grade 3 farmland. At Burtonwood, however, the former United States Airbase, well known for its involvement in the Berlin Airlift, was still in use as a stores depot. Earlier, the site had been considered for development as a 'Lancashire' international airport, but the proposal had been ruled out due to mining subsidence. Later advice, however, indicated that this had largely ceased and the decision was taken to align the motorway along the redundant main runway.

Croft Interchange

At Croft, where a major interchange would be required at the junction with the M6, various alternative layouts were considered. Significant factors were the very heavy traffic movement between Liverpool and the south, and the drainage of the area. The final design allowed for easy curves with a design speed of 70 mph for the major turning movements, and 40 mph on the slip road loops. In view of the extensive area of land required for the Interchange, certain parts within it were to be provided with access, so that they could continue in agricultural use. Other parts were to be used for the disposal of unsuitable excavated material, and landscaped.

East of Risley, the proposed route under consideration traversed Holdcroft Moss, Irlam Moss and Barton Moss, within the area generally known as Chat Moss. Whereas Holdcroft Moss is a virgin raised peat bog, the other parts of the area contain highly-productive market-garden land, where it was of prime importance to minimise the impact of the motorway.

It was known that peat would be encountered up to a depth of about 20 feet. The only feasible way of constructing the motorway across this area was to remove the peat down to the underlying clay, in order to ensure a stable formation. The critical question, however, was whether the drainage system of the motorway, at such a level, would be able to discharge under gravity. Investigations showed that this could be achieved by laying a long outfall connecting into the Manchester Ship Canal.

The Manchester-Liverpool Line had been constructed across Chat Moss by Stephenson in the 1850s and, according to local 'folklore', it had been built on 'cotton', implying that bales of the material had been used to stabilise the formation. In actual fact, the story relates to the financing of the project due to the prosperity of the textile industry during that period, with Manchester as the commercial centre and Liverpool as its port. There was some evidence, however, that fascines had been used in the construction.

If settlement takes place in the operation of a railway, it can be dealt with by 'ballasting' under the sleepers in order to adjust the levels. Any deformation of the surface of a motorway can, however, create a potential hazard for high-speed traffic and cannot be remedied in a similar manner.

This section of the motorway was to terminate at the Eccles Interchange which had been substantially completed in the Contract for the construction of the M602.

It was apparent that if major drainage outfalls, certain earthworks and several bridges, could be completed in advance of the main contract works, the period for the completion of the motorway would be reduced. The first advance contract, which involved the construction of an 84-inch-diameter concrete pipe outfall 1,267 yards long, from Barton Moss to the Ship Canal, began in February 1970.

At Tarbock, an interchange with the proposed Liverpool Outer Ring Road, M57, was to be constructed, and from there to Risley, the main Contract for the construction of 13½ miles of dual three-lane motorway began in September 1971. The works also included two-level interchanges with A57 and A49, in addition to the major interchange with the M6.

Eccles Interchange under construction

The construction of 36 bridges was required, including a viaduct over the West Coast Main Line railway. The ground adjacent to this bridge had very poor bearing capacity and pulverised fuel ash was used for the approach embankments, constructed under an advance contract.

At Croft, the Contractor acquired land for a borrow pit adjacent to the site of the motorway, from which 2½ million cubic yards of Bunter Sandstone was extracted without having to use existing roads for haulage.

The length of motorway between Tarbock and Croft was opened to traffic in November 1973 and a service area was later provided at Burtonwood.

Meanwhile, the main Contract for the construction of the difficult six miles of dual three-lane motorway between Risley and Eccles began in April 1972. Advance works contracts had already been carried out in order to provide access along the line of the motorway. These included drainage outfalls and the excavation of unsuitable material through Holcroft Moss, most of which was a raised peat bog unsuitable for agriculture. It was side-cast to tips on either side of the motorway cutting, which were not allowed to encroach to within 100 feet of the top of the slope. In the very wet areas, where the peat had a moisture content of 1,400 per cent, a stable slope of 1 in 3 could not be achieved and buttresses of imported material had to be constructed.

Twelve bridges were required, including Barton Moss Railway Bridge carrying the main Manchester-Liverpool Line over the motorway and designed by British Rail. The works also included the completion of the Eccles Interchange and bridges at Risley for a future junction of the proposed Orford/Risley Expressway.

On completion, in August 1974, there was a continuous length of the M62 in use from Tarbock through into Yorkshire.[*]

Work had begun on the 3½-mile dual three-lane carriageway Section of the motorway between Queens Drive and Tarbock in October 1973.

Due to the urban character of the area at the western end, it was necessary to demolish over 150 houses and small shops, together with two public houses, a warehouse and other miscellaneous buildings. This was required in order to accommodate not only the motorway but also a 'braided' type of interchange alongside and over a length of three-quarters of a mile, between Queens Drive and Bowring Park, where a conventional two-level junction was to be provided.

With a complex urban road system, and two railway lines passing through the area, a large number of structures was required. In addition to two viaducts, 10 other bridges, seven subways, and two major retaining walls had to be constructed, together with the reconstruction of several existing bridges.

The 594-feet-long Bowring Park Viaduct which carries the motorway over minor roads has six spans of twin segmental trapezoidal post-tensioned box beams.

Between Bowring Park and Queens Drive the motorway is in cutting, with residential property on the south side supported by long retaining walls. The extended height of the walls provide a noise barrier and, in the case of some properties, noise insulation was also provided.

Queens Drive is a heavily trafficked Inner Ring Road of Liverpool. A 1,030-feet-long viaduct carries Queens Drive over the terminal junction of the motorway in seven spans. The single segmental trapezoidal post-tensioned box beam is supported on tapering elliptical piers.

[*] Lancashire-Yorkshire Motorway M62, Croft to Worsley Section, Opening Brochure, 22 August 1974, NWRCU/Lancashire Sub-Unit (Preston Record Office).

The two viaducts were technically demanding to construct. A travelling gantry was used to lift the units of the Queens Drive Viaduct, each weighing up to 55 tonnes. Calculations carried out on site had to allow for both vertical and horizontal curvature, and superelevation. As the viaduct was constructed in the summer of 1976 when temperatures reached 32°C, exceptional difficulties were experienced. In the event they were positioned on the temporary works to a tolerance of less than one quarter of an inch in any direction.

Queens Drive Viaduct

With the considerable amount of pedestrian movement in the Queens Drive area, four of the subways were constructed in the Interchange and particular attention was given to landscaping the approaches.

A long length of Queens Drive was widened and a new carriageway involved the construction of a bridge over the Manchester-Liverpool Line. Bowring Park Road and Broad Green Road were also widened. In addition to this work, over three miles of link roads, slip roads and side road diversions were constructed.

It was recognised that such major works carried out in a largely urban area would cause difficulties for local residents. A member of the supervisory staff was, therefore, permanently allocated to deal with any complaints which might arise.

East of the Bowring Park Interchange and through to Tarbock, the design and construction was that of a conventional dual three-lane rural motorway. Provision was, however, made in the earthworks in cuttings and embankments to accommodate future four-lane carriageways.

The completion of the works in November 1976 marked the end of the construction of the M62 across Lancashire, which had begun 10 years earlier.

7   The Rochdale–Oldham Motorway A627(M)

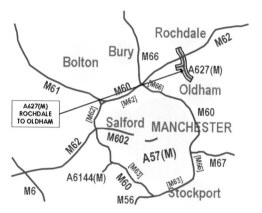

The A627(M) was built as a 'Principal Road motorway' linking the towns of Rochdale and Oldham with the Lancashire-Yorkshire Motorway M62, and with each other.* As distinct from a 'Trunk Road motorway' for which the Minister is responsible, a Local Authority is the 'Highway Authority' for such a motorway, with the project normally attracting a 75 per cent grant from Central Government. The length between the M62 and Chadderton was, however, considered to be of sufficient importance to warrant a 100 per cent grant, as a 'potential Trunk Road'.

In December 1958, the Minister of Transport suggested that the Local Authorities within each of the major conurbations outside London should investigate and formulate proposals for its long-term highway requirements. This led to the setting-up of a consortium of the Local Authorities in the sub-Region known as SELNEC (South East Lancashire and North East Cheshire). It included the Councils of the Counties of Lancashire and Cheshire, together with the City Councils of Manchester and Salford and the County Borough Councils of Rochdale and Oldham, all of which were Highway Authorities in their own right.

The need for links to the County Boroughs of Rochdale and Oldham from the motorway system had been envisaged in the 1949 Road Plan for Lancashire. In a Report of a Committee of SELNEC published in December 1962, a Rochdale-Oldham Route was included as a firm proposal to be incorporated in a future programme.

It was agreed that the Lancashire County Council would design and supervise the construction of the road on behalf of the three Highway Authorities. The net cost, after payment of the grants, was to be shared on the basis of the actual measured work carried out within each Authority's area.

From Broadway A663 in Chadderton, the proposed route ran north under a roundabout connecting with the local road system, including an all-purpose dual carriageway link into Oldham. Descending into a valley, it then climbed to an interchange at Slattocks, with a motorway link to the A664 in Middleton. After reaching the junction with the M62, where provision was to be made for a future fly-over, the motorway was to descend to a terminal roundabout with links to the A664 and A58 in Rochdale.

* Rochdale-Oldham Motorway A627(M) (W.M. Johnson MBE), year 2000. Personal impressions (Preston Record Office).

83

Although involving only a comparatively short length of four miles of dual two-lane motorway and seven miles of dual carriageway all-purpose road, the scale of the earthworks was to be considerable. There were to be eight underbridges, five overbridges, three pedestrian subways, extensive retaining walls and a railway overbridge designed by British Rail.

The statutory procedures began in February 1968 and, although there were several objections to the Compulsory Purchase Order, the procedures were completed, tenders were invited and construction started in March 1970 with a contract period of 25 months.

Situated in the foothills of the Pennine range, the route necessitated sizeable cuttings in extremely variable glacial materials. As a result of the site investigation, the Contract envisaged that, of the total requirement of over 1½ million cubic yards of filling material for embankment construction, all but 80,000 cubic yards could be provided from suitable material excavated from the site; 1.1 million cubic yards of material was predicted as being unsuitable for re-use.

The winter prior to the start of the Contract had been exceptionally wet. In some of the cuttings there was 'suitable' clay and 'suitable' sand in close proximity. Separately, they could be used as 'fill' but, when mixed in excavation during a period of several months of exceptionally wet weather, they became totally unusable.

The fact that this was a Local Authority contract enabled the County Surveyor, as the Engineer, to negotiate with the Contractor the most economic means of dealing with the problem. If the project had been carried out for the Ministry, it would have been necessary to obtain approval for the measures which were adopted and serious delay and disruption would probably have occurred, with a consequential excessive increase in cost.

The deficit in suitable material would normally have led not only to the need to import expensive substitutes, but also to the use of land for extra tips, which would have been difficult and expensive in the semi-urban environment. By negotiating new rates, the Contractor was reimbursed for the cost of digging borrow pits for about 200,000 cubic yards of material near the site, which were subsequently used for the disposal of unusable material.

Additional material was 'created' by lowering the profile of the motorway in locations where it was aesthetically possible, and where the underlying material was of good quality.

Agreement was also reached on the use of draglines and wagons rather than rubber tyred scrapers, in order to facilitate the separation of different materials.

In all, a deficiency of some 500,000 cubic yards, representing one-third of the estimated total of suitable excavated material, was made good.

The most dramatic manifestation of the earthworks difficulties occurred at the Slattocks Interchange. The proposed cutting was particularly

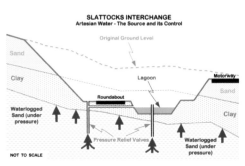

Slattocks Interchange
– landscaped lagoon

wide at this point, to accommodate the junction roundabout and its attendant slip roads. There were three well-defined strata sloping down from east to west. An upper layer of good sand 30 feet thick covered a layer of good clay of the same thickness. It was intended that the roundabout carriageway should be located in the clay.

Below the clay was a layer of sand and silt of unknown depth, which was saturated and, due to the slope, under considerable pressure. With the removal of some 50-feet depth of sand and clay the artesian pressure forced upwards the clay at the bottom of the excavation. This became known as the 'Slattocks Gusher'. A temporary system of well points and pumps, linked together around the perimeter of the roundabout, had to be installed to enable the completion of the Interchange.

A permanent 'safety valve' consisting of 11 well heads was installed. Three within the roundabout were then incorporated in a landscaped lagoon, which also collects water from other sources – a unique feature in a motorway interchange, which later was designated as a Site of Special Scientific Interest.

There was considerable variety in the design of the bridges. In general, the ground conditions required the use of piled foundations. However, for two bridges over Thornham New Road the bearing capacity was improved by means of the 'Vibroflotation' technique.

The Cripplegate Lane Footbridge was of steel box-girder construction. In view of national concern at the possibility of the failure of such structures, the Bridge was subjected to design checks but no remedial work was considered to be necessary.

The motorway was opened to traffic in January 1972,[*] three months early, and in view of the difficulties which were experienced, it was a considerable achievement.

* Rochdale-Oldham
Motorway A627(M),
Official Opening
Brochure, 7 January
1972, Lancashire County
Council (Preston Record
Office).

8   The Mancunian Way A57(M)

The Mancunian Way, nearly two miles in length, included the first section of truly urban motorway to be constructed in the Region.

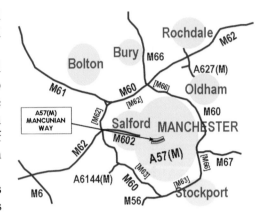

It is a lateral road along the southern fringe of the central area of the City of Manchester. Its primary purpose was to carry the traffic, much of it commercial, moving between the industrial areas on the east side of the Conurbation through to Manchester Docks and Trafford Park. Formerly, most of this traffic had to pass through the centre of the city and, in consequence, caused considerable congestion.

A further important function of the road was to act as a distributor between the heavily trafficked main radial roads south of the city centre.

It was the intention that it would form part of a comprehensive network of urban motorways envisaged in the SELNEC (South East Lancashire and North East Cheshire) Highway Plan of 1962.

The early proposals for the route were formulated in 1959, following traffic surveys carried out by the then City Engineer and Surveyor. It was decided that the road would have to be elevated on the section from west of Medlock Street to just east of Sackville Street, a length of approximately 1,400 yards. This was the only practicable way of providing the necessary grade separation at the closely spaced intersections of the motorway with Medlock Street, Cambridge Street, Oxford Road and Brook Street, all of which are important radial routes.

The City Council was the Highway Authority for the scheme and the design of the ground level roads, service diversions, drainage and landscaping was carried out by the City Engineer and Surveyor. G. Maunsell & Partners, Consulting Engineers, were appointed to undertake the design of the elevated structure and the supervision of the construction of all the works.

The statutory procedures for the other motorways in the Region were undertaken in accordance with the requirements of the various Highways Acts applicable at the time. In contrast, the Corporation promoted a Parliamentary Bill to authorise the construction of the Mancunian Way and this received Royal Assent in 1961.

The project was carried out in two stages. Work on the first stage, which involved the construction of a 950-yard length of all-purpose dual

Mancunian Way,
elevated section

* Corporation of
Manchester Link Road
17/7, Report on Elevated
Structure, January
1963, City Surveyor/G.
Maunsell and Partners
(Preston Record Office).

carriageway east of the A6, started in November 1963. It was opened to traffic in November 1965.

The second stage, between the A6 and the A56, was designed as a motorway and construction commenced in December 1964.* It included the elevated section, which is a prestressed concrete structure 3,232 feet 6 inches long between the end abutments. Of the 32 spans, 28 are each 105 feet, two are 60 feet to accommodate ground-level features, and the eastern and western spans are 97 feet 6 inches and 75 feet long respectively.

Between Cambridge Street and Brook Street the layout changes from dual two-lane to dual three-lane carriageways. With a lane width of 11 feet, the overall width of the eastern part of the structure is 79 feet, and elsewhere 61 feet. Ramped connections from the local road system are provided at Cambridge Street and Brook Street.

The main carriageways were designed for a speed of 40 mph and to have a minimum radius of 1,500 feet and maximum superelevation of 1 in 35. The maximum gradient was to be 1 in 25, and 1 in 19 on the intermediate ramps where the minimum radius was 109 feet, both made necessary by the need to accommodate the basic geometry of the existing ground-level road network.

The bedrock is predominantly Bunter Sandstone of Triassic age, but over a short length adjacent to the West Manchester Fault the bedrock is Manchester Marl of Permian age. The rock is overlain by glacial drift varying in depth from about eight to 47 feet, the depth being greatest near the middle of the alignment.

The standard foundation consists of two reinforced concrete bored piles and a linking pile cap under each column. The two piles, placed transversely to the main centre line of the structure, provide a 'couple' to resist the high lateral moments due to eccentric live loading, bearing restraint, and centrifugal and wind forces. The smaller longitudinal moments from friction are counteracted by the piles, in bending. The piles are between 3 feet and 4 feet 6 inches in diameter and are belled-out in the solid sandstone bedrock. The maximum base diameter of seven feet was used in the region of the West Manchester Fault, where the piles were founded in marl. Before each pile was cast, the footing was visually inspected and in many cases in-situ plate-bearing tests were carried out to confirm the suitability of the rock to withstand the design loading.

The reinforced concrete columns are of rectangular solid section, tapering on the longitudinal sides and vertical on the transverse faces. They are monolithic with the pile caps.

The main structural element is a hollow box spine beam with the top slab cantilevered out on both sides. Over 85 per cent of the superstructure is constructed with precast concrete units of uniform cross section. The transition section between the two- and three-lane parts of the structure is formed with in-situ concrete, and includes the ramps which carry a single traffic lane.

In contrast to the Hammersmith Flyover, when three basic types of precast unit were used for the beams, cantilevers and deck slabs, the functions of all three were combined in a single unit. As a result, both the casting and erection were simpler and more economic.

The joints between the segments were of in-situ concrete of three-inch nominal thickness to allow for irregularities in the casting of the units and some latitude in erection.

After positioning the units on staging and the completion of jointing, Freyssinet multi-strand prestressing cables were threaded through pre-formed ducts within the webs. The extremities of the superstructure, including the intermediate ramps, are terminated in solid reinforced concrete end blocks which formed effective anchorages for the main prestressing cables. An embossed copper waterproofing membrane was laid over the entire carriageway area followed by a 2¾-inch-thick double layer of hot-rolled asphalt surfacing.

The bridge over the River Medlock was constructed with a deck of standard precast prestressed beams spanning 38 feet 7 inches.

The 18 pedestrian subways included in the scheme were designed as reinforced concrete box culverts with the walls finished in glazed tiles.

The section of motorway between the A6 and the A56 was opened to traffic in March 1967.

The traffic islands beneath the elevated section were extensively landscaped in order to provide attractive secluded rest areas for local residents. Areas flanking the road along its entire length received similar treatment.

The 'Mancunian Way' was officially opened by the Rt Hon. Harold Wilson MP, on 5 May 1967,* the second time a section of motorway in the Region had been opened by the Prime Minister in office.

* Mancunian Way, Opening Brochure, 5 May 1967, Manchester City Council/ G. Maunsell and Partners (Preston Record Office).

9 The Eccles–Salford Motorway M602

9.1 Eccles By-pass

East of Warrington, the A57 is a county road and passes through the centre of the Borough of Eccles, to the boundary with the city of Salford. The 1949 Road Plan for Lancashire included a proposal for improving the road in the borough to a dual two-lane standard, but it was recognised that this would require extensive property demolition.

In the early 1960s, it was considered that it would be preferable to by-pass the town centre as an extension of the proposed South Lancashire section of the M62, and that this should be designed as a motorway. As an alternative route for traffic using the A57, it was to be a motorway for which the County Council, as the Highway Authority, would be responsible.

The alignment of the proposed dual three-lane By-pass, which is 1¾ miles long, was largely determined by the locations of the junctions at each end, and the requirements for the future extension of the motorway eastwards through Salford. At the western end of the By-pass, the location of the Eccles Interchange with Stretford-Eccles By-pass was fixed within small limits, since it had to be north of the Manchester-Liverpool Line to avoid an Eccles Corporation housing site, which extends up to the south side of the railway.

Any northward movement of the Interchange was impracticable because of the close proximity of the Worsley Court House Junction on M62. Because of the heavy volumes of turning traffic anticipated at the Interchange, it is of a 'free-flow' type with traffic joining the main motorway after outgoing traffic has left it. The area required for the Interchange was to be kept to the minimum, but it still occupied some 69 acres of land.

Towards the eastern end, the By-pass was located immediately adjacent to the north side of the railway, which reduced severance and provided the most suitable location for a roundabout with links to the existing A57 and A576 near the Salford City Boundary. This location was confirmed by the agreement of the City Council, a Highway Authority in its own right, for the continuation of the route into Salford along the north side of the railway. The roundabout was well placed for distributing traffic leaving the

By-pass on to A57, and A576, in addition to providing a direct connection between the By-pass and Eccles Town Centre.

Between the two extremities, the route chosen for the By-pass took advantage of the existence of semi-derelict land between existing development, where very little modern property was affected. Of the 353 houses which would have to be demolished for the By-pass, 293 were constructed before 1914. In addition, two churches, 47 shops, two public houses and a small number of other premises would be similarly affected.

At its eastern end, the By-pass would be in cutting at about the same level as the railway, in order to interfere as little as possible with the amenity of the area. To the west of Wellington Road, however, the motorway had to be raised above ground in order to provide headroom over the Bridgewater Canal and side roads, and extensive embankments would be required.

There was considerable opposition when a route through Eccles was disclosed, but after the County Surveyor had explained the proposals to a special meeting of the Eccles Borough Council's General Purposes Committee in July 1962, the Borough Council approved them in October 1962.

At the time, concern was expressed about the difficulties which would be experienced by the owners of properties affected by the scheme in the period prior to its implementation, particularly in regard to the houses. In December 1962, the County Highways and Bridges Committee agreed that the County Council would purchase any properties affected

Eccles By-pass

by the scheme, which were offered to the County Council. This enabled property owners to make arrangements for alternative accommodation, as and when suitable premises came on to the market.

Some 214 houses, nine plots of land, six lock-up shops, five shops with living accommodation, two factories, nine flats and eight other properties were purchased by the County Council under this arrangement. Largely as a result of this, there were only nine objections to the Compulsory Purchase Order when it was advertised in September 1967, following the admission of the scheme to the then Ministry of Transport's Principal Road Programme in 1966. A Public Inquiry into these objections was held in March 1968 and the Order was confirmed in October of that year.

The layout for the By-pass provided for dual three-lane carriageways, 8 feet 4 inches-wide hard shoulders, 6 feet-wide verges, and a 13 feet 8 inches-wide central reserve. Additionally, an eight-inch-wide edge line was to be provided along each side of the dual carriageways.

The detailed design was in hand before any standards had been laid down by the Ministry of Transport for the layout of motorways in urban areas, and the widths of the central reserve and hard shoulders were to be greater than those adopted later.

The entire route of the motorway overlies rock which is covered by glacial and post-glacial deposits, and an extensive soil survey showed that the area covered by the Interchange is sited on a deep pre-glacial valley which deepens considerably towards the west. The glacial valley is filled with a deep deposit of Lacustrine Clay overlaid by Boulder Clay, with thin deposits of sand and gravel. Overlying this was a poor clay of exceptionally low shear strength, which for the greater part of the Interchange was overlain by a band of sand and gravel, with the water table only about 18 inches below ground level.

As the Interchange is wholly on embankment, rising to a height of over 30 feet, it was necessary, where the poor clay outcropped at ground level, to excavate this material completely and refill with rock excavation, a total of 50,000 cubic yards being involved.

Where there was sufficient depth of sand overlying the poor clay, it was found to be impossible to build a stable embankment by using filling material having low density and certain defined physical properties. These requirements were met by the use of unburnt colliery shale and pulverised fuel ash, of which over one million cubic yards was used as filling in the Interchange alone. Where the embankments were at maximum height, they were formed entirely of pulverised fuel ash.

As the motorway extends eastwards from the Interchange the underlying rock is Manchester Marl, with occasional bands of limestone, overlying which is stiff Boulder Clay varying from 10 to 30 feet in thickness. For the last half mile at the easterly end of the motorway, the Bunter Sandstone outcrops near ground level. There was roughly a balance between 'cut' and 'fill', and of the 450,000 cubic yards of material which was suitable for re-use, about half was Bunter Sandstone.

Unsuitable excavated materials from cuttings and below embankments were deposited within the boundaries of the Interchange, and elsewhere, for landscaping purposes.

The severance of side roads by the motorway necessitated the construction of major foul sewer diversions, the most important of which was the main foul sewer for Eccles. This crosses the line of the motorway at the point where the cutting in sandstone is at its deepest, and this diversion required the construction of 1,000 feet of 54-inch-diameter tunnel at depths up to 40 feet. The tunnel is lined with precast concrete segments and passes under the Manchester-Preston Line. On a section of the tunnel adjacent to the parish church, dating back to the 12th century, the use of explosives as a means of excavation in the sandstone was prohibited, and hand excavation had to be resorted to.

Enclosed footbridge

A total of 26 bridges was required, including seven in the Eccles Interchange. Future mining subsidence was expected in this area and jacking facilities were provided in the decks.

One of the most significant structures is the Regent Railway Bridge, carrying the link road from Regent Street to the By-pass and passing over the railway near Eccles station. It is a single-span bridge varying in width from 87 feet to 143 feet, comprising Preflex steel beams encased in concrete with spans up to 79 feet.

In addition to the bridges a large number of retaining walls was required varying in length up to 2,500 feet and in height up to 30 feet. These are generally of reinforced concrete cantilever construction, with some lengths on piled foundations.

Special treatment has been given to the exposed face of the concrete wing walls to some of the overbridges and retaining walls, by facing with precast concrete blocks, whilst the faces of other bridges and retaining walls have been treated with coloured textured 'Pyrok' or 'Ceramitex'. The colours of the mosaic tiling used on the subways to the roundabouts at the eastern end of the By-pass were chosen in consultation with the Borough Surveyor of Eccles.

In an advance works contract, Thirlmere Aqueduct bridge was built over the Stretford-Eccles By-pass to carry the diverted water mains of Manchester Corporation in the Interchange area.

Work began on the main Contract in December 1969 and included not only the construction of the By-pass but also the whole of the Eccles Interchange, with the exception of the surfacing of those carriageways which would later connect into the South Lancashire Section of the M62.

Although the site of the Interchange was rural in character, the operations in its construction around the heavily trafficked Stretford-Eccles By-pass were governed by the over-riding necessity for the traffic flow to be unimpeded.

The necessity for road and pedestrian traffic to be maintained throughout the construction of the roadworks was another difficult problem for the Contractor. This was particularly so because the line of the By-pass crossed nine north-south roads in a heavily built-up area requiring a large number of bridges to be built.

It was necessary for the close integration of bridgeworks relative to the excavation of the cuttings, in order to comply with the detailed requirements of the Contract. These also specified the extent of the diversions to be completed before closing existing sections of road and the need for certain crossings over the route of the By-pass to be kept open at all times. Within a length of 1½ miles of the By-pass, there were no fewer than 13 separate side road diversions.

A further requirement was for the site to be used for the movement of construction traffic wherever possible, and for the use of existing roads to be kept to a minimum. For example, the Contractor constructed a temporary retractable bridge across the Bridgewater Canal, thus enabling heavy earth-moving plant to be used for the haulage of bulk excavation.

When the By-pass was opened to traffic in November 1971,[*] it was the first truly 'urban motorway' to be built within the Administrative County of Lancashire, and its construction presented many problems not normally associated with 'rural motorways'.

9.2   Extension: Eccles to Salford

It was envisaged that the construction of the Extension of Eccles By-pass through the City of Salford would be carried out shortly after the By-pass was completed in November 1971. The statutory procedures had begun in 1970, undertaken by the City Council as the Highway Authority. However, little further progress was made prior to 1 April 1974 when Local Government Reorganisation took place. The Greater Manchester Metropolitan County Council was then created and became the Highway Authority.

The decision was taken to proceed with the scheme and the firm of G. Maunsell & Partners, Consulting Engineers, was appointed to undertake the design and supervision of construction of the dual two-lane carriageway section of motorway.

[*] Eccles By-pass M602, Official Opening Brochure, 3 November 1971, Lancashire County Council (Preston Record Office).

Originally, it was intended that the motorway would extend as far as the proposed Manchester and Salford Inner Ring Road. However, when this was deleted from the SELNEC Highway Plan, which had been prepared in 1962, it was decided that the M602 should be terminated at a roundabout at Cross Lane, Salford. Subsequently, Regent Road running eastwards from the roundabout was improved to a dual carriageway standard, thereby providing an improved route to connect with the Mancunian Way.

The 2¼-mile-long route runs for almost its entire length on the north side of the world's first passenger railway line, which was opened for business in 1830 between Manchester and Liverpool. Its westbound carriageway was to utilise land occupied by the former 'slow lines' of the railway. At its western end, the route was separated from the railway by the goods lines leading in-and-out of land owned by the Manchester Docks Company.

The scheme required the construction of four bridges carrying side roads over the motorway and the adjacent railway. It was necessary to demolish a footbridge over the railway, and to replace another with a new bridge spanning both the railway and the motorway.

At the Cross Lane Interchange the roundabout was to be built over the railway, requiring two bridges. An existing 150-year-old bridge over the railway had to be refurbished to provide, along with four subways, pedestrian routes 'through' the terminal roundabout.

The vertical alignment of the side road crossings was severely restricted by adjacent property and the need to provide the maximum possible clearance over the railway, for possible future electrification. In general, precast prestressed concrete beams were used in the superstructures.

The most significant bridge is Cross Lane West, with a length of some 550 feet of which 400 feet is fully enclosed, thereby producing a tunnel effect. Consequently, British Rail insisted on lighting being provided for inspection and maintenance purposes. The lower part of each column was to be surrounded by a large diameter concrete pipe set in mass concrete to provide an impact barrier.

As the motorway was to be approximately at the level of the railway for the greater part of its length, an in-situ reinforced concrete retaining wall/sound barrier was to be built along the north side of the motorway. It would be provided with a 6 feet 6 inches-high parapet to screen the properties. Over one mile long, the wall was to be sloped back

Eccles-Salford Extension. Retaining Wall under construction.

at an angle of 1 in 5 to reduce the reflection of traffic noise to properties on the south side of the railway. Noise 'deadening' was to be achieved by means of a regular pattern of deep vertical grooves in the battered face. In addition, retaining walls were required to support the motorway, as it rose above rail level towards Cross Lane.

It had been stipulated that there should be a minimum clearance of 14 feet between the northernmost rail and the boundary fence of the motorway. No open excavation was to be closer to the railway track than a line drawn from the sleeper ends at 45° to the horizontal. Thus abutments and piers adjacent to the railway were supported on bored piles which also had the advantage of avoiding disturbance by upheaval or vibration.

Although designed for the construction of dual two-lane carriageways initially, provision was made for future widening to provide dual three-lane carriageways.

The motorway drainage was designed on the basis of three outfalls, using existing culverted watercourses. However, considerable difficulties were experienced with several old Victorian brick sewers, due to their positions not being accurately recorded.

The Greater Manchester Metropolitan County Council was the Highway Authority, but the project was to be financed by a 100 per cent grant from the Department of Transport as a 'potential Trunk Road motorway'.

Before construction of the main works, and in order to minimise traffic disruption on local roads, it was decided to build bridges to carry Stott Lane, Weaste Road, Derby Road and Langworthy Road over the line of the motorway. The existing railway bridges on these roads were reconstructed at the same time. In addition, a new drainage outfall to the Manchester Ship Canal was to be constructed in order to upgrade the surface water outlet from the western section of the motorway. The design of the canal outlet had to be such as to limit the velocity of the discharge to a level that would not affect the steerage of passing ships. Designs were prepared by 'Maunsell' and advance works contracts were awarded, on which work began in 1980, the 150th anniversary of the opening of the passenger railway line.

Tenders for the main Contract were invited with alternatives of flexible and rigid carriageway construction. In the event, the accepted tender provided for flexible construction, and work began in January 1981.

Property demolition had already been carried out under separate contracts let by Salford City Council. However, it was found that most of the properties had cellars in which demolition material, e.g. brick, timber, and plaster, had been dumped. It was necessary to remove it, as otherwise an acceptable standard of compaction could not be achieved.

There was more 'unsuitable' excavation than expected, because of extensive soft areas above and below formation, particularly under the westbound carriageway, which was to be built over the former 'slow lines' of the railway. When in use, the 'slow lines' had been provided with 'railway' drainage, but when British Rail decided to remove the two tracks, maintenance of the drainage ceased. The original site investigation had been undertaken in 1970, not long after British Rail had discontinued use of its 'slow lines', and in the intervening 11 years the drainage had 'clogged' and the clay strata below the original railway trackbed became saturated. The soft areas above and below formation of the eastbound carriageway probably occurred as a result of earlier property demolition which left the ground exposed for several years, resulting in water table changes.

The Contractor programmed to carry out earthworks to formation level, for the western third of the Contract, in the first season. A major delaying factor arose due to difficulties met at the outset, when attempting to locate the existing main sewers crossing the site, to the east of Gilda Brook. A similar but less delaying problem occurred in the eastern third of the Works where the Pendleton Interceptor Sewer had to be relocated before major earthworks could begin in that section.

To the east of Stott Lane, a watercourse had been culverted, both to the north and the south of the line of the motorway. It was necessary to establish its condition downstream, as far as the outfall into the Ship Canal. It was found that at one point a partial roof collapse of the brick culvert had occurred, which restricted flow. Remedial action had to be taken before the culverted sections were required to provide the surface water outlet from the western half of the motorway.

In view of the proximity of the motorway to the railway, and the limited verge width, a continuous tensioned corrugated beam safety barrier was provided, where the distance between the back of the hard shoulder and the nearest rail is less than 30 feet. Should the motorway be widened in order to provide the third lanes to the carriageways, it would be replaced by a concrete barrier.

Clearly the use of an existing 'corridor' for the M602, by building alongside the railway, had considerable merit, in eliminating the severance of the community, which would have otherwise occurred. However, it had the effect of creating many difficult engineering problems in such an intensively developed urban area.

The motorway was completed and opened to traffic in December 1982. From the Cross Lane roundabout, Regent Road, A57, was upgraded to a dual carriageway standard to connect with Mancunian Way, and Trafford Road, A5603, was widened through to White City.

The effect was a general renewal and upgrading of this part of Salford with the Council selling most of its blocks of flats to housing developers who refurbished them for private sale. The redevelopment of the former Manchester Docks into Salford Quays, and the success of the Trafford Park Development Corporation in revitalising the Trafford Park Industrial Estate, led to an influx of 'new money' and work opportunities.

10 The Liverpool Outer Ring Road M57

M57
THE LIVERPOOL
OUTER RING ROAD

A proposal for a Liverpool Outer Ring Road, extending from Sefton Town in the north to Gatacre in the south, was included in the 1949 Road Plan for Lancashire. It was to comprise lengths of new all-purpose road together with the substantial widening of existing roads.

During the following two decades, however, massive industrial and housing development began to take place, particularly on the 'Lancashire' periphery of the Merseyside Conurbation. Kirkby grew from a small village to a town with a population of 68,000, the population of Aintree and Maghull doubled, and housing estates proliferated in both Liverpool and Bootle. Major new industries moved into the area, for example, the Ford factory at Halewood and, at Seaforth Docks, large container facilities were built.

Having regard to the development which was taking place, and the consequent generation of new traffic and traffic patterns, a joint committee of the six major Highway Authorities in the Merseyside Conurbation undertook the Merseyside Traffic Survey in 1962, which showed the urgent need for greatly improved road facilities in the Lancashire area.

The County Surveyor then proposed a completely new line for the Liverpool Outer Ring Road, aimed at interconnecting the major radial roads, which included the projected Liverpool-Preston and the South Lancashire motorways. It would also serve the major growth and development areas within the county.

The new route would enable the Ring Road to be built to 'motorway standards', with grade-separated junctions. Subsequently it was designated M57. The proposal was accepted by the Merseyside Highways and Traffic Committee in its Report published in 1965, and was incorporated in the Consultants' Report on the Merseyside Land Use and Transportation Survey. In the latter, the Ring Road was not only considered a necessary part of the road network, but it was recommended that a start on construction should be given the highest priority.

It was the intention that the motorway would run from a junction with Liverpool-Southport Trunk Road, A565, in Thornton, and be clear of the development at Netherton. It would connect with the A59 Trunk Road where, on open land between Aintree and Maghull, a major interchange would form the junction with the proposed Aintree-Skelmersale Motorway. Continuing in a south-easterly direction, there would be a junction with the East Lancashire Road, A580. Skirting Knowsley Park it would pass through a gap between built-up areas to a junction with Liverpool Road, A57, which would provide connections for Huyton, Prescot and St Helens. It would then extend to Tarbock, where an interchange with the South Lancashire Section of the M62 was to be constructed. Beyond this point, it was envisaged that the Ring Road would be continued as far as the Speke-Widnes Road, A562.

Although the 14-mile route passed through a densely populated urban area, only five dwelling houses would have to be demolished to accommodate the construction of the Ring Road. To a large extent, this was due to the existence of the Green Belt and the ready acceptance of the Planning Authorities that the construction of a motorway was not incompatible with it.

As a 'Principal Road motorway', the Lancashire County Council was the Highway Authority for the scheme, which attracted a 75 per cent grant from the Department of the Environment. Its implementation, therefore, was dependent on the timing of its inclusion in the Department's programme and, in order that an early start could be made on at least some part of the construction, it was decided that the scheme should be phased. Priority was given to the Section between the A59 and A580, primarily for the movement of industrial traffic to and from Seaforth Docks, and referred to as Phase 1. Apart from the terminal junctions of this Section, a two-level interchange was to be provided at Ribblers Lane, to serve Kirkby.

Following detailed investigation and preliminary design work, the statutory procedures were completed in 1969, without undue difficulty. The design and supervision of the construction of two bridges to carry railways over the motorway was undertaken by British Rail, and both were the subject of advance contracts.

Work began on the main Contract in April 1970 and, although it provided for earthworks and structures to be built to the ultimate dual three-lane layout, it was intended that, initially, the motorway would only have dual two-lane carriageways. After the Contract had been awarded, however, it was agreed that, having regard to the forecasts of increased traffic, the third lanes would be constructed at the outset.

The Contract involved the construction of 11 structures, the most important being Radshaw Nook Bridge, carrying the northbound slip road of the motorway over the East Lancashire Road, a four-span continuous structure 218 feet long and curved in plan to a 424-feet radius. All the bridges are supported on piled foundations.

Site investigations indicated glacial Boulder Clay overlying relatively soft Bunter Sandstone. In the vicinity of the River Alt, however, alluvial

Radshaw Nook Bridge

sands were encountered. Adjacent to the river, areas of peat with rotted trees were found below the sands, in what may have been former water-courses. On the approach to the East Lancashire Road, the clay was overlain by 'blown' sand.

Approximately 70 per cent of the motorway was constructed on embankment, the largest being between Spencers Lane and the crossing over the Leeds-Liverpool Canal. Most of the imported filling was of unburnt colliery waste from old pit heaps in the St Helens area. A total of almost 1½ million tons was used, thus making a useful contribution to dealing with dereliction. Tests proved that the material was free from the risk of spontaneous combustion, but its use was not permitted within 44 inches of the surface of the motorway.

At the A580, the connection consisted of two slip roads for movement to and from the north only, with the intention that the major portion of the interchange would be constructed in Phase II. Phase I was completed two months early, and was opened to traffic in April 1972.[*]

Meanwhile, in March 1972, work began on the main Contract for Phase II, which involved the construction of six miles of dual three-lane motorway between the East Lancashire Road, A580, and the M62 Interchange at Tarbock. It included a further interchange at the junction with Liverpool Road, A57, at Prescot.

Further advance contracts for two bridges carrying railways over the motorway had already been awarded by British Rail. The construction of 20 other bridges was required, the largest being Knowsley Wood Bridge, carrying the Ring Road over the A580 in two spans each of 120 feet, and with a superstructure of steel plate girders.

Many service diversions were needed, including three 40-inch-diameter trunk water mains serving Liverpool from reservoirs at Rivington. A spoil heap of excavated material from a former open-cast coal site was shaped to form the approach embankment to a railway crossing, and shallow mine workings, probably dating from the early 19th century, were rafted over.

Provision was made in the Contract for the two-mile section between the A57 and Tarbock to be completed at the same time as the section of the M62 between the Interchange at that point, and the M6. These two lengths of motorway were opened to traffic in November 1973 thereby enabling traffic using the M62 to gain access to the centre of Liverpoool via the A57 route, in advance of the completion of the M62 between Tarbock and Queens Drive.

* Liverpool Outer Ring Road Phase I, A59 to A580, Official Opening Brochure, 5 April 1972, Lancashire County Council (Preston Record Office).

Phase II of the Ring Road was completed in March 1974,* shortly before Local Government Reorganisation, when the former Lancashire County Council went out of existence. Its opening to traffic was the final episode in a long series of such events, covering the considerable mileage of motorway for which the Council had been directly responsible, both as the Highway Authority and as the Minister's Agent Authority. It was considered to be fitting that the Liverpool Outer Ring Road was a 'county motorway' lying within the administrative area of the new Merseyside County Council.

In due course the M57, connecting with the M58 and the M62 respectively, became part of the Trunk Road Motorway Network and the responsibility of the Minister of Transport, as the Highway Authority.

Regrettably, no immediate progress was made towards the completion of the remaining parts of the Ring Road, as originally intended. It took nearly 20 years before construction began on the extension from the M62 Interchange at Tarbock to the Speke-Widnes Road, A562. Completed in March 1996, it was designed as a high standard all-purpose road with a two-level interchange connection to the A562, but it was not a 'motorway'.

Although it is believed that there is a strong case for extending the existing Ring Road from the M58/A59 Interchange at Maghull to a junction with the Liverpool-Southport Road, A565, in Thornton, no action had been taken by the year 2000.

* Liverpool Outer Ring Road Phase II, A580 to A57, Official Opening Brochure, 27 March 1974, Lancashire County Council (Preston Record Office).

11   Preston Northern By-pass M55

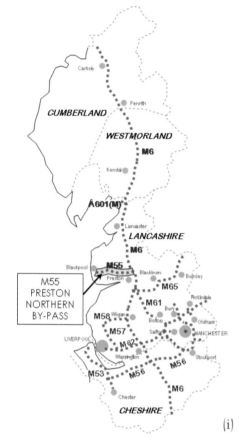

The Road Plan for Lancashire 1949 included a number of '2nd Group Routes', with one of their functions defined as connecting large towns to a '1st Group Route'. A 'link' to Blackpool from the proposed North-South Motorway was such a route, with the intention that it should be designed and constructed as a 'motorway'.

When the Preston By-pass section of the M6 was constructed in the late 1950s, its northern end connecting it with the A6 south of Broughton was planned to be the first part of the 'link', and filling was placed between the slip roads of the junction, for this purpose.

In 1963, traffic problems were becoming so severe in the area that Lancashire County Council, Preston and Blackpool County Borough Councils and other Local Authorities in the Fylde instructed their Surveyors to produce a joint Report putting forward a reasoned case for the early construction of the Blackpool Link, as the route was then called. Supporting statements from the Chief Constables of Lancashire and Preston were included and the Report stressed the following points:

(i)   The increase in leisure time, car ownership, and the much easier access to the area brought about by the completion of the M6 south of Preston, was causing congestion in the town.

(ii) The Fylde roads, in particular the A583 Trunk Road, were more frequently overloaded and the position was steadily deteriorating.

(iii) As a result of (i) and (ii), many accidents were occurring and it was estimated that the construction of the proposed motorway could save over 500 accidents per year including 17 'fatal' in the Fylde area and in Preston.

(iv) The Preston-Lancaster Section of M6, under construction at that time included, at Broughton, the first three-level interchange to be built in Britain. It was designed to provide a connection for the Blackpool Link.

Following the submission of the Report to the Ministry in March 1964, the County Council was authorised to proceed with surveys and preliminary design work, as the Minister's Agent.

In the same year, a re-appraisal of the traffic plans within Blackpool was carried out, which led to a change in the terminal point for the route from East Park Drive to Peel Hill. As a result the route westwards from the proposed junction with Fleetwood Road, A585, north of Kirkham was amended. Subsequently, the railway line from Kirkham to Blackpool South was closed, and a further variation was made in the alignment of the route, in order to utilise a length of the disused track bed.

On the formation of the North Western Road Construction Unit in April 1967, the responsibility for carrying out the preparatory work for the Scheme passed to the Lancashire Sub-Unit.

In early 1969, a Feasibility Study was carried out into proposals for an east-west By-pass of Preston. It considered three proposals:

(a) Preston Northern By-pass, extending to the Fylde Coast,
(b) Preston Southern By-pass, and
(c) Preston Western By-pass

The Study Report* published in September of that year concluded that, whereas the full network of By-passes would be required by 1980, Preston Northern By-pass merited the highest priority.

The Report had highlighted the high incidence of very serious and fatal accidents on the roads leading to the Fylde Coast. Since January 1959 a total of 376 fatal accidents had occurred within the Study area. With a high number of the accidents occurring within Preston itself, it accounted, to some extent, for the change which had taken place in the naming of the route.

After the consideration of possible alternative lines, the motorway, now designated M55, was included in the Minister's Firm Programme in October 1971, and the statutory procedures were begun. The scheme did not involve the demolition of a single habitable dwelling and the number of objections was comparatively small. However, Public Inquiries were held during 1972 and the statutory procedures were completed without undue difficulty.

The project included the construction of approximately 11 miles of dual three-lane carriageway motorway, and a ½-mile length of dual two-lane carriageways through the Broughton Interchange.

The completion of the Interchange with the A6 at Broughton involved the construction of two slip roads to the west of the existing roundabout. To the east of A6, the existing slip roads required amendment to provide a four-lane weaving section for eastbound traffic and a separated collector-distributor road for weaving westbound traffic. The existing Trunk Road, A6, forms part of the national high load route network, on which headroom at bridges must be higher than normal. The number of high loads using the A6 through Broughton each year is very limited. Consideration was given to the most economical way of providing the required headroom

* East-West By-pass of Preston Feasibility Study, Final Report, September 1969, NWRCU/Lancashire Sub-Unit (Preston Record Office).

and it was decided to construct a depressed route through the centre of the roundabout for use by high-load vehicles only. The alternative was to raise the level of the motorway, which would have involved a considerable additional expense in raising the viaduct and approach embankments, constructing additional retaining walls, lengthening the new slip roads and steepening the grades of the existing slip roads.

The scheme also included the construction of a standard two-level interchange with the Kirkham-Fleetwood Road A585 at Corner Row, and slip roads connecting to Preston New Road A583 at Peel, where bridges carrying the roundabout were to be provided in readiness for the extension of the road westwards, at a later date.

M55/A6 Interchange under construction

In total, 21 over-bridges, nine under-bridges, the widening of an existing under-bridge, a reinforced concrete box culvert, a farm underpass, two pedestrian subways, and two retaining walls, were required.

The design of the over-bridges varied, depending upon the services and the class and width of road which they carry. Three have decks of continuous Universal beams composite with reinforced concrete deck slabs and five bridges have decks comprising precast prestressed concrete inverted tee-beams with diaphragms and composite deck slab. Eight of the bridges, including three occupation bridges, are of three-span type with reinforced concrete cantilever side spans and precast prestressed concrete box beams in the centre suspended span. Two of the bridges are of four-span type comprising simply supported precast prestressed concrete box beams.

The most significant under-bridge is the viaduct crossing the existing Broughton Circle roundabout junction with Garstang Road A6. Almost 400 feet long, it comprises three suspended spans of precast prestressed concrete box beams, reinforced concrete frames for the intermediate supports and reinforced concrete slabs cantilevered from the abutments.

The bridging of the Preston-Lancaster Canal posed a stability problem due to the deep-seated peat layers under and adjacent to the crossing, particularly on the west side. To keep the peat excavation and embankment away from the canal, it was decided to incorporate an additional span in the bridge, which consequently has two equal spans of precast prestressed concrete shear-connected box beam construction, the land span of which, on the west side, also serves as an occupation bridge.

Considerable standardisation was achieved by the use of precast concrete deck beams and the extensive use of elliptically shaped and rounded columns of equal size, which allowed standard shutters to be used. The standardisation of fascia detail permitted precasting, with a consequential high standard of finish.

The first contract to be awarded was for the construction of the bridge carrying the motorway over the West Coast Main Line, in order that it could be completed in advance of its electrification. Work began in September 1972 and the early completion of the bridge in July 1973 had the added advantage of providing access along the line of the motorway for use by the main Contractor.

Tenders were invited for two separate main Contracts, east and west of the Preston-Lancaster Canal. In the event, the same Contractor was successful in being awarded both, and began work in May 1973.

The deposits of peat, which occur in many low lying or poorly drained areas, are remnants of the larger concentrations covering much of the Fylde in historic times. They have largely vanished as a result of the combined effects of natural erosion and agricultural drainage. In six areas along the route of the motorway, the peat had to be removed completely, and backfilled to 12 inches below original ground level with imported free-draining material.

The largest of the areas at Mythop Moss extended over a length of 4,000 feet where the peat, which reached a depth of over 30 feet in places, was underlain by soft alluvial silt and clay. The total volume of peat excavated in this area was almost 400,000 cubic yards and the sand used as backfill was obtained from a borrow pit which was opened up between the existing and disused railway lines.

Material for backfilling was obtained from a nearby disused airfield at Inskip, where the runways were broken up and the land returned to agriculture.

In addition to the removal of peat, some 2¼ million cubic yards of other excavation was necessary; 1¾ million cubic yards of selected filling was required, the majority of which had to be imported from quarries up to 20 miles away.

In May 1974, work began on a further Contract for the diversion and widening of the existing Broughton to M6 southbound slip road over a length of almost one mile. Structural work included the extension of an existing reinforced concrete box culvert and the partial reconstruction of two over-bridges.

BAC Jaguar on M55

* M55 Preston Northern By-pass, Opening Brochure, 3 July 1975, NWRCU/Lancashire Sub-Unit (Preston Record Office).

† 'The Blackpool Motorway M55' (W.M. Johnson MBE), year 2000. Personal impressions (Preston Record Office).

Shortly before the M55 was due for completion, arrangements were made in conjunction with the Ministry of Defence, and the British Aircraft Corporation, for a Jaguar G R Mark 1 aircraft, from the Warton (Lancashire) Airfield, to land on the afternoon of Saturday, 26 April 1975, on the road base of a section of carriageway near Weeton. After fitting four of the RAF's latest cluster bombs, it took off from the motorway. The purpose was to demonstrate the Jaguar's ability to land and take off in short distances.

The motorway was opened to traffic in July 1975.*

In 1971, the County Council and the Blackpool County Borough Council had jointly submitted to the Department of the Environment a proposal for a road known as the Squires Gate Link Road. It was to be an all-purpose road from the terminal roundabout of the M55, utilising a further one mile of the disused railway track bed, and would serve Blackpool South Shore and the Airport by means of Squires Gate Lane. It would also connect with the A574, a main route between Blackpool and Lytham St Annes.

In the same year, it was proposed that a further road should be constructed along the full length of the disused railway leading into the centre of Blackpool, and to be known as the Central Railway Route.

The two roads would each have a different function, but would be complementary to each other. Initially, priority was given, by the County Council, to the Squires Gate Link Road, but the Central Railway Route, subsequently to be named 'Yeadon Way', was constructed first and opened to traffic in January 1986. It provided a direct connection into major coach/car parking areas on the site of former railway sidings, with a capacity equivalent to 6,000 cars.

The construction of Squires Gate Link Road, and the dualling of Squires Gate Lane, were completed in May 1995.†

12 Bury Easterly By-Pass M66 and A56 Extension to M65

12.1 Bury Easterly By-pass M66

Route 9 in the Road Plan for Lancashire 1949 was described as 'tapping the industrial area of East Lancashire north of Manchester'. It was intended to replace the A56 as far as the northern termination of the proposed Bury By-pass. It would then follow the existing A56 Trunk Road to Edenfield, and the A680 corridor to its junction with Route 8 near Whalley. Haslingden would be by-passed. Burnley and Blackburn traffic would connect with the route at Edenfield and Haslingden respectively.

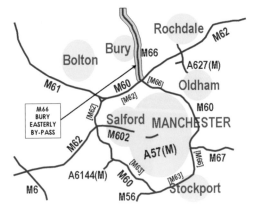

It was included within the category of 'Express (1st Group) Routes'. They would all have dual carriageways and almost 50 per cent of the total length would be designed and constructed to 'motorway standard'.

At its southern end, the first section of the route was the one-mile length of the proposed Middleton Link which subsequently was to become part of the Manchester Outer Ring Road M60. From an interchange with the proposed Yorkshire Branch Road which was later designated the Lancashire-Yorkshire Motorway M62, the three-mile section to a junction with the A58 at Heap Bridge was to be known as the 'Bury Easterly By-pass Southern Section'.

The six-mile-long 'Northern Section' was to extend as far as the southern end of the proposed 'Edenfield-Rawtenstall Level Crossing By-pass' at a junction with the A676. In the event, it was the first part of Route 9 to be constructed. In February 1962, the By-pass was included in the Minister's Programme, with the Lancashire County Council acting as the Agent Authority for the design and the award of the construction contract.

Apart from by-passing the level crossing in the centre of Rawtenstall, the scheme also included a connection to the A680, known as the Haslingden Link.

As a high standard dual two-lane carriageway road with grade separation, limited access, and only a small number of footpath crossings, the extra cost of a design for the 3½-mile-long By-pass conforming with full 'motorway standards' would have been comparatively small. Regrettably the Ministry would not agree to the County Council's recommendations in that respect.

The line of the By-pass, as shown in the Road Plan, was to the east of Edenfield. It was, however, moved to the west of the village in order to produce a better alignment.

The statutory procedures were completed without the need for a Public Inquiry.

Early in 1967, tenders were invited by the County Council, for return to the North Western Road Construction Unit (NWRCU) on 3 April, only

Middleton Link from M62

two days after the Unit was formed. As this was the first of the Units to be established, the Contract for the construction of the By-pass was the first in the country to be administered under the new arrangements.

Work began in June 1967 and the By-pass was opened to traffic in July 1969.

In November 1969, the Final Report of the North East Lancashire Project Study was published. It included a proposal for an east-west route, the subsequent Calder Valley Motorway M65. The effect on Route 9 was to move its northern terminal eastwards from Whalley towards Padiham, by-passing Accrington and Clayton-le-Moors, and abandoning proposals for widening the A680 through the two towns, as envisaged in the Road Plan. As a result, Route 9 would become of greater importance as a direct link between two motorways, the M62 and the M65.

Meanwhile, several alternative lines were considered for the by-passing of Bury and those to the west of the town were discounted. The statutory procedures for the Southern Section began in the early 1970s based on a line similar to that in the Road Plan, and there were no serious objections. However, as a result of comments made at the time, an under-bridge was provided between the M62 and the A58 to allow for a future link to serve industrial development at Pilsworth.

A Contract for the construction of this Section of dual three-lane carriageway motorway was awarded by the NWRCU and work began in February 1973. It was completed and opened to traffic in August 1975.

Meanwhile, progress had been made on the Northern Section in that it was included in the Programme in November 1971 and a Public Inquiry was held in the following year. One of the major objections to the proposal came from an industrial firm regarding the loss of available space for expansion, which the By-pass would cause. An alternative line was investigated and agreed, but the statutory procedures had to be recommenced and it was not until early 1975 before they were satisfactorily completed.

From the A58 Interchange at Heap Bridge the Route followed a line which had been protected since the 1930s, when a large housing estate was being built. At that time, it was intended that the By-pass would be a dual two-lane all-purpose road. Designed as a motorway in the early 1970s, however, it was to have grade separation, restricted access, and a consequently higher profile, requiring the construction of retaining walls through the estate.

Because of the limitations imposed by the development, it was necessary to minimise the width of the 'land-take' along this length. By lessening the width of the central reservation, the hard shoulders and the verges, an overall reduction of over 12 feet was achieved, without departing from the standard width of the carriageways. The height of the 'fence' walls on the top of the retaining walls was increased progressively to assist in noise reduction.

For a length of almost one mile north of the housing estate the gradient was 2.85%, justifying the provision of a climbing lane for slow-moving goods vehicles on the north-bound carriageway.

Where the By-pass crossed Manchester Road, A56, at Ramsbottom, south-facing slip roads were to be provided. That part of Route 9, which was to be designated M66, terminated at the southern end of the Edenfield/Rawtenstall By-pass some two miles to the north, where the construction of north-facing slip roads were to form, in effect, a split-diamond junction.

Over the whole length of the By-pass surface deposits of glacial drift lie over the solid rocks of the Carboniferous system. The regional dip of the rock is to the south-west but the beds are subject to much local faulting and folding. In a few areas, mainly in valley bottoms and poorly drained hollows, there are local deposits of peat and recent alluvium.

The Route crossed the ridge carrying Walmersley Old Road, within a cutting up to 50 feet deep, where the drift was very thin and almost all in rocks of the Millstone Grit series. It was found that the stability of the east side of the cutting was affected by the presence of a thick bed of permeable gritstone overlying impermeable mudstone. With the strata dipping towards the cutting, water percolating through the gritstone would be held up by the mudstone and its pressure was likely to provoke a slope failure. In order to avert this danger, drains were to be installed in the slope by boring horizontally a distance of 100 feet and installing perforated plastic pipes in the boreholes.

North of Walmersley Old Road the Route enters the Irwell Valley and runs along its eastern slope. The valley was once occupied by a glacial lake (Lake Irwell). When the ice retreated at the close of the glacial period, the lake was drained and the lowering of the water level caused many landslips in the soft Lacustrine clay on the valley sides. These are notorious, and easily reactivated by civil engineering works.

The Route was carefully chosen, by taking advantage wherever possible of the strength of the underlying Millstone Grit where this was near the surface, and by avoiding very high cutting or embankment slopes on side-long ground.

The scheme required the construction of five under-bridges, 10 over-bridges, two footbridges, five subways and five long retaining walls.

The bridge piers, bank seats and abutments and the retaining walls were all to be of reinforced concrete construction. Columns of elliptical cross-section, without cill beams, were chosen wherever possible to provide a light and uncluttered appearance.

The most significant structure was the four-span Manchester Road Bridge, carrying the A56 over the motorway, with a severe skew. With spans of 85 feet, 105 feet, 85 feet and 98 feet, the superstructure consisted of nine continuous welded steel plate girders, and a reinforced concrete deck slab.

The superstructures of the other bridges were designed in either reinforced or prestressed concrete, using precast beams, in most instances.

In addition to a conventional drainage system, provision was made for channels to be constructed in the rock cuttings, with the same depth as that of the carriageway construction in order to avoid excessive excavation. Concrete lined open 'ditches' at the back of the hard shoulders served a dual purpose by acting as a 'rock-catcher' to prevent loose rocks rolling on to the carriageway.

Following the award of a Contract, work began in August 1975.

The earthworks involved a total of 2.3 million cubic yards of excavation, of which 650,000 cubic yards was in rock. Some 1.1 million cubic yards was required for the construction of embankments.

There was no active mining in the area but there were records of old coal workings. Where these were found within 30 feet below road level, they were dealt with either by excavation and back-filling, by grouting, or by capping with reinforced concrete slabs.

In the cutting at Bolton Road roundabout, where Lacustrine deposits occur, buttresses of rockfill were constructed in the eastern slope in order to provide stability in an area where much flatter slopes would otherwise have been necessary.

The cutting at Sheep Hey is in the Fletcher Bank Grit with very little overlying drift. Because of the nature of the rock and the flat bedding, it was found possible to design the side slopes to a very steep 4 in 1 angle. Blasting was required to excavate the cutting and a pre-splitting technique was specified to obtain an even appearance to the rock face. Rock bolting was employed to tie back individual blocks which, upon inspection, appeared capable of movement. Bands of shale or poorly cemented rock were faced with rubble masonry to prevent erosion by weathering.

In addition to the provision of noise barriers, where the motorway is close to residential property, a number of buildings received insulation treatment.

The Northern Section of Bury Easterly By-pass was completed and opened to traffic in May 1978.[*]

12.2   A56 Extension to M65

The further extension of Route 9 beyond the northern end of Edenfield-Rawtenstall By-pass was carried out in stages. Following a Public Inquiry held in 1976, work on the construction of the 2½-mile-long Haslingden By-pass, to the west of the town, began in June 1979. A high standard all-purpose dual carriageway road, it had restricted access and occupied part of the disused track-bed of the former railway line between Helmshore and Accrington. At its northern end, at the junction with the A680, only a surface level roundabout was constructed without any provision for upgrading to full grade separation. It was completed and opened to traffic in December 1981.

Meanwhile, the construction of the Northern Section of Accrington Easterly By-pass had begun in August of that year. This one-mile length provided a link between the A679 and the Hyndburn to Burnley Section of the M65, both of which were opened to traffic in December 1983. The construction of the three-mile-long Southern Section involved heavy earthworks, particularly in the northern Peel Park cutting. Starting in February 1984, the Contract was completed in July 1985, 10 months ahead of programme, and Route 9 between M62 and M65 became fully operational.

[*] Bury Easterly By-pass (Northern Section), Opening Brochure, May 1978, NWRCU/ Lancashire Sub-Unit (Preston Record Office).

13   The Aintree–Skelmersdale Motorway M58

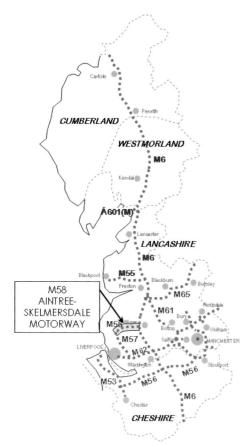

The Road Plan for Lancashire 1949 contained proposals for improvements to the road network in the Southport and Ormskirk area, which included Route 215 connecting Wigan to the A570 Trunk Road at Bickerstaffe. This incorporated a section of the Wigan-Ormskirk Road, A577, and included proposed by-passes of Up Holland and Skelmersdale.

On confirmation of the choice of Skelmersdale for the site of a New Town, in the early 1960s, the line of Route 215 was drastically revised to form a continuous new route south of the New Town, and a junction with the M6 at Orrell. At the same time, investigations were carried out into possible routes for its extension.

Eastwards through South Wigan it was the intention that the route should connect with the proposed M61 and continue beyond, into Bolton. Referred to as Route 225 in the Road Plan, the scheme was the subject of preliminary design, to the extent that, in the construction of the M61 in the late 1960s, the Ministry of Transport agreed to the inclusion of a bridge under the motorway at Westhoughton, to allow for a future interchange.

Westwards, it was considered that the route should be extended through to Aintree, to a junction with the Liverpool-Preston Trunk Road A59 and the proposed Liverpool Outer Ring Road.

Designed for an eventual population of 80,000, and as an 'overspill' development, it was expected that there would be substantial traffic flows between the New Town, Liverpool, Bootle and Crosby. The proposed route would also relieve the seriously congested A59 through Ormskirk and Burscough, by providing an alternative for traffic to and from the north, especially heavy vehicles serving the Dock complexes of Merseyside.

In 1966, the Aintree-Skelmersdale-M6 Route featured in the County Council's campaign, 'Lancashire Needs'. Subsequently, it appeared in the Government's White Paper, 'Roads for the Future' published in May 1970, as an integral part of the national inter-urban road system.

Meanwhile, in 1964, work had begun within the New Town and one of the first requirements was to by-pass a section of the A577, and to open up the proposed industrial area. This was to be achieved by the construction of a new two-mile-long road along the line of the proposed Aintree-M6 Route between Glenburn Road and Stannanought Road. Starting in May 1966, it was to be known as the Regional Road and would form the 'backbone' of the future road system of the New Town. However, due to restrictions on grants from central Government, the standard was limited to that of a single two-lane carriageway all-purpose road when it was opened to traffic in March 1968. Only minimal work was to be carried out at the junctions with the internal roads.

As Skelmersdale developed, it became increasingly urgent to connect the New Town to the M6. A detailed scheme was prepared by the Lancashire County Council incorporating, within the design of the interchange, the existing Edgewood Hall Bridge, which had been constructed to carry the M6 over the line of the proposed Route 215. On the east side of the M6, there was to be a link between the interchange and the A577, which would enable traffic to by-pass Up Holland.

Junction with M6 at Orrell

Extending from the eastern end of the Regional Road at Pimbo, through to the M6, the construction of the Up Holland By-pass section of the Route began in 1968. As a County road, the County Council received a grant of 75 per cent of the cost, from the Ministry of Transport.

Although only a dual two-lane carriageway all-purpose road, it was envisaged that, in due course, it would be upgraded, with the addition of third lanes and the provision of hard shoulders. An extruded asphalt kerb was, therefore, provided at the outer edges of the carriageways and a 'positive' drainage system was installed.

Two bridges were required at the crossing of minor roads, the most significant being Moor Road Bridge with a single span of 158 feet. Six eight-feet-deep steel girders carry a nine-inch-thick reinforced concrete deck slab. The existing M6 Winstanley Park Railway Bridge over the Wigan-Up Holland Line had to be widened on each side to carry the slip roads connecting with the By-pass.

Four old mineshafts, with a maximum depth of 240 feet, were encountered. These had been filled by the previous mine owners but grouting was carried out to fill any voids, prior to 'capping'.

The By-pass was opened to traffic in October 1970.[*]

* Skelmersdale and Up Holland By-pass, Skelmersdale Link to M6, Official Opening Brochure, 1 October 1970, Lancashire County Council (Preston Record Office).

In 1972, the Minister of Transport agreed to the Route being designated as a Trunk Road and, in the following year, the Regional Road was upgraded by the provision of a second two-lane carriageway, and hard shoulders. Further upgrading of the whole of the length from Glenburn Road to the M6 was undertaken in 1977 when it became a dual three-lane 4½-mile Section of the M58.

The statutory procedures for the remaining eight miles of the motorway began in 1971. These were the subject of a Public Inquiry in September 1973, which was inconclusive, and it was adjourned for a period of a year. Subsequently, the procedures were completed satisfactorily. The work was to be carried under two contiguous Contracts but tenders were not accepted until 1978, both being awarded to the same Contractor. Construction began in the April of that year.

Apart from the terminal interchanges at Aintree and Glenburn Road, the Contracts included the building of intermediate interchanges at the junctions of A506, Melling, and A570, Bickerstaffe. The A506 is an important route serving the large residential and industrial area of Kirkby, which had developed rapidly after the Second World War. This Interchange was, however, to be uni-directional, allowing only for traffic movement to and from the east, i.e. Skelmersdale and M6.

The section of the motorway between Melling and Glenburn Road was to have dual three-lane carriageways. Between Maghull and Melling, however, only two-lane carriageways were to be provided, but the 'land-take' allowed for future widening in order to accommodate the third lanes at a later date.

At Aintree, part of the Maghull Interchange, as it was known, had already been constructed to connect the Liverpool Outer Ring Road M57 with the A59. In the development of its design to accommodate the M58, allowance had to be made for the possibility of extending the M57 to the west, to connect with the A565.

The two-year Contracts included the construction, or alteration, of a total of 27 bridges, with the decks mainly formed of prestressed concrete beams. The most significant structure is Wood Hall Railway Bridge, carrying the Walton Junction-Preston Line over the motorway and slip road. With three continuous skew spans of approximately 130 feet, 90 feet and 135 feet, British Rail designed and supervised its construction. Apart from the crossing of side roads and minor watercourses, other bridges were required to carry the motorway over the Leeds and Liverpool Canal, and a slip road over the River Alt.

A major diversion of the River Alt in both culvert and open channel was necessary. This involved the construction of a reinforced concrete structure 500 feet long.

The main drainage included a coffer-dam crossing of the Leeds and Liverpool Canal, for both a culvert and outfall pipe, and a thrust bore was driven beneath the railway line to accommodate a 42-inch-diameter pipe.

During the period of the Contracts, it was considered necessary to redesign part of the Maghull Interchange. Whereas traffic on the A59 passing through the Interchange would normally negotiate the roundabout, it was found that this was causing severe congestion at peak hours. It was decided, therefore, to construct a carriageway across the roundabout and provide traffic signal control. Although it was intended that this facility should only be brought into operation at times of congestion, it became a permanent feature. For this reason, and delays due to adverse weather and difficult earthworks problems, the Contractor was granted an extension of time.

Work on the two Contracts was completed during 1980, and the length of the motorway open to traffic was extended through to the junction with the A570 at Bickerstaffe in June, and to Aintree in September, of that year.

At the time of Local Government Reorganisation in 1974, the proposals of Lancashire County Council for Route 225, which would extend the motorway through to Bolton, had been transferred to the Greater Manchester Metropolitan County Council. Despite representations which were made to the Ministry of Transport emphasing the importance of the scheme, little progress had been made before the Metropolitan County Council went out of existence.

Subsequently, the Department of Transport accepted responsibility for the proposal and appointed Consulting Engineers to investigate possible alternative alignments. In 1989, Public Consultation was carried out into three routes for the construction of a 'high standard all-purpose road' – not a 'motorway'. None of these would have utilised a bridge carrying the M61, which had been provided specifically for the future interchange between the two motorways.

The Preferred Route, which would connect with the A58 near its junction with the M61 at Chequerbent, was the subject of a Public Inquiry held in October 1994/February 1995. The Secretary of State accepted the Inspector's recommendations regarding this route and the statutory procedures were completed, but the scheme was withdrawn from the Trunk Road Programme in 1996.

It was decided, however, that the line of the route should still be protected against development, and the responsibility for the scheme was passed to the Local Authorities. This seems surprising, as an eastwards extension of the M58 would be of considerable benefit to the north-west region, and relieve the very heavily trafficked sections of the M62 within the Manchester Conurbation.[*]

* Aintree-Skelmersdale –M6 Motorway M58 (W.M. Johnson MBE) November 2000. Personal impressions (Preston Record Office).

14   Hyde By-pass and Denton Relief Road M67

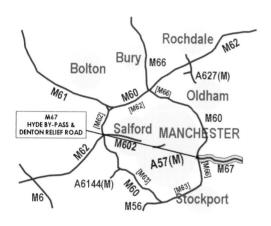

The A57 Trunk Road from Denton to Mottram-in-Longendale had been seen to be in need of improvement for many years and proposals for its upgrading go back to the inter-war period. In 1965 the Ministry of Transport appointed Sir William Halcrow & Partners to report on a route selected by the County Surveyor of Cheshire and this led, in stages, to the development of the design to partial 'urban' and partial 'rural' motorway standards. Its place in the system of motorways around Manchester is that of a radial route in an easterly direction from the Manchester Outer Ring Road, to which it would eventually be connected via the proposed Denton Relief Road. It was the intention that, in due course, the motorway would be extended as an improved route through to Sheffield.

The three-mile-long Hyde By-pass section of dual three-lane motorway, M67, was the first part to be constructed. From a grade-separated junction with Manchester Road, Denton, it was to pass through a mainly urban area to the junction of the A57 and the A560 near Mottram. The horizontal alignment was severely constrained by buildings of industrial or social importance and by reservoirs at Godley. A grade separated split-diamond interchange was to be provided to give access to Hyde town centre.

The existing ground to be traversed by the By-pass falls from its eastern end for some two miles at a 1 in 30 gradient. The line crossed several narrow, 30- to 50-feet-deep steep-sided valleys, in addition to that of the River Tame. The site investigation indicated the presence of Boulder Clay and some alluvium in the Tame valley.

The designed profile for the By-pass required a 20-feet-deep cutting at the western end and embankments with a maximum height of 45 feet at the river crossing. Elsewhere, it was to be predominantly in cutting, with a maximum depth of 50 feet where it was to pass under the Manchester-Sheffield Line.

It was estimated that approximately one half of the excavated material would be suitable for embankment construction.

Although no active mining now takes place in the area, it was known that some was carried out within living memory and mineworking investigations and treatment, where necessary, were to be included in the Contract. These included the filling of a known shaft to a drift mine, just east of the River Tame, and the location of a suspected mineshaft on the centre line of the motorway.

Before work on the high embankments was to be allowed to commence, a two-feet-thick layer of granular material was to be laid as a 'starter layer'. A six-month waiting period was to be included in the Contract to allow for initial settlement and dissipation of pore pressures, after the first stage fill had been placed.

The By-pass required the construction of eight bridges. The most significant is that over the River Tame. Supported on reinforced concrete columns founded on cast in-situ bored piles, continuous steel girders carry a composite deck over three spans of 74 feet, 105 feet and 74 feet.

The design and supervision of the construction of the two railway bridges over the By-pass was undertaken by British Rail.

Two pedestrian subways and two culverts of reinforced concrete box construction were also required. To minimise the land-take in the urban area, substantial lengths of retaining wall up to a maximum height of almost 40 feet were to be constructed in the cuttings.

Denton Relief Road

The navigable Peak Forest Canal had to be diverted through a new 360-feet-long reinforced concrete channel, and culverted under the By-pass.

Construction work began in May 1975, with a series of advance contracts followed by a main Contract. Due to the difficulties encountered in working within the urban area, requiring major service diversions, the By-pass was not completed and opened to traffic until March 1978.[*]

Meanwhile, work had begun on the construction of the Denton Relief Road, M67, the westwards extension of the Hyde By-pass.[†]

Passing through the heavily built-up centre of the town of Denton, the 1½-mile length of dual three-lane carriageway Section of motorway deviates to the north, away from the A57. Mainly in cutting to a maximum depth of 30 feet, it is then carried on embankment to be almost coincident with the A57, before passing over the Heaton Norris-Guide Bridge Railway line. Slip roads continue westwards to join the split dual carriageways of the A57.

A two-directional grade separated Interchange serves the town centre. Of the 650,000 cubic yards of excavated Boulder Clay to be taken from the cutting, only 90,000 cubic yards was required as filling to embankments.

Seven bridges were required and high retaining walls were provided to support the faces of both the cuttings and embankments.

The bridge at Denton station has four separate decks, carrying the motorway, two slip roads, and one carriageway of the diverted A57, over the railway.

A 33-inch-diameter outfall drain, 1,000 yards long, was laid under an advance works contract, which was completed in 1975. Major water mains up to a maximum diameter of 36 inches were diverted prior to re-laying on the bridges over the motorway.

Work on the main Contract began in July 1978.

Similar difficulties to those experienced in the construction of Hyde By-pass had the effect of delaying the opening of the Relief Road until September 1981.

[*] M67 Hyde By-pass Motorway, Explanatory Brochure, February 1978, NWRCU/Sir William Halcrow and Partners (Preston Record Office).

[†] M67 Motorway, Denton Relief Road, Explanatory Brochure, May 1980, NWRCU/Sir William Halcrow and Partners (Preston Record Office).

15 The Mid-Wirral Motorway M53 and A55 Extension to the Welsh Border

15.1 The Mid-Wirral Motorway M53

In the 1960s, Vauxhall Motors decided to build a car factory at Hooton, Ellesmere Port, on the site of a disused airfield. However, the existing road access was totally inadequate.

A new road network was required within the immediate area, to serve the development. Not only was it essential for the supply of raw materials, and as a reasonable means of access for employees, but it was required also for the delivery of finished vehicles to markets in all parts of the country and abroad.

The site was close to Ellesmere Port itself, at the western end of the Manchester Ship Canal, and near to the docks at Birkenhead and Liverpool.

In particular, access was needed to the A41, the major road between Chester and Birkenhead.

In view of the employment which the factory would bring to the area, the Cheshire County Council was keen to assist in the development. Following negotiations with the company it was agreed that a new dual two-lane carriageway road would be constructed from a junction with the A41 at Hooton, and a junction with the A5032 immediately north of Ellesmere Port, both of which would be grade separated. The latter would link directly into the site of the new factory and its cost would be met by the company.

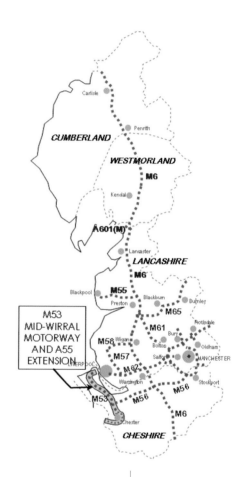

Both the factory and the 2½-mile-long road, known initially as the Hooton Industrial Road, were built concurrently by the same Contractor.

Although primarily serving the needs of the factory when completed in 1968, it soon became apparent that there was an expanding need for even better facilities. It was decided, therefore, to extend the road southwards, through Ellesmere Port for a further 2½ miles, as far as the A5117 and to provide grade separated junctions. On completion of this section, in 1975, and upgrading to a dual two-lane carriageway standard, the whole length was designated as the M531, the first 'County motorway' in Cheshire.

Meanwhile, in 1965, G. Maunsell and Partners, the firm of Consulting Engineers, was appointed by the Ministry of Transport to carry out a location study for a new route serving the Wirral Peninsula generally. It was to commence from the southern end of the 2nd Mersey Tunnel (Wallasey-Liverpool), at Bidston, and terminate in the Hooton-Sutton area.

Parliamentary powers for the construction of the 2nd Mersey Tunnel had been granted in 1964 and work on a pilot tunnel had commenced early in 1966.* In their Report submitted in the August of that year, the Consultants recommended that the new route should be a dual three-lane motorway from the new tunnel approach road in Wallasey to connect with the Hooton Industrial Road, which was then under construction.

It was further recommended that, in due course, the route should be extended further southwards across the A5117 to a connection with the A41 near Backford.

The proposed road was then designated the M53 and, in 1967, the firm was appointed to undertake the detailed design of that part of the route north of Hooton.

Following a Public Inquiry, the statutory procedures were completed and a Contract for its construction was awarded, which included provision for a future interchange at Hooton to accommodate the recommended extension.

The works commenced in July 1969 and included the construction of four interchanges at Moreton, Woodchurch, Clatterbrige and Hooton, along its nine-mile length.

The site investigations along the route had shown predominantly Boulder Clay overlying Pebble Beds and Bunter Sandstone with some Keuper Marl at the northern end. Low-lying ground in the Fender Valley has deposits of soft peaty clay and silt up to 25 feet thick.

It was recognised at the design stage that, for a length of one mile between Upton Road and Woodchurch, the soil was low-quality alluvium of considerable depth and that special requirements should be specified. These included pre-drainage, the restriction of heavy plant, dry-weather operations only, and the use of selected materials. All material, whether in cuttings or under future embankments, was removed for 2 feet 6 inches below formation level and replaced with rock layers.

In the areas of severed land inside the loops of the Moreton Spur connecting roads, the Contractor excavated borrow pits which were reinstated with unsuitable material.

Rock blasting was forbidden in the area adjacent to Clatterbridge Hospital but it was found to be possible to excavate the rock by 'ripping'.

At Moreton, a spur road designed and constructed to 'motorway standard' provided the link to serve the Upton/Moreton area. The layout divided the heavy commuter traffic from that using the motorway, by

* Mid-Wirral Road 'Report & Recommendations on the Route and Design of the Road', August 1966, Ministry of Transport/G Maunsell and Partners (Chester Record Office).

means of exceptionally long slip road connections with relatively easy curves. This was possible because of the low agricultural value of the low-lying area of the Fender River Valley.

The design of the Woodchurch Interchange was unusual and, at that time, the only one of its type in the country. It is, in effect, a three-level interchange fitted into a two-level site, by having an elongated roundabout with rising gradients. Features controlling the design were the limited headroom under, and in close proximity to, a railway; the Fender river flood water levels; a nearby block of flats; and the limited availability of land due to new development.

Compared with a compact three-level interchange, the adopted design saved about 800,000 cubic yards of imported filling and 500 feet length of viaduct.

A total of 41 bridges was required and, with the exception of two post-tensioned segmented spine bridges, they all comprised precast pretensioned concrete beams. There are two viaducts of eight and ten simply supported spans.

Woodchurch
Interchange

A piled raft formed the base construction of over a mile of carriageway with a total area of 42,000 square yards in the Fender Valley, where peat and silty alluvial sands reached depths of up to 20 feet. The 13-inch-thick reinforced concrete slab was supported on driven cast in-situ piles varying in length from 35 to 50 feet at 14 to 16 feet centres. It was necessary to form a shallow embankment as an essential prerequisite to the piling in order to provide access over the bad ground for plant and materials.

Although the cost was high, it showed a considerable saving compared with the alternative of peat excavation and replacement with imported filling.

The Contract was completed in February 1972, following the opening to traffic of the first 'bore' of the 2nd Mersey Tunnel, in June 1971.*

The Consultants had recommended that the extension through to Backford, which would provide a by-pass of the A41 and give traffic relief for Sutton, should continue as part of a phased programme of construction. Clearly, however, the upgrading of the route through Ellesmere Port, as the M531, made the prospect of this being achieved in the foreseeable future very unlikely.

The M531 was further extended by a County Council contract for the construction of a seven-span viaduct over the A5117 roundabout and a one-mile length of dual two-lane carriageway motorway to link in to the Interchange with the M56 at Stoak. This was completed, together with the adjoining length of M56, in March 1981.

Work on the construction of the final section of the Mid-Wirral Motorway, which was to be numbered the M53 throughout the whole of its length, began in June 1980. From Stoak Interchange, it extended over

* M53 Motorway Cross Lane to Hooton, Official Opening Brochure, 1 February 1972, NWRCU/G Maunsell & Partners (Chester Record Office).

a length of almost three miles to connect with the A56 at Hoole Village, on the outskirts of Chester.

It required the construction of four under-bridges and two over-bridges, the most significant being a four-span crossing at the Shropshire Union Canal.

Alternative tenders had been invited by Cheshire County Council for flexible and rigid construction, for the dual two-lane carriageways. In the event, the lower of the tenders, involving concrete construction, was accepted. The Contractor elected to lay the 11-inch-thick reinforced concrete slab for each carriageway, with its adjacent hard shoulder and central reserve edge strip, in a single 38-foot width, between fixed forms.

For most of its length, the motorway was to be on shallow embankment less than six feet in height, the main exception being at the southern end where it reached 25 feet.

In order to ensure the uninterrupted progress of the SGME concreting train, it was necessary to complete all the structures and side road diversions in the first 12 months of the Contract. Sections of flexible construction were to be provided at the under-bridges.

The concreting train was required to lay the slabs in two layers, with the upper three-inch thickness in air-entrained concrete. Using limestone aggregate, construction joints were to be spaced at 20-feet intervals.

The laying of the concrete slabs for the two carriageways was carried out in 12 and nine working days respectively. The maximum length laid in a single day was nearly 1,800 feet.

This section of motorway was opened to traffic in July 1982.

15.2   The A55 Extension to the Welsh Border

As long ago as 1924, there were proposals for a 'ring road' around Chester and by the 1930s the north-eastern section had been completed. Although some progress was made in furthering the scheme during the 1940s, it was not until 1961 before an Order was made relating to a route for a southern section of the 'ring road', as a diversion of part of the A55 and later to be known as Chester Southerly By-pass.

It was envisaged that the By-pass would extend from the A41 Whitchurch Road, east of Chester, through to Broughton in North Wales. Based on predicted traffic flows, it was considered that the section between A41 and A483, Wrexham Road, should be designed to 'motorway standards' to form an ultimate link into the national motorway system via the proposed M53 and M56 routes.

Following extensive Public Consultation, and negotiations between the Department of Transport and the Welsh Office, the statutory procedures were completed in September 1972, following a Public Inquiry.

The Orders were, however, only in respect of an 'all-purpose road' and not a 'motorway', although it was the publicised intention to apply a Special Road Order on opening, in order to restrict its use.

The most significant features in the design and construction of the 6½-mile-long dual two-lane carriageway By-pass were the River Dee Crossing and the problems associated with alluvial deposits to the west of the river, and across the Balderton Marsh area.

The By-pass was completed and opened to traffic in December 1976, when the Secretary of State for Wales announced the timetable for the completion of the dualling of the whole of the A55 from Chester to Holyhead. This represented a major investment in North Wales and a commitment to provide an improved link to the Port of Holyhead, serving Ireland.

There was, however, the 'Missing Link'. For many years there had been serious problems of traffic congestion on that section of the A41 between the eastern end of the By-pass and the A56, north of Chester.

Although the road has dual carriageways, it has many junctions and sub-standard visibility where it crosses railways and a canal. Carrying a large volume of industrial and tourist traffic to both Chester and North Wales, the situation was exacerbated by the completion of the M53 in 1982.

Work on the construction of the three-mile dual two-lane carriageway all-purpose 'Missing Link', under a Cheshire County Council contract, began in October 1989. With grade separated interchanges at M53/A56, and A51 at Vicars Cross, and at the connection with the Southerly By-pass, a total of 14 bridges was required.

Its completion in June 1991 achieved the objective of providing a continuous high standard route into North Wales. It is regrettable, however, that, at a comparatively minor increase in cost, it was not designed and constructed as a 'motorway'.

16   The North Cheshire East-West Motorway M56

16.1   Introduction

The need for a high standard modern road south of the River Mersey between the Merseyside and Manchester Conurbations was foreseen many years ago. Such a road was included in the Chapman Plan for Cheshire published in 1947, and the County Development Plan of 1958 defined a line agreed between the County Council and the Ministry of Transport.

At its eastern end, the proposed road was to be an extension of Princess Parkway, in the City of Manchester, and was included in the proposals of the South East Lancashire and North East Cheshire (SELNEC) Authorities, published in 1962. It would be part of the local motorway system and complementary to the network of national motorways of which the M6 is the principal north-south route west of the Pennines.

The main functions of the proposed motorway were to:

(a)   provide an improved means of communication between North Wales, the Wirral part of the Merseyside Conurbation, and the Manchester Conurbation,

(b)   cater for the development of industry in North Cheshire and

(c)   connect both Conurbations to the M6.

The County Council was of the view that it should be independent of the existing road system and grade-separated throughout. In November 1963, the Minister of Transport announced the inclusion of the Extension of Princess Parkway through to Bowdon in the Trunk Road Programme for 1967-1968. In the following year the Helsby-Frodsham By-pass Section at the western end of the route was also included in this programme, but a date was not specified.

The early work on route location and preliminary design was carried out by the County Council, and was fully described in 'The Blue Report'. In locating a line for the proposed road, the following main issues were considered:[*]

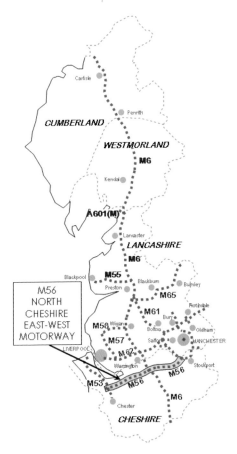

*North Cheshire Motorway M56, Hapsford/Wythenshawe, Explanatory Brochure, 1970, Ministry of Transport/Cheshire County Council (Chester Record Office).

(i)   Between Hapsford and Preston Brook, the alternatives of a 'marsh' crossing through deep peat deposits and a 'hill' route across attractive countryside necessitating steep gradients and rock excavation.
(ii) The crossing of the River Weaver, and the Weaver Navigation Canal.
(iii) The effect on the development of Runcorn New Town.
(iv) The need for a connection to the Runcorn-Widnes Bridge.
(v)   The interchange with the M6.
(vi) The future connection to the proposed Sale By-pass.
(vii) The provision of a link to Manchester Airport.

In April 1967, the scheme became the responsibility of the North Western Road Construction Unit, with the Cheshire Sub-Unit undertaking the design and supervision of construction.

A traffic study, undertaken by the County Council, had shown that, within four years, the A56 through Helsby and Frodsham would be carrying more than three times its capacity. Over 30 per cent of the daily traffic flow between Hapsford and Daresbury consisted of medium and heavy goods vehicles.

There was strong support from local action groups for immediate progress being made on the scheme. On one occasion, the car in which the then Prime Minister, the Rt Hon. Sir Alec Douglas Home MP, was travelling on the A56 was stopped in Helsby. Irate residents demanded the early construction of a by-pass of Helsby and Frodsham.

16.2   Hapsford to Preston Brook

It was finally decided that the section of the route by-passing Helsby and Frodsham should cross the marshland to the north and, following the completion of the statutory procedures, a major advance works contract began in May 1968.

There were two peat deposits 9,000 feet and 4,000 feet long with maximum depths of 30 feet and 18 feet. It was the intention, in the Contract, to remove 1.3 million cubic yards of the peat by hydraulic means and replace it with sand from a nearby deposit. However, the Contractor chose to carry out the work in a more conventional manner, using 'drag lines' excavators. Sandstone was excavated from a nearby outcrop and used as filling, the resulting hole being back-filled with the peat.

The Contract also included the construction of the 490-feet-long seven-span Helsby Junction Viaduct over the Ellesmere Port to Helsby Line, and a branch line. The works were completed in December 1970.

During the same period, a further Contract was awarded for the construction of the Weaver Viaduct. Designed by Husband and Company,

Consulting Engineers, it is 3,186 feet long, with a 222-feet span over the Weaver Navigation Canal, and a 125-feet span over the River Weaver. The canal crossing has anchor spans and cantilevers of six cast in-situ box beams, stiffened transversely with reinforced concrete diaphragms. Both the 125-feet-long suspended span, and the river crossing, are of prestressed beam and slab composite construction with transversely stressed diaphragms. There are 30 approach spans each of 90 feet. The reinforced concrete piers are founded on 17-inch-diameter driven cast in-place piles up to 70 feet long through alluvium to underlying Boulder Clay and Keuper Marl.

Weaver Viaduct

The Contract also included the construction of a haul road alongside the viaduct, and temporary bridges over the Canal and the River for use by the motorway Contractor. Progress on the Contract was severely disrupted by labour disputes which bedevilled the whole of the construction industry in Merseyside and North Cheshire for the following 10 years. It was, however, completed in September 1970.

Under separate advanced contracts, three bridges carrying railway lines were designed and the construction supervised by British Rail. Of these, two are similar 300-feet-long 'tied-arch' bridges, the superstructure consisting of a main span of 207 feet and side spans of 44 feet. The central span comprises two parabolic arch ribs 34 feet 9 inches in height, and joined at the crown. The prestressed concrete deck slab is suspended from the arches by four-inch-diameter mild steel bars at 10 feet centres.

Tied-arch railway bridge under construction

Sutton Fields Farm Bridge was also constructed in advance, to carry an occupation road and large diameter ICI brine mains. It was vital to ICI's activities, in the area, that the mains were fully operational at all times.

Work on the main Contract for the eight-mile length of dual three-lane carriageway motorway began in December 1969. It included the construction of the two terminal interchanges at the ends of this section of motorway, where it was to connect with the A5117 at Hapsford and the A56 at Preston Brook. In addition, an intermediate junction with the

A557 at Clifton provided a link with Runcorn New Town.

A total of 18 further bridges was required, additional to those within the advance Contracts. They, and those required for the Contracts which were to follow, were designed by the Sub-Unit under a policy of bridge standardisation. It had three aims: to reduce costs of construction by standardisation of components; to increase the productivity of the design engineers; and to establish a characteristic appearance. This led to the development of the 'Cheshire' beam which uses standard formwork of constant cross-section throughout, the mould being filled with concrete to different levels for the various lengths of beam. The manufacture combines the advantages of both pre-tensioning and post-tensioning.

The Contract was, in effect, split into two distinct parts, either side of the Weaver Viaduct. To the west, the finished level across the marshes was generally about 10 feet above ground level. The embankments were to be formed of non-cohesive material separated from the 1.5 million cubic yards of excavation from deep cuttings in Keuper Waterstones and Boulder Clay, to the east of the viaduct. This was to be transported over the temporary bridges crossing the waterways.

However, due to the labour disputes, which affected progress in the construction of certain of the structures, the earthworks were disrupted and a borrow pit was opened up in a sand deposit on the marsh section. The surplus excavated material was stockpiled on the line of the motorway to the east of Preston Brook, as advanced works for the future extension.

The length of motorway between Hapsford and Clifton was completed and opened to traffic in February 1971, thereby achieving the objective of by-passing Helsby and Frodsham. The Section was finally completed in September of the same year.

16.3   Bowdon to Wythenshawe

The Minister of Transport had given priority in the Trunk Road Programme to the Extension of Princess Parkway, in Manchester, through to Bowdon, in Cheshire. This included the proposed Bowdon to Wythenshawe Section of the M56.

The risk of subsidence due to salt mining restricted the location of the motorway to a narrow band north of Rostherne. From a junction with the A556 Trunk Road, the route passed to the south of Bowdon and Hale, to a junction with the A538, north-west of Wilmslow. Between this point and a terminal interchange at the junction with the A560, an intermediate interchange was to be built for a dual two-lane carriageway motorway link, directly serving Manchester Airport.

A total of 24 structures was required spanning railways, canals, the River Bollin and various side roads. The contract for the construction of the 6½-mile Section of dual three-lane carriageway motorway began in July 1969.

From the River Bollin, through Wythenshawe, Keuper Marl is close to the surface and the designed profile required a long cutting in this area. The total of 2.5 million cubic yards of excavation proved to be very difficult, due to the poor quality of the material, and the need to use as much as possible in forming embankments. On one length of embankment, an extra layer of cement-bound granular material was laid, in order to strengthen the formation.

Alternative forms of carriageway construction had been offered to tenderers. A semi-flexible base of a seven-inch thickness of dry-lean concrete and a three-inch thickness of dense bituminous macadam was the choice in the lowest tender.

Wilmslow Road
Interchange

As a major part of the line of the motorway had been located to pass through estate coverts, in order to reduce farm severance, little landscaping treatment was required. In Wythenshawe, however, where the route had been protected against development for many years, unsuitable excavated material was used to form protective mounding, which had the additional advantage of providing noise baffles for adjoining residential property. This Section of the M56 was completed and opened to traffic in January 1972.

16.4   Preston Brook to Bowdon

Two alternative routes were investigated for this section of the M56. It had always been envisaged that it would cross and join the M6 at the already constructed A50 Interchange, at Lymm. However, it was later recognised that the capacity of this junction, and of Thelwall Viaduct, would be the cause of future problems from the traffic growth which was expected.

A new 'motorway to motorway' interchange sited further to the south was, therefore, considered. In due course, the route which was published, as the first stage in the statutory procedures, provided for the connection with the M6 approximately 3,000 feet south of the existing A50 Interchange.

The scheme, which was the subject of a Public Inquiry held in July 1970, provided for the construction of the 11½ miles of dual three-lane carriageway motorway; the completion of the Interchange at Preston Brook; an interchange at Stretton to connect with the A49 and A559;

an interchange with the M6; and slip roads to connect with the A556 at Bowdon.

As the Warrington New Town Development Corporation envisaged a new north-south road joining the M56 at Stretton, it supported the proposals.

The route passes through agricultural land and the former Stretton Airfield. It was located to avoid property. Demolition was limited to two cottages, a disused chapel which was being used as a potato warehouse, and a gatehouse/bungalow.

The Cheshire Plain, which it crosses, is generally well-covered with boulder clays and their associated Middle Sands. Keuper Waterstones approach the surface in places. It was expected that, in the deep cuttings which would be required to achieve the designed vertical profile, the sandstone, siltstone and mudstone would be reusable, if protected from the weather.

The new Lymm Interchange was designed without a direct free-flow motorway link from M6 south, to M56 east, and vice versa. East-bound traffic would be signed to leave the M6 at the A556, the next junction to the south, and travel along the A556 to Bowdon. Movement in the reverse direction would use the same route.

Of the 26 bridges required for this length of the motorway, 21 were designed with a similar type of deck using prestressed precast concrete beams. The edge beams are 'troughs', and on

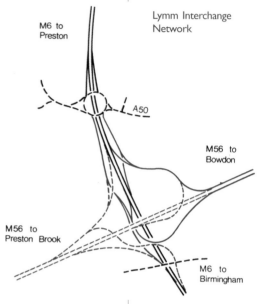

Lymm Interchange Network

M6 to Preston

A50

M56 to Bowdon

M56 to Preston Brook

M6 to Birmingham

Lymm Interchange

the over-bridges these were to be used as service bays. A novel feature was the use of precast concrete parapet plinths which almost entirely eliminated the need for temporary formwork.

The bridge with the longest span was required to carry the motorway over a slip road. With a large skew, and sight-line requirements, a 108-feet span was required, which was a length in excess of the maximum for a beam transported by road. A design for a simply supported post-tensioned concrete deck of cellular construction was therefore adopted.

Following a further Public Inquiry into the Compulsory Purchase Order, a favourable decision was given.

The construction of the motorway was to be carried out under two Contracts, separated along the eastern boundary of the M6. Alternative tenders were invited for rigid, composite and flexible carriageway construction. In each case, the accepted tender provided for fully flexible construction, and work began in October 1972 on both Contracts.

The excavation in cuttings produced sufficient suitable material for the embankments, and the design allowed for the use of the better materials at formation levels. The Waterstone was, therefore, placed as a 'capping layer' on embankments, and in some cuttings to a minimum construction depth of 18 inches. This construction depth provided enough protection for frost-susceptible materials. Extensive landscaping was included in the Contracts, using excavated unsuitable materials, shaped and mounded throughout the Scheme, with particular attention given to the Lymm and Bowdon Interchange areas.

The motorway between the M6 and Bowdon was opened to traffic in December 1974,* followed by Preston Brook to the M6 in July 1975.

16.5   Hapsford to Lea-by-Backford

'The Blue Report' had identified the need for the M56 to be extended westwards from Hapsford towards Queensferry, and the scheme was included in the Minister's Trunk Road Preparation Pool, in March 1968

As a first stage, a Preliminary Report was prepared in November of that year on the investigations which had been carried out into the proposal for an extension as far as Little Stanney. At this point, it would connect with the proposed extension of the Ellesmere Port Motorway, M531.

It was envisaged that, in due course, it would be extended further, to cross the proposed Dee Barrage. Until this was constructed, however, M56 traffic would cross the Dee at either Queensferry or via the proposed Chester Southerly By-pass.

In August 1969, a second Report was prepared justifying the extension as far as Dunkirk, on A5117, at a point between the A41 and A540

* North Cheshire Motorway M56, Preston Brook to Bowdon Section, Opening Brochure, 16 July 1975, NWRCU/Cheshire Sub-Unit (Chester Record Office).

junctions. It was considered that the improvement of the existing route was not practicable. Apart from the fact that it had been built across peat deposits and subsidence was still evident, nearby there were extensive oil refineries, pipelines, and a recently constructed sewage treatment works. The statutory procedures which were commenced in 1973 were in respect of proposals for:

(a)   The completion of the Hapsford Interchange by the addition of west facing slip roads

(b)   Dual three-lane carriageways from Hapsford to Stoak,

(c)   the M56/M531 Stoak Interchange, and

(d)   Dual two-lane carriageways from Stoak to Dunkirk.

The Public Inquiry which was held in January/February 1974 also examined the proposals of the Cheshire County Council to extend M531 southwards to the A56 at Hoole Village. Following a favourable decision, three separate Contracts were awarded. In March 1978 work began on the construction of:

(i)   the three-mile-long section of motorway between Hapsford and Stoak, which included two overbridges and an underbridge at the crossing of the River Gowy and

(ii)   the Stoak Interchange which included lengths of side and link road, and seven bridges over the Chester to Ellesmere Port Canal and the link roads.

In the flood plain of the River Gowy, a large quantity of peat was removed and replaced by sandstone from a quarry which was opened up specifically for the purpose.

Progress on the Stoak Interchange Contract was severely affected by the labour disputes, such that completion over-ran by 34 weeks. Under the third Contract, the construction of the remaining two-mile length of motorway, between Stoak Interchange and the A5117, began in September 1978. It included bridges to carry the motorway over the A41 and the Chester to Birkenhead Line. A third bridge was required to carry the A5032 over the motorway.

The Contractor took up the option of submitting an alternative tender based on the construction of the carriageways in concrete using the 'slip-form' method. This was the only section of the M56 to have this form of construction. In the relatively short length involved, the concreting was completed within nine days.

The delay in the completion of the Stoak Interchange prevented the opening of the length of the motorway, beyond Hapsford. However, by March 1981, the whole of the 35 miles of the M56 from Lea by Backford through to the junction with the M63 (M60) at Sharston had been completed, and was in use.

17 The Calder Valley Motorway M65

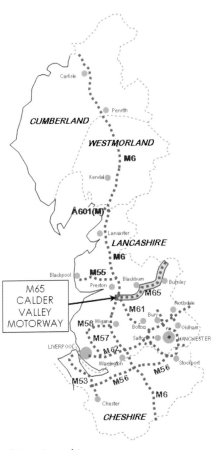

* North East Lancashire Project Study, Final Report, September 1969, Lancashire County Council/Blackburn and Burnley County Borough Councils (Preston Record Office).

† Calder Valley Route M65 Motorway, M6/M61 to Burnley Section, Route Location and Design (S Coleman), October 1998, NWRCU/ Lancashire Sub-Unit (Preston Record Office).

17.1 Introduction

Proposals for a new route along the Calder Valley did not feature in the Road Plan for Lancashire 1949. Several reasons account for this, chiefly

(i)   it was envisaged that the Liverpool-Leeds Trunk Road A59 along the Ribble Valley, to the north of the Calder Valley, would be improved by the provision of local by-passes of places such as Clitheroe and Whalley, and

(ii) historically the textile manufacturing towns of North East Lancashire had a close relationship with Manchester, as the commercial centre for the industry and, therefore, improved north-south communications were of greater significance.

In 1967, the Ministry of Housing and Local Government commissioned a study to assess the effect of the proposed Central Lancashire New Town upon the towns of the Calder Valley, extending as far as Colne. The Report on this study, known as the 'Impact Study', was published in 1968. It indicated the need for a new route connecting the towns lying between Colne and Blackburn, with the New Town, and with the national motorway system.

Following publication of the Report,* the Lancashire County Council and the Blackburn and Burnley County Borough Councils jointly carried out the 'North East Lancashire Project Study' (NELPS). Completed in 1969, it recommended the construction of the route, now known as the Calder Valley Motorway M65.

In 1970, the Minister of Transport accepted responsibility for the proposal as far as Burnley, in that it would supersede the existing A59/A6119/A677/A679 Trunk Road route. At Rose Grove, Burnley, the A646 Trunk Road extended that route in a south-easterly direction into Yorkshire.†

Between Burnley and Colne, the A56 passing through Brierfield and Nelson was the existing main traffic route along that part of the Calder Valley and, as a Principal Road, it was the responsibility of the two local

Highway Authorities, the Lancashire County Council and the Burnley County Borough Council. It was agreed, however, that the preparation and design of that Section of the proposed M65, which would supersede the A56 along the valley, would be undertaken by the County Council.

North-east Lancashire has a long history of industrial development. Even the agricultural areas between the closely-spaced communities frequently conceal legacies of past mining, quarrying and tipping. The nature of the terrain made it difficult to select a line which would provide a route designed to the required motorway standard and cause the least interference with existing land uses. In consequence, it was necessary to align the motorway in close proximity to the East Lancashire Line and to the Leeds and Liverpool Canal, often using derelict land and areas of poor ground previously avoided by developers.

17.2 Burnley–Colne

The preliminary design began in November 1971 and, in due course, it was agreed that the proposed line of the route should be protected against development. The scheme was given potential Principal Road status, which meant that it would qualify for a grant from Central Government of 75 per cent of the cost.[*]

The statutory procedures, which included the submission of a Planning Application, commenced in January 1973. The standard adopted in the design was for dual three-lane carriageways, which were considered to be necessary for the whole of the route. However, following the publication of the proposals in May of that year, advice was received from the Department of Transport that, as the capacity figures for design had been revised, it was considered that dual two-lane carriageways would suffice.

It was suggested, to the Department, that the scheme should proceed as intended, but with only two-lane carriageways constructed in the first instance and, in the light of the experience gained on the Preston By-pass, the bridges should be designed to allow for future widening. The proposal was totally rejected by the Department and in the circumstances, particularly in regard to the issue of grant, the County Council had no alternative but to accept the ruling. In consequence, it was necessary to recommence the statutory procedures for a Scheme designed to the lower standard.

In February/March 1974 a Joint Public Inquiry was held to consider objections submitted in respect of both the County Council's proposals for the Burnley to Colne Section and those of the Department for the Hyndburn to Burnley Section. Unfortunately, it was not until late 1975 that the Secretary of State gave a favourable decision. Meanwhile, following Local Government Reorganisation in April 1974, the County Council had become the sole Local Highway Authority.

* Calder Valley Motorway, Burnley to Colne Section, Preparation and Design (J.B. Firth), March 2000, Lancashire County Council (Preston Record Office).

For many years it had been the policy of the County Council to purchase property affected by an approved highway scheme, when requested by the owner. Burnley Borough Council had decided to adopt the same policy and, therefore, a great deal of property had been purchased before the County Council proceeded to make a Compulsory Purchase Order.

With the completion of the statutory procedures, the County Council was able to start on the construction of the motorway between Burnley and Colne by the award of the first contract in August 1976. It is significant that work did not commence on the Department's Hyndburn to Burnley Section until some five years later.

Primarily due to uncertainty as to the availability of finance, particularly grant from central Government, which was only issued on a 'year to year' basis, the County Council decided that the project should be undertaken in three main sections.

The 3½-mile Burnley to Brierfield Section was constructed under five contracts. Three advance works contracts were undertaken with the principal objective of

(a) providing direct access to the line of the motorway from the A56 at Brierfield, thereby minimising the use of existing roads by construction traffic, and

(b) constructing key bridges, in particular, the Clifton Aqueduct required to carry the Leeds and Liverpool Canal over the motorway.

Construction works at Gannow Top showing Clifton Aqueduct

Work on the first main Contract, which began in March 1978, included the completion of the Brierfield Junction, and major bridgeworks of which the most significant is the four-span Montford Viaduct. Along the valley, and close to the river known as Pendle Water, the motorway was to be constructed mainly on embankment. The underlying weak material was known locally as 'Bible Clay', being laminated clay separated by silt and resembling the leaves of a book. The embankments were, therefore, constructed under controlled conditions using lightweight material such as pulverised fuel ash.

The construction of two interchanges was included in the second main contract. The full-movement Burnley Barracks Interchange was to be constructed in an area formerly occupied by old terraced property. It included a diversion of Padiham Road, a roundabout on each side of the motorway and a system of pedestrian subways. Apart from major services which needed to be diverted, a unique feature was the 1,200-feet-long Gannow Tunnel carrying the Leeds and Liverpool Canal and passing under the area. This was the subject of inspection and close monitoring by British Waterways engineers who were concerned at the possibility of damage being caused.

In the 50-feet-deep cutting required for the motorway, old shallow mine workings were encountered. Half a mile to the north, Crow Wood Junction was to be constructed immediately north of a bridge carrying the motorway over the River Calder, with slip roads leading to and from the Colne direction only. It provides a direct link into Burnley town centre. For a comparatively short length of motorway, the bridgeworks were extensive, with 10 under-bridges and six over-bridges.

Montford Viaduct

The Burnley to Brierfield Section of M65 was completed and opened to traffic in October 1981,[*] providing considerable relief to Burnley and parts of Brierfield. These urban areas had suffered from congestion and a serious traffic accident record for many years.

In the light of the experience gained earlier, an advance earthworks contract began in November 1981 on the Brierfield to Nelson section. With similar ground conditions, the lower layers of embankment were constructed with carefully controlled rates of filling.

A start on the main Contract for the 1¼-mile continuation of the motorway through to Reedyford, Nelson, was made in August 1982.

Special ground treatment involved the installation of a series of six-feet-diameter rock-filled piles, 50 feet deep.

The construction of two bridges completed the Brierfield Junction and the access to a major industrial estate development at Lomeshaye. A three-span bridge over a side road and two pedestrian underpasses were also constructed.

Major accommodation works included replacement bowling greens, and the pavilion of Nelson Cricket Club, where the slope of the adjoining motorway embankment provided new terracing.

The work was completed and this section was opened to traffic in December 1983.[*] The temporary slip road connection to the A682, Scotland Road, at Reedyford, had the effect of enabling traffic to by-pass Nelson town centre.

The programming of the construction of the 1½-mile-long Nelson to Colne Section was influenced by two major factors. Firstly, the availability of finance and secondly, the timing of the provision of replacement facilities

* Calder Valley Motorway M65, Burnley-Brierfield Section, Opening Brochure, 14 October 1981, Lancashire County Council (Preston Record Office).

M65 passing through
Nelson. Brierfield
Junction is in the
background and the
Cricket Ground in the
right foreground.

* Calder Valley Motor-
way M65, Brierfield-
Nelson Section, Opening
Brochure, 9 December
1983, Lancashire County
Council (Preston Record
Office).

† Calder Valley
Motorway M65, Nelson-
Colne Section, Opening
Brochure, 16 September
1988, Lancashire County
Council (Preston Record
Office).

for Reedyford Hospital which was on the line of the motorway, and due for demolition.

It was necessary to divert Reedyford Road, as part of the works involved in the construction of the major Reedyford Interchange. This could be achieved without any direct effect on the hospital, although passing through its grounds. The road diversion was the subject of the first of two advance works contracts beginning in March 1985.

The second Contract, starting in April 1986, involved the construction of two bridges at the Barrowford Locks of the Leeds and Liverpool Canal. Both the motorway, and the diverted Barrowford to Colne road, were to be carried over the locks.

Due to delays in obtaining possession of the Reedyford Hospital site, the first main Contract, which began in November 1986, was only in respect of the works between Barrowford Locks and the terminal roundabout at Greenfield, on the outskirts of Colne. From this junction, an all-purpose dual carriageway link road known as the Whitewalls Diversion provided a connection to the Burnley to Colne road, A56. The roundabout was designed to allow for the construction of a further link road connecting with North Valley Road to enable A56 traffic, to and from Skipton, to by-pass Colne town centre.

The final Contract beginning in May 1987 involved the construction of the Reedyford Interchange, and the motorway through to Barrowford Locks, which required a three-span bridge over Colne Water. The ground conditions were similar to those experienced in the other contracts carried out along this part of the Calder Valley. The special measures which had been adopted to deal with the problem were repeated.

Within the Interchange, pedestrian movement is segregated from the vehicular traffic routes by a network of footways passing through open aspect subways or via a spiral ramped footbridge.

By the time this last Section of the six-mile-long motorway between Burnley and Colne had been completed and opened to traffic in September 1988,† it had taken over 12 years from the start of the first contract. Eleven separate construction contracts were undertaken, with a number of different contractors successful in competing for the work. This required very careful programming by the County Council and its staff, in order to

ensure that there would be no overlap in terms of access and the possession of the various parts of the site. In the event, there were no serious
difficulties and the effect was the construction of an important section of
the M65, at an economic cost. Whereas the main source of finance was
grant from central Government, the County Council was also successful in
obtaining assistance from the Regional Development Fund of the European
Economic Community, and a loan from the European Investment Bank.

In contrast, the programming of the Trunk Road sections of the
M65 between M6/M61 and Burnley was not influenced by financial
considerations, which meant that the construction could be carried out
under comparatively few major contracts.

The County Council always held the view that the Calder Valley
Route should be continued eastwards from Colne and, to that end, pro-
tected a route against development through to the county boundary on
A6068. However, due to its wider national and inter-regional significance,
the County Council considered that the proposal should be adopted as a
Trunk Road scheme.

Reedyford Footbridge
under construction

17.3 Whitebirk–Burnley

The line of the six-mile-long section of the Calder Valley Motorway
between Hyndburn and Burnley was established following the Joint Public
Inquiry held in 1974. As a Department of Transport scheme, the statutory
procedures were the responsibility of the North Western Road Construction Unit, with the Lancashire Sub-Unit carrying out the detailed design
and supervision of construction.

The route lay south of the River Calder, and north of the East Lancashire Line along the section beyond Huncoat. The Leeds and Liverpool
Canal follows the natural contours along the valley. In consequence, the
construction of the motorway necessitated the provision of a number of
canal bridges and diversions of the waterway.

From the Hyndburn Interchange roundabout towards the western end
of the section, a short length of link road was to connect with the A678.
The completion of the Burnley Barracks Interchange by the construction of
the west-facing slip roads was to form the eastern terminal. Intermediate
interchanges at Huncoat and Hapton were to give access to and from the
A679 Trunk Road. Not only would the Huncoat Interchange allow for the
connection of the Accrington Easterly By-pass as a northerly extension of
the M66 and Haslingden By-pass, but also the proposed Shuttleworth Hall
Link leading towards Padiham and into the Ribble Valley. At Hapton, a
'half-junction' would enable traffic on the A646 Todmorden/Burnley Trunk
Road route, and travelling to and from the west, to use the motorway
via a short length of the A679. It was considered, therefore, that only

two-lane carriageways were necessary beyond the Hapton Interchange, in conformity with the layout on the County Council's section of the motorway between Burnley and Colne. From Hyndburn to Hapton, the motorway was to have dual three-lane carriageways.

In 1980, the decision was taken, by the Government, to abolish the Road Construction Units. It was the intention that the work load of the Sub-Units should be transferred to Consulting Engineers and, in the case of the Lancashire Sub-Unit, it was to be the firm of Babtie Shaw and Morton. By early 1981, the detailed design and the preparation of contract documents for the Hyndburn to Burnley Section was nearing completion. In order to avoid delay in proceeding with the project, the County Council made representations, requesting that the Council should be appointed as the Agent Authority for awarding the Contracts, with the County Surveyor acting as the Engineer supervising the construction. This proposal was accepted.

The works, which began in August 1981, were carried out under two separate Contracts, east and west of the Huncoat Interchange.

Between the Hyndburn Interchange and the Accrington to Whalley Road, A680, 'Bible Clay' was encountered, similar to that experienced in the Burnley to Colne Section. Special measures were adopted in the construction of a major embankment. An extensive temporary traffic diversion was necessary at Whalley Road to allow the construction of the bridge carrying it over the motorway where it passed through a cutting.

Major earthworks involved traversing the northern slope of Whinney Hill in a rock cutting with a maximum depth of 80 feet. Part of the area had been quarried for many years to win shales for brick making and the excavations had been backfilled with domestic waste. Elsewhere, compensation had to be paid to a brick manufacturing company, for the loss of quarrying rights.

'Rock catchers' were constructed behind the hard shoulders on both sides of the motorway in order to prevent any loose rock from the faces of the cutting rolling on to the hard shoulders and carriageways.

The brook at the bottom of Altham Clough had to be culverted prior to the construction of a 60-feet-high embankment. The watercourse passed through a culvert under the adjoining Canal and was in a poor structural condition. The opportunity was taken, by British Waterways, to carry out extensive repairs while access from the motorway site was available.

The eastern side of Altham Clough had been used for many years as a tipping site for colliery shale, containing fragments of coal. The material was accepted for use as a filling material, but it was recognised, from the smoke and acrid fumes exuding from the tip, that slow combustion was taking place. The extraction of the shale by excavators, dump trucks and motor scrapers became a hazardous operation as, when the material was exposed to the air, heat, flames and smoke were generated. However, several hundred thousand cubic yards of the shale were used in constructing embankments by placing it in thin layers separated by clay. The environmental benefit was considerable.

Where the canal impinged on the route of the motorway or the approach to the Huncoat Interchange, it was necessary to divert the Canal over a length of one quarter of a mile, by the construction of a reinforced concrete trough. The Canal had to be kept open to traffic throughout the operation.

The presence of the 200-year-old Gannow tunnel entailed very complex structural work in the vicinity of the Barracks Interchange.

Of the bridges required for crossing the Canal between Huncoat and Burnley, the most significant was a five-span structure which also crossed a railway line. A further major diversion of the canal was also required.

The crossing of the Green Brook Valley required the construction of an embankment 70 feet high, utilising nearly 30,000 cubic yards of excavated chemical waste.

The whole of the length of the motorway between Hyndburn and Burnley required the construction of a total of 17 vehicular bridges, three footbridges, three major culverts, and several large retaining walls. In addition, three piped crossings under the Canal had to be provided.

Advance contracts had been carried out, involving the demolition of property. It was a requirement that dressed masonry from the traditional terraced housing of the area should be stored for re-use. Bridges and walls were faced with this material to ensure that the new structures were in keeping with the local environment.

The two main Contracts were completed at the same time, and the Hyndburn to Burnley Section was opened to traffic in December 1983,* concurrently with the Brierfield to Nelson Section.

Meanwhile, in April 1980, the Minister of Transport had announced that, as the Central Lancashire New Town had not developed as rapidly as anticipated, the M6/M61 to Whitebirk Section of the Route could not be justified. It was considered that following a proposed improvement of the existing all-purpose A59/A677/A6119 route, to the north of Blackburn, this would be adequate as the link between the M6, at Samlesbury, and Whitebirk. The Minister confirmed, however, that preparation and design work for a section of dual three-lane carriageway motorway between Whitebirk and Hyndburn should proceed.

The obvious location in which to site the Whitebirk Interchange, a large roundabout, was in the vicinity of the junction of the A6119, Whitebirk Drive, and the A678, Blackburn to Rishton road.

The selected 2¼-mile-long route through to the Hyndburn Interchange ran generally in an eastwards direction, and south of the A678. In deep

Excavation in colliery shale tip

Huncoat Interchange under construction, showing the diverted canal

* Calder Valley Motorway M65, Hyndburn-Burnley Section, Opening Brochure, 9 December 1983, NWRCU/ Lancashire Sub-Unit/ Lancashire County Council (Preston Record Office).

cutting, it passed through the edge of the Rishton golf course, under the East Lancashire Line and the Leeds and Liverpool Canal, before crossing the valley of the River Hyndburn, where high embankments would be required on the approaches to the river bridge.

The proposals also included the diversion and dualling of a section of Whitebirk Drive, and the construction of the all-purpose Hyndburn Link Road leading from the Hyndburn Interchange into Accrington.

A Public Inquiry, which commenced in November 1980, was repeatedly disrupted by 'environmental objectors' and, in the event, the long-awaited favourable decision was not given until 1982.

Much of the early design work had been carried out by the Lancashire Sub-Unit of the NWRCU but, in September 1981, the scheme was transferred to Babtie Shaw and Morton.

Following the completion of the detailed design, a Contract was awarded. The construction began in January 1983, with that firm responsible for the supervision of the work.

The adverse ground conditions required special measures, in order to ensure the stability of the major earthworks, namely extensive supplementary drainage in cuttings and rock fill toe trenches to embankments.

Three crossings of the Canal and two crossings of the railway required bridgeworks. The design and supervision of the construction of the structure carrying the railway over the motorway was undertaken by British Rail.

The most significant bridge is the Dunkenhalgh Aqueduct carrying the canal over the motorway. The abutments were founded on very large diameter bored piles, installed under bentonite. The heavily reinforced post-tensioned concrete trough, forming the deck, was cast on the ground, which was later excavated for the motorway cutting below.

The completion and opening of this Section of motorway between Whitebirk and Hyndburn, in December 1984,[*] had the immediate effect of relieving Accrington, Rishton and Clayton-le-Moors of a considerable volume of heavy traffic.

17.4   M6/M61 to Whitebirk

The recommended highway network in the Final Report of the North East Lancashire Project Study (NELPS), published in 1969, included a 'Fast Route' as its backbone. From the intersection of the M6 and the M61 the proposed route for a dual three-lane motorway ran eastwards to the heart of Blackburn to be integrated into the future plans for the town. Beyond the town centre it passed through to Whitebirk, and further east, along the Calder Valley as far as Colne.

[*] M65 Calder Valley Route, Whitebirk-Hyndburn Section, Opening Brochure, 19 December 1984, Department of Transport/Babtie Shaw & Morton (Preston Record Office).

In 1972, the firm of consulting engineers, Howard Humphreys and Partners, was appointed to carry out the design of the route between Riley Green and Whitebirk, which included the section through Blackburn. The Lancashire Sub-Unit of the NWRCU assumed responsibility for the detailed design of both the section between M6/M61 and Riley Green, and that from Whitebirk to Burnley.

It was intended that the preparation, design, statutory procedures, and construction would be completed by 1978, but this optimistic programme did not allow for the full implications of new requirements for public participation in road planning. It was decided, therefore, by the Department of the Environment, that there should be extensive Public Consultation into a number of possible routes, between M6/M61 and Hyndburn.

Of the six routes examined, the Sub-Unit carried out the initial route location and assessment for four of them, identified by the colours, red, yellow, purple and green. The consulting engineers concentrated on the complex blue and brown routes passing through Blackburn town centre. Whereas, it was intended that four of the routes would be constructed to 'motorway standard', the yellow and green routes would be 'all-purpose' roads only.

The first of its kind in the UK, the Public Consultation, which took place in Spring 1975,* involved the distribution of several thousand copies of a document inviting participants to complete a questionnaire commenting on the alternatives. An exhibition was held for several days at six different locations.

The County Council as the Local Highway Authority, together with all the District Councils in North East Lancashire, except Blackburn Borough Council, supported the 'motorway standard' brown route. It was feared, however, that the majority of the members of the public would opt for the green route, as it affected the least number of properties and avoided the urban parts of Blackburn.

The Secretary of State did not announce his decision that the 'all-purpose' green route had been selected until the autumn of 1977. This route to the south of Blackburn had been rejected at an early stage in the NELPS, and did not feature in the Report of the Study. With a relatively low economic rate of return, the scheme was removed from the National Roads Programme in 1980, when design work was suspended.

Strong representations continued to be made against these decisions, which culminated, in late 1983, in a major deputation to the Minister of State for Transport led by the County Council and supported by Members of Parliament, and representatives of all the Local Authorities in North East Lancashire.† By that time sections of the Calder Valley Route beyond Whitebirk had already been completed or were under construction to motorway standard.

* Calder Valley Route M6/M61 to Hyndburn, Choice of Route, May/June 1975, NWRCU/Lancashire Sub-Unit/Howard Humphreys and Partners (Preston Record Office).

† Calder Valley Route M6/M61 to Whitebirk, comparison between a scheme to upgrade the existing Trunk Road route and the proposed green 'B' route, 9 December 1983, Lancashire County Council (Preston Record Office).

In 1984, the Secretary of State accepted the case that had been made and, in due course, design work was resumed for a 'motorway standard' road on an alignment similar to the green route. With the abolition of the Sub-Unit, Howard Humphreys and Partners assumed design responsibility for the whole of the Section,* which became known as the Blackburn Southern By-pass.

Detailed design work began in 1989 for the 13-mile-long By-pass, and Public Inquiries were held in February 1990 and November 1991.

It was to have mainly dual two-lane carriageways, with some lengths constructed with three-lane carriageways. All the structures were, however, to be designed to allow for future widening.

There were to be two major three-level interchanges connecting with the M6 and the M61, and a free-flowing junction with the completed section of the M65 to the east of Whitebirk. Of the four other interchanges providing

M6 Interchange

links to major roads, three were to be located on radial routes to the south-west and south of Blackburn. It was envisaged that the improvement in communications would enhance the opportunities for developing major industrial sites on the southern periphery of Blackburn, and in nearby Darwen.

The works were to be undertaken under two main Contracts to the west and east of Stanworth, starting in March 1994 and March 1995 respectively. However, alterations to public utility services were carried out under advance contracts involving major items: the Thirlmere Aqueduct, and 440kV National Grid and other high voltage overhead lines.

In an area where there had been no substantial level of objection to the motorway, the arrival of 'protesters' at the start of the first main Contract affected progress. They established bases in abandoned buildings and trees, and caused delay and disruption to both Contracts. The provision of security guards also involved considerable additional costs.

In carrying out the earthworks there was a massive shortfall of 'site-won' filling material, with the main deficit at the eastern end of the project. In all, over three million cubic yards of imported fill were needed for the two Contracts, the main source being a borrow pit near Brindle, which raised considerable opposition from local residents.

There were three major rock cuttings, near Stanworth Farm, at Guide, and at Stanhill. The motorway passed between a line of 440kV pylons and the listed building of Stanworth Farm. Forming the almost vertical sides of the cutting presented a particular challenge. Elsewhere, it was necessary to cap two old mineshafts, and an ancient tramway tunnel, last used in 1850, was found while excavating a cutting.

Where the motorway passed through an area known as Earcroft, an underground system of stone soughs was encountered. These carried water

* M65 Blackburn Southern By-pass (J.M.T. Clunas), March 2000. Personal recollections (Preston Record Office).

to nearby cotton mills and a system of thrust-bore tunnels was installed to pick up and discharge the flow. At Feniscowles, special measures were necessary to prevent the water supply to a paper mill drawn from the River Roddlesworth from being contaminated by run-off from the motorway.

A large number of structures was required. Of the total of 46 bridges, there are four major viaducts. Two carry the motorway over the M6 and the M61, within the Interchanges, and the others cross steep-sided valleys. At Stanworth Woods, the spectacular 1,000-feet-long structure is over 100 feet above the valley floor. It was incrementally launched by the Contractor in order to reduce the damage to trees in the valley below. In addition to a further 15 under-bridges, there are 20 over-bridges, one of which carries the Blackburn-Manchester Line. Of the four footbridges which were constructed, a unique lattice girder bridge at Brimmicroft carries both a public foot-path and a stream over the motorway.

Stanworth Woods
Viaduct

Throughout both the design and the carrying out of the construction, particular attention was given to environmental matters. These included the pre-contract relocation of plants, and extensive planting on the completion of the works.

In addition to the extensive use of mounding, the first use in Britain of transparent screens on two over-bridges had the effect of reducing traffic noise on adjacent property.

The Blackburn Southern By-pass Section of the M65 was opened to traffic in December 1997.*

It is regrettable that, from the opening of the first section of the Calder Valley Motorway between Burnley and Brierfield, in October 1981, it took a further 16 years for the M65 to be finally connected to the national motorway system. It is recognised that financial restrictions during that period and the time taken to complete the statutory procedures were material factors. It would appear, however, that the extensive Public Consultation exercise, and the resulting delays in the decision-making process as to how the project was to be taken forward, were the major reasons why the aspirations of the population of north-east Lancashire were not realised at an earlier date.

* M65 Blackburn Southern By-pass, junctions 1-6, Opening Brochure, December 1997, Highways Agency/ Howard Humphreys and Partners (Preston Record Office).

18 Major Influences Affecting the Development of the Motorway Network in the Region

18.1 The Effect of Periods of Financial Restraint

In acknowledging the other demands for public expenditure, particularly during the post-war period, it is accepted that it would have been unreasonable to expect a continuing high-level of financial resources to be made available in order to meet a long-term programme of motorway construction, irrespective of how that was determined.

However, 'short-term' financing created many difficulties in the development of the network, which led to much valid public criticism in regard to the poor rate of progress on some of the major projects undertaken in the Region.

The most striking example of 'piecemeal' programming was the construction of the Manchester Outer Ring Road. Subsequently designated as the M60, earlier sections were numbered M62, M63 and M66. Referred to in the Road Plan for Lancashire 1949, it took 40 years from the opening of the first section to its completion in the year 2000. Within this extended period, there became a need for increased traffic capacity which required the widening of several of the earlier sections and the introduction of higher standards of layout for those constructed later. As a result, the variation in the number of traffic lanes throughout the 35-mile length, together with the exceptionally high frequency of the interchanges, created an abnormal amount of weaving traffic movement. The provision of a satisfactory system of signing throughout the whole of the Manchester conurbation has been a massive undertaking.

Financial constraints had the effect of influencing the location of some of the motorways by basing the alignment on a series of by-passes, each of which would produce immediate benefits when constructed separately. For example, the M6 through Lancashire and Cumberland was developed in this way, but such an approach was often open to the criticism that the construction of one section prejudged the alignment of adjoining sections, in advance of the statutory procedures.

In Cheshire, however, the alignment of the M6 was influenced by the need to connect with the Lancashire section at the proposed crossing of the Manchester Ship Canal, and with the Staffordshire section located to the west of the Stoke/Stafford conurbation. A further factor was the need to avoid the salt subsidence areas around Northwich.

To some extent, the limited availability of finance led to the adoption of the principle of undertaking 'advance works' contracts to deal with major obstructions along the line of a section of motorway. Not only did this enable tenderers to programme the works more efficiently, thereby reducing costs, but it gave the opportunity for smaller firms to compete for the smaller contracts. The effect was, undoubtedly, a lower overall cost of construction.

Once a financial commitment had been made in respect of the Trunk Road motorways, and those Local Authority motorways financed by specific grants, contracts could be entered into and payments made without difficulty. However, with the introduction of Transport Supplementary Grant (TSG) in 1974, which was only issued on an annual basis, the Local Authorities concerned were placed in a difficult position. If a major motorway contract was awarded by a Local Authority, there was no guarantee that TSG would be forthcoming beyond the first year. This accounted for the large numbers of contracts involved in the construction of the Burnley-Colne Section of the M65 and required considerable skill on the part of the staff of the County Council in regard to programming.

The method of financing the four New Towns within the region enabled the Development Corporations to undertake major roadworks on a scale which was in marked contrast to the programming of those motorways intended to serve them. For instance, the first stage of the construction of the Aintree-Skelmersdale Motorway, M58, was opened to traffic in 1966, but a further 14 years elapsed before it was completed and Skelmersdale New Town became fully connected to the national motorway system.

18.2   Route Location and Public Consultation

During the early stages in the development of the motorway network in the region, the County Councils took a leading role in route location. There was, therefore, close public involvement in this function through the elected members not only of the County Councils, but also of the Councils of the County and non-County Boroughs, and the Urban and Rural Districts, which were consulted at all stages.

The routes of the main motorways were, in the main, self-evident and 'shadowed' the traditional transport corridors. Skill was required in siting the junctions in optimum locations to gain access to and from the main urban areas.

When selecting alternative alignments for detailed investigation, many factors were involved. As a legacy of the Industrial Revolution, the region possessed many areas of dereliction, and maximum use was made of redundant land, thus providing twofold benefit. Slag and chemical waste heaps could be levelled, moss land drained, redundant airfields utilised and wherever possible poorer quality farmland traversed. They were located with a view to minimising the severance of farm units, and the disruption to public utilities, and to cause the minimum impact on areas of redevelopment. However, in south Lancashire, it was important to avoid potential coal mining subsidence and, in Cheshire, areas subject to subsidence due to salt extraction. In the post-Beeching era, wherever possible, use was to be made of redundant railway land, and this was of particular benefit in urban areas.

The required skill in route location involved blending all these factors, and many others, into an alignment which was direct, would meet all engineering criteria, and was economical in cost. The objectives included the provision of a road which had a smooth free-flowing alignment both horizontally and vertically, a reasonable balance of cut and fill and positive drainage. The whole package had to cater for the efficient collection and distribution of existing and predicted traffic and be economical in cost.

Even in the 1950s and '60s, high priority was given to the environmental impact of a scheme and, when a motorway skirted a residential area, its profile would be purposely depressed wherever possible to contain traffic noise and visual intrusion. This was often coupled with the provision of noise mounds and screening. The aesthetic impact of the road was also important, and a great deal of effort was made to provide interesting and pleasing structures. Inevitably there were areas of contention and these often occurred at the interface between motorway connecting roads and built-up areas. Where property could not be avoided, routes were aligned through housing clearance areas, again providing twofold benefit. From the outset every effort was made to maximise benefit and minimise impact.

Based on technical advice from their officers, the elected members of the councils were able to make a judgement as to the merits of each case in the interest of their particular community, without being unduly influenced by vociferous minorities. The importance of public relations was recognised and once a proposal had been agreed, public meetings were held at which a detailed presentation would be given and any views expressed would be taken into account before the scheme was finalised for the purpose of the statutory procedures.

In Lancashire, where the County Council, in respect of both its own motorway schemes and those for which it acted as the Agent Authority of the Secretary of State for Transport, special measures were adopted in the more rural areas. Farmers' 'surgery' meetings were organised in conjunction with the National Farmers Union at a venue local to each proposed motorway. The farmers affected were invited to attend at half-hour intervals and by reference to plans of the proposals discussion took place with an open exchange of information. Farm boundaries and methods of farming were identified, which enabled the full impact of the proposed motorway to be considered. Follow-up meetings were then held at the farms, as necessary and, when accommodation works had been agreed, they were invariably endorsed by the District Valuer. In Cheshire, however, negotiations with landowners and tenants were undertaken jointly by the engineers and a representative of the District Valuer. Elsewhere in the region, e.g. in Cumberland, the negotiations were carried out entirely by the District Valuer following early investigation by the design engineers.

The resulting effect was to minimise objections and avoid the need for Public Inquiries.

It was unusual for a number of alternatives to be presented for public comment at the same time, as it was considered that this would not only lead to confusion but have the effect of creating widespread 'blight' on all the properties identified as being affected.

In July 1973, the Department of the Environment issued details of new procedures for Public Consultation, which demanded that any viable routes, although rejected, should be included. The proposals for the section of the M65 between the M6/M61 and Hyndburn became the subject of the first exercise of its kind in the UK, when the public were consulted in the summer of 1975 on six alternative routes through the centre and to the north and south of Blackburn. It was a massive and costly operation involving the issue of 40,000 pamphlets and booklets containing a questionnaire to enable members of the public to express their choice of route. The task facing the Department in analysing the results of a great deal of divided opinion was considerable and a period of over two years of uncertainty elapsed before a decision was made on the preferred route. Similar procedures were adopted for M63 and M66 around Stockport, which had the effect of reducing the number of objections at the Public Inquiry.

The EC Directive on 'the assessment of the effects of certain public and private projects on the environment' (85/337/EEC) which was adopted by Government and effective from July 1988 had a major impact on route location and design procedures. The directive formalised consultative procedures, many of which had been in operation for some years, and included statutory requirements for staged environmental assessments. For every highway project, a number of alternative routes had to be designed and assessed in detail for formal justification purposes. Whilst it had always been the practice to consider all possibilities, 'non-starters', in highway terms, could be discarded at an early stage, thus saving unnecessary work.

Environmental matters had to be given top priority. The proposed route of a highway now became heavily influenced by proximity not only to property, but to woodland, hedgerows, ponds, rivers and canals, wetlands, flora and fauna and other important environmental sites. Similarly, the profile of a road was to be determined by environmental considerations; e.g., screening from view by depressing the alignment, even though 'trapped valleys' might be introduced. Cut/fill quantities could be thrown completely out of balance, thereby increasing overall costs and causing environmental problems elsewhere at 'offsite' sources of imported fill material and landfill sites. Anomalies could arise when farm severance was exacerbated because a pond or copse had to be protected or an unsightly slagheap could not be utilised because it had been colonised by a rare wild orchid.

To what extent the earlier motorways would have complied with these requirements is not known. The much higher cost involved, both in preparation, design and construction, would, however, have led to the construction of a reduced overall mileage of motorway and less benefit to the community as a whole.

18.3 'Land-take'

In the case of the early motorways the need to contain the 'land-take' to the minimum arose from two major influences. Firstly, the importance of food production ensured a form of 'protection' for agricultural land, particularly that classified as having a 'high grade'. Secondly, there was concern that objectors to a Compulsory Purchase Order would have strong justification for challenging the acquisition of any land not absolutely necessary to accommodate the motorway.

This had a number of adverse effects, for example:

(i)   the slopes of cuttings and embankments were designed too steeply, which led to slips both during construction and when the motorway was operational,

(ii)   with no provision for working strips, and land for temporary diversions, the Contractor was left to negotiate with land owners who might earlier have been subjected to the compulsory purchase of their land and, therefore, were not amenable to further approaches, and

(iii)   whereas it was possible to carry out landscaping on odd plots of severed land acquired by agreement, it was mainly confined to tree and shrub planting on the slopes of cuttings and embankments, as additional land could not be purchased compulsorily.

With subsequent changes in agricultural policy, and consequent new legislation, there was a more realistic approach to 'land-take' in the later stages of the development of the motorway network.

18.4   The North Western Road Construction Unit (NWRCU)

During the early stages of carrying out the Trunk Road motorway programme in England, its overall management, including the work involved in the necessary statutory procedures, was centralised in the London HQ of the Ministry of Transport.

For many years Agent Authorities had undertaken the design of trunk road schemes of varying magnitude and the awarding of construction contracts, on behalf of the Ministry. This practice was followed in respect of a number of motorway projects, in those counties where the County Council had the staff resources available.

Elsewhere, firms of consulting engineers were appointed to carry out the design and supervision of construction, but the contracts were awarded by the Ministry. In the 1960s, however, it became clear that, with the increased work load arising from the escalation in the programme, new arrangements were necessary and, in due course, six regional Road Construction Units were established, as a partnership between the Ministry and certain of the County Councils.

In April 1967, the first of the units was formed in the North West (NWRCU), covering the counties of Cheshire, Cumberland, Lancashire and Westmorland. With its HQ in Preston, it was staffed jointly by civil servants, and local government officers seconded from the Lancashire and Cheshire County Councils, the two participating County Councils.

Drake was appointed its Director, and the County Surveyors of Lancashire and Cheshire acted, part-time, as the Chief Engineers of Sub-Units. Members of staff were allocated to the Sub-Units to undertake the detailed design and the day-to-day supervision of construction of motorway projects within those counties. The various contracts were awarded by the NWRCU, with the Director appointed as the 'Engineer'.

Under the overall control of the Director, Cumberland County Council continued to act as the Minister's Agent Authority for the design and supervision of the construction of the M6 within that county. For schemes in other parts of the Region – for example, the M6 in Westmorland, the Mid-Wirral Motorway, M53, and sections of the M63 (M60) – Consulting Engineers had already been appointed and continued to fulfil their traditional role.

Bearing in mind that the Minister was the Highway Authority for the Trunk Road network, with all that this entailed in terms of public accountability, the NWRCU was, in many respects, very successful. During the 14 years of its existence a large number of motorway projects was completed, and it is unlikely that this achievement could have been realised under the previous system of control exercised by the Ministry.

The statutory procedures were, in general, dealt with speedily, but it is suggested that the decline in the influence of the participating County Councils, as they ceased to operate as Agent Authorities, may have been detrimental. In the past, they had been closely involved in the process of route location and public consultation, to the extent that a great deal of support for the various proposals was often generated with minimal objection. Although there was a link through the County Surveyors acting as Chief Engineers of the Sub-Units, the County Councils tended to distance themselves from the contentious issues. It is recognised, of course, that the growth of the 'anti-motorway' lobby did not encourage active participation in the promotion of schemes.

Unfortunately, the Director had only limited involvement in terms of the programming of schemes in the national context, where political and financial considerations dominated. There was an emphasis on the careful timetabling of the preparation and design of each scheme. The notorious '39 Steps' which had to be taken, were 'milestone' events and formed the basis on which a schedule of key dates was produced. In due course, it became the practice to prepare a Critical Path Network which would be used for that purpose. Having adopted such a disciplined approach, it could be very frustrating following a Public Inquiry, to have to wait an indeterminate period for the Minister's decision, before the last stage of inviting tenders could proceed. There was often the feeling that financial constraints might be the cause. Such factors failed to recognise the desirability of being able to award a major Contract, normally of two years' duration, no later than the end of a calendar year. By enabling the Contractor to mobilise his resources for a substantial start on the works in the following early spring, it ensured the availability of two full summers for construction.

There was a considerable degree of delegation from the Director to the Chief Engineers of the Sub-Units. However, they did not have the same level of authority in supervising the works, as they would have had under 'Agent Authority' contracts or as that enjoyed by the Consulting Engineers. Although this anomaly existed, it was fortunate that the good working relationships which existed between successive Directors and Chief Engineers did not materially affect the management of the Contracts.

At the outset, it was realised that the RCUs would have a limited life. With a reduction in the national road programme, and a new Government taking office in 1979, with a policy of privatisation, the decision was taken to 'wind-up' the units. The Sub-Units were to be disbanded and their workload transferred to firms of Consulting Engineers. The HQs of the RCUs were to be absorbed into the Ministry's normal organisation.

Regrettably, the recommendations which were made to the Minister, that the operation should be 'phased-out' gradually, were not accepted. It was substantially completed by 1981, at a considerable cost. Inevitably, there was a measure of disruption in proceeding with schemes in course of preparation due to the 'break-up' of many of the teams of experienced engineers, as staff were transferred or made redundant. Fortunately, in isolated cases where the statutory procedures had been completed and tenders were to be invited, the Ministry agreed to the supervision of construction being carried out by the relevant County Council, on an Agency basis.

With the demise of the RCUs very few Trunk Road motorway projects were undertaken by Agent Authorities. In the 1990s, the responsibility for the programme was passed to the newly formed Highways Agency, which employed Consulting Engineers entirely and Agent Authorities ceased to be involved in the development of the motorway network.

18.5   The Design of Bridges

The design loading for the bridges of the early motorways was set out in a Ministry Memorandum. Designers within the various organisations undertaking the work within the Region were, however, given considerable freedom to choose the types of bridge to be provided and, in consequence, there was a great deal of innovation.

In recognition of the anticipated difficulties of providing access for the future maintenance painting of steel structures over a 'live' motorway, there was a preference for concrete superstructures. For spans of up to about 50 feet, a deck with a shallow construction depth could be achieved using pretensioned prestressed beams placed side by side, and in-filled with concrete. Bridges of this type were ideal for carrying side roads over a motorway. There were, however, no standard beam sections available at the time and, in Lancashire, a considerable amount of development work was undertaken before the design of an 'in-house' standard beam was finalised. Later, beam cross sections developed by the Cement and Concrete Association in conjunction with the precast concrete manufacturers were used.

Steel was preferred for the major multi-span structures, such as Barton High Level Bridge and Thelwall Bridge, carrying motorways over the Manchester Ship Canal. With the production of the new Universal Steel Beam in the late 1950s, however, steel became competitive for the medium span overbridges. The design of a large number of bridges was required for the Warrington-Preston Section of the M6, in a relatively short time. A range of standard designs was evolved for the spans and skews necessary for most of the bridges, to form a composite form of construction with a reinforced concrete deck slab. This led to the use of a variety of colours in the painting of steel over-bridges to enhance the aesthetics of the motorway in Lancashire, and relieve drivers of monotony. Other adverse effects of standardisation were reduced by the use of differing facework treatment to abutments and piers.

By contrast, in Westmorland, a different approach was taken in the design of the bridges for the M6 through the spectacular scenery of the eastern fringe of the Lake District. It was considered that much interest and relief was afforded to the motorway user by the varying alignment, and the terrain. It was believed that, from an aesthetic point of view, a continuity of appearance was desirable, provided that it was practical and that it did not distort the engineering choice. There was, therefore, a preference for three-span overbridges of in-situ reinforced concrete side spans and cantilever arms, with precast prestressed suspended spans. This gave uninterrupted access for construction traffic along the line of the motorway.

In addition to standard precast prestressed beams considerable use was made of Preflex beams for the M6 bridges in Cumberland. On the Penrith-Carlisle Section many of the bridge decks were of trapezoidal steel box construction.

In Cheshire, in the 1960s there was a recognition that, due to the rapid build-up of motorway preparation work, particularly for the proposed M56, there was a need to consider two specific aspects of bridge design. The aims were to increase the productivity of the staff involved and achieve a reduction in capital cost. Some form of standardisation was, therefore, desirable. As a result of a statistical analysis carried out into the incidence of various spans, skews and loadings, a decision was made as to the choice between concrete and steel, or composite decks.

Comparative studies indicated an economic preference towards concrete, with greater development possibilities in the medium span range by the use of prestressed concrete. This led to the development of the 'Cheshire' standard beam of which a novel feature is that a proportion of the steel tendons are deflected to slope upwards towards the ends. A standard mould of constant cross section is used, being filled to such a level as to suit the particular length of beam.

With the exception of those bridges with short spans, there was comparatively little scope for standardisation in the design of the under-bridges, within the region. The crossings of roads, rivers, railways and canals, and in the interchanges where curved structures were necessary, led to a wide variety in the design. An increasing number of major concrete bridges was constructed, such as that carrying the Mancunian Way, the Weaver Viaduct, and the River Eden Bridge.

A large number of under-line railway bridges was required, all of which were designed and the construction supervised by British Rail. Mainly in concrete, the superstructure of the bridges was invariably constructed alongside the track and 'slid' into position during possessions.

It is evident that, compared with the other Regions, the appearance of the motorways throughout the North West has been materially enhanced by the high standards of the designs and the quality of the workmanship in construction.

18.6   Earthworks and Carriageway Construction

Design engineers, and those preparing contract documents for motorway projects, have always had the difficult task of interpreting site investigation data for two significant purposes.

Firstly, to try to obtain a balance of 'cut' and 'fill' in the earthworks which, due to the various factors controlling the vertical profile, is, in effect, an impossibility. It should be the objective, therefore, to utilise as much of the excavated material as possible, in the construction of embankments and to reduce both the amount of material to be taken to 'tip' and the quantity of imported filling. This requires an assessment of the amount of 'suitable' excavated material, as a prime consideration in order to prepare a fair and realistic contract.

Secondly, it is necessary for a judgement to be made as to the characteristics of the 'formation' likely to be achieved following the completion of the earthworks, in order to decide on the form of carriageway construction. With the exception of chalk, the north-west Region contains almost every type of the materials to be found in the UK. The glacial clays, however, caused some of the greatest problems.

When the Irish Sea ice sheet finally withdrew to the west, the Cheshire Plain was 'left' predominantly with glacial clay till covering the 'soft' Triassic rock series of sandstones, Marls and mudstones from which the characteristic red brown till had been derived. Subsequent fluvial deposits added to the former interglacial actions to produce extensive pockets of well-sorted granular material.

Typically the glacial till has in excess of 80 per cent silt size material providing relatively rapid drainage characteristics. Consequent upon its relatively high permeability it has the propensity for relatively quick softening of the material once overburden had been removed. It was, therefore, important for suitable material to be protected until required and then, once excavated, to be formed without delay, placing cohesive material separately from granular. A typical 'rule of thumb' for earthworks suitability was that cohesive fills up to 25 feet high could be formed with adequate factors of safety, using moisture contents not exceeding 1.3 x plastic limit.

The sandier and siltier clays of Lancashire were difficult to test for plastic limit. A simple criterion was adopted for suitability based on the moisture content not exceeding 0.5 liquid limit, this test being far less susceptible to human error. Problems were experienced with the stonier till in North Lancashire and Westmorland when used in embankments. The solution involved the use of drainage layers and a controlled rate of filling.

In the construction of the M6 through Westmorland, the Boulder Clay was found in both shallow deposits and in drumlins. The site investigation had indicated that a high proportion of the material would be too wet to place and compact in embankments, in the normal manner. A trial length of embankment, using the wet Boulder Clay in a layered form of construction, was completed in imported filling material and left to consolidate under its own weight. The method proved to be successful and long lengths of embankment were constructed in this way, with control exercised using instrumentation. Periods of at least four months elapsed before pavement construction was allowed to start.

Throughout the region, the mixing of sands and clays in embankments also created problems. While the materials used in isolation were 'suitable', water displaced from the sand into the mixed material resulted in the fill becoming too wet to compact.

Successive revisions of the Ministry of Transport 'Specification for Road and Bridge Works' and the methods of preparing the 'Bills of Quantities' for use in contracts for motorway construction, attempted to deal with the earthworks problem. The best of intentions of both the design engineers, and the contractors faced with the task of programming the work and the choice of plant were, however, all too often frustrated by the characteristics of the materials which were encountered, and the climate of the North West.

Whilst at the site investigation stage, in-situ CBR values in excess of 20 were often recorded within the glacial till, rapid softening of this moderately overconsolidated material upon excavation and exposure produced effectively, CBR values around the 3 mark. This became a standard yardstick in the North West for pavement design within cuttings where softening was anticipated. The appreciation of such effects may have been the significant factor in avoiding subgrade failures which occurred elsewhere.

Concurrently with this consideration was the introduction of a layer of selected 'hard' granular material at formation level to increase the CBR value. The innovation of using a relatively low-cost material not only reduced the design pavement thickness but provided a platform from which the contractor could complete the installation of drainage, whilst also allowing construction to continue when the relatively high northern rainfall might otherwise have required a cessation of work. Initially known as a 'sub-grade layer', it subsequently became known as a 'capping layer'.

Once such a layer had been introduced, it was considered necessary to aim for an optimum of sub-grade reaction to achieve an efficient pavement design. The Plate Bearing Test was, therefore, used either at formation level or at the top of the sub-base in order to 'prove' the construction. This in-situ test had the advantage of catering for prevailing weather conditions, and a re-test allowed the evaluation of temporary pore-pressure water build-up. Such pavement design philosophies, first developed in the North West to deal with the particular ground and weather conditions, were subsequently adopted nationally.

The fluvioglacial sorting which had laid down relatively uniformly graded 'rounded' sands over much of the Region had not produced the best fine aggregate for production of the then new 'hot-rolled asphalt' mixtures. Similarly the generally low strength of some of the local rocks made this unsuitable for coarse aggregate use.

Although pre-existing recipe specifications had been satisfactory for early traffic the rapidly increasing design life expressed in MSA (million standard axles) required better technical approach if problems of fatigue and plastic deformation were to be avoided. Beginning, therefore, with qualitative tests on soundness, strength and frictional properties, pioneering work was undertaken in Cheshire which gradually led to 'Marshall Properties'. Initially 'Marshall' design was used for the optimisation of particular raw material mixtures, but this rapidly developed into the 'full-blooded' Cheshire specification based on Marshall quotient, minimum binder content and maximum void content.

Pleasingly, most of these early concepts can be found in the latest drafts of the harmonised European (CEN) standards for higher categories of asphalt design. With such standards it may be truly said that asphalt mixtures can be properly designed for today's traffic.

19 The Benefits to the Region

19.1 Traffic and Road Safety

The opening of a section of motorway has the immediate effect of removing traffic from the network of roads in the area through which it passes.

It is, of course, inappropriate to attempt to generalise as to the extent of that effect. Every case is different, but a feature of the motorways in the North-West Region has been the ability to attract a large proportion of heavy vehicles, both serving the industries of the area and passing through it on inter-regional routes such as the M6 and the M62.

The value of a motorway, in traffic terms, is demonstrated when it is necessary for it to be closed due to a major accident, or for exceptional maintenance reasons. Fortunately, this only occurs very infrequently, but the effect on the alternative traffic routes can be dramatic.

The motorways of the Region have provided much-needed increased traffic capacity to cope with the industrial regeneration which has taken place, following the post-war decline in activity in many of its traditional industries.

It has often been said that 'good roads are the essential extensions of the production lines of industry'. The savings in both travel-time and vehicle operating costs, which the motorway network has brought to the Region, have been vital in enabling it to remain competitive.

Whereas it was a characteristic of the Region for workers to live in close proximity to their place of employment, the redundancies of recent years have required the labour force to adopt a flexible approach in 'job-seeking'. The Region's comprehensive system of motorways has assisted in that respect.

It is an indisputable fact that motorways are safer than any other class of road. The transfer of traffic from inadequate roads to a motorway can reduce road accidents over a wide area. However, to quote a simple example of the effect, there were 146 injury accidents on the length of the A6 during the 12 months prior to its being superseded by the 13½-mile Preston-Lancaster Section of the M6. Following the opening of the motorway in January 1965, there were 60 accidents on the A6 and 23 on the M6 in the succeeding 12 months.

By 1968, after the Preston By-pass Section of the M6, Britain's first motorway, had been in use for 10 years, the accident rate in terms of injury accidents per million vehicle miles was 0.248, compared with 0.58 on the superseded length of A6 through Preston.

The traffic and road safety benefits of the motorways to the Region as a whole are considerable.

19.2 Economic

In the period immediately post-1945, Britain's primary economic objectives were reconstruction and exports. It was the time when 'Britain's bread hung by Lancashire's thread' and the greater part of Britain's re-emerging motor car industry, newly released from the war effort, was destined for overseas markets. The post-war boom was soon overtaken by the urgent need to tackle re-housing, clearance and renewal, dereliction, town centre redevelopment and a myriad of social and economic problems. The first tentative steps towards a system of town and country planning had been taken in the 1930s but the Town and Country Planning Act of 1947 provided a formalised framework for a whole raft of interwoven policies to deal with these issues. The opportunity was taken to integrate them with the national commitment to build a network of motorways capable of speeding-up the movement of raw materials and manufactured goods throughout the country.

The Local Authorities in the Region took a leading role, with the opening of Preston By-pass in 1958, as the first stage in the construction of the M6. At its intersection with the East Lancashire Road, A580, at Haydock, the Lancashire County Council purchased land for the development of an industrial estate to attract new growth industries and compensate for jobs lost in declining heavier industries based on the South Lancashire Coalfield. In the event, the Haydock Industrial Estate developed from 1959, predominantly as a regional warehousing, store and distribution location. Haydock, at a point free from the congestion of Manchester and Liverpool, attracted a large number of businesses serving markets across much of Northern England.

Stretford-Eccles By-pass had been completed in 1960 (then numbered the M62) as the first stage of the projected Manchester Outer Ring Road. Its primary purpose was to ease traffic conditions in the vicinity of the large Trafford Park Industrial Estate and the notoriously congested crossing of the Manchester Ship Canal at the Barton Swing Bridge.

Part way along the M61 at Wingates, Westhoughton, the County Council initiated proposals for the development of a new industrial estate to provide jobs for a rapidly growing population. The chosen site lay close to the intersection of the motorway with a proposed new road route, the A5225 Wigan, Hindley and Westhoughton By-pass, linking the Bolton area south-westwards to Merseyside.

The East Lancashire Road, A580, between Liverpool and Manchester, had featured strongly in the economic development of Lancashire and the region, since it was opened in 1934. A major advance at the time, it was already beginning to prove inadequate within little more than 20 years, and was upgraded throughout to a dual carriageway standard by the early 1960s. Much of its traffic was to and from the port of Liverpool and it also served large industrial estates at Kirkby and Knowsley. Although the dualling brought some benefit, Lancashire County Council considered it essential that a motorway be built across South Lancashire, the better to connect the Region's two major conurbations.

From the early 1960s onwards, New Towns were designated within the region at Skelmersdale, Runcorn, Warrington and in Central Lancashire. On the Wirral Peninsula, Ellesmere Port was given the status of an Expanding Town. Able to offer a combination of Development Area grants, New Town infrastructure and housing, they attracted new industry on a large scale.

Skelmersdale, within the Merseyside 'Travel to Work' Area, with its high unemployment, experienced rapid growth. Initially it was connected to the M6 by an all-purpose road completed in 1970, but this was later upgraded and became part of M58. Extensive employment areas were developed at Gillibrands, Pimbo and Stanley. It successfully weathered the closure of its two largest new factories (Courtaulds and Thorn Electrical in 1976/77 with 2,400 redundancies) and over the following 20 years, assisted by UK and European funding, proceeded to fill virtually all of the original designated sites. Much of its success is attributable to the M58 which provided a fast link from the M6 through to Seaforth Docks in Liverpool and the Liverpool Outer Ring Road, M57.

The South Lancashire Section of the M62 and the M56, North Cheshire Motorway, running on roughly parallel east-west alignments to the north and south of the Mersey/Manchester Ship Canal corridor and both intersecting with M6, endowed the Warrington New Town with superb accessibility to the national motorway network. As a result, from the 1970s, Warrington became a by-word as a business growth point and one of Britain's most successful locations for inward investment, attracting many new projects notably in the warehousing, distribution and service sectors.

The Runcorn-Widnes Bridge, which was opened to traffic in 1961, superseded a suspended transporter bridge with a capacity of only 1,500 vehicles per day. Although not part of the motorway network, it was the first bridge crossing of the River Mersey upstream from the mouth of the estuary and led to a rapid expansion in the chemical industries in the two towns. Further investment was attracted by the construction of the M56 which was routed to pass through the southern part of the Runcorn New Town, with a direct link to the new Bridge.

At Ellesmere Port, a spur road from the A41, known initially as the 'Hooton Industrial Road' which was built by Cheshire County Council, enabled Vauxhall to establish its new car factory and create several thousand jobs in an area of high unemployment. It subsequently became part of the M53.

Central Lancashire New Town inherited a robust existing economy based on companies including British Aerospace, GEC, Leyland Trucks and many others. Not an area of high unemployment, it was unable to offer Development Area grants like Skelmersdale, but succeeded in its objective of attracting a wide range of investment due to its attractive environment and position, at one of the focal points of Lancashire's motorway network at the junction of M6/M61. Within the Designated Area a network of local distributor roads linked large new residential sites and major employment areas such as Walton Summit, North Preston (Eastway), and Moss Side (Leyland), to the motorway system. Development of the former Courtaulds factory site at Red Scar, Preston, was given further impetus by the provision of direct access to the Preston By-pass section of the M6 by the provision of a new interchange at Longridge Road B6243, and numbered 31A.

With the completion of M62 through into Yorkshire in 1971, the County Council commenced feasibility studies for a major industrial site alongside the motorway, at Milnrow. Development of important existing industrial estates at Pilsworth in Heywood, and at Stake Hill in Middleton, accelerated as a result of improved accessibility, by the connection of the M66 and the A627(M) with the M62.

Blackpool, famous for its Tower, illuminations, three piers, huge stock of hotel and boarding house accommodation and as the venue for party political and other national conferences, has for long been Britain's premier seaside resort, attracting over 20 million visitors per annum representing spending power of over £500 million in the local economy. The M6, and the M55 completed in 1975, brought in even more visitors by providing a fast route to the Fylde Coast, by-passing Preston. At the end of the M55, Yeadon Way provides a direct route into Blackpool via extensive car and coach parks. The Squires Gate Link Road, built with assistance from the European Regional Development Fund, gives Blackpool South Shore and Lytham St Annes, including Blackpool Airport, access to the motorway system. By the 1970s an acute shortage of land for employment purposes was threatening to stultify the economy of the Fylde Coast and approval was given for a large new sub-regional site, the Blackpool-Fylde Industrial Estate, to which it has direct access to the M55 via the Squires Gate Link. The road infrastructure also facilitated development, for commercial purposes, of land surplus to the operational requirements of Blackpool Airport.

The M55 also brought about improved accessibility for the roll-on/ roll-off Irish Sea container service operating from the port of Fleetwood.

Container lorries on the national motorway system are able to leave M55 at Junction 3, north of Kirkham, and travel to Fleetwood along the A585 which itself has been provided with a number of by-passes and improvements.

For the ancient city of Chester and for North Wales, tourism is also an important industry. In fact, the Welsh Tourist Board has declared that it is almost impossible to overstate its importance to the Welsh economy. A key feature contributing to its increasing success has been the continuing development of the motorway system, in particular M6, M56, M53 and the continuation of A55 south of Chester into North Wales, which have opened up those areas to the populations of Merseyside, Lancashire, Greater Manchester and beyond.

It was, of course, not the only industry to benefit. There is ample evidence of other commercial and industrial development in Cheshire and North Wales, examples being the huge Deeside Industrial Park just over the Welsh border and developments at Wrexham and Mold along the A55, all providing employment after the decline of the coal and steel industries in those areas. The new developments were varied and imaginative and included the prestige Chester Business Park (4,500 employees) and Cheshire Oaks retail outlet on the edge of Ellesmere Port, all built close to motorway connections. A later example was a prestige office development at Daresbury Park located at the M56/A56 junction.

Another primary requirement for business, especially foreign investors, is a fast road link to a major, international airport. M56 provides such a link and has contributed to the success of the Manchester Airport. Although it aimed to increase the use of rail from 10 per cent in 1992 to 25 per cent by 2005, the predominant means of access will still be by road for cars, taxis, buses, coaches and vehicles using the freight-handling facilities. The effect on the regional economy of the UK's largest airport outside the south-east is almost incalculable but its growth, assisted by its position on the motorway network, particularly M56, M60 and M6, results in its supporting 35,000 jobs in the Region, with a forecast of a further 50,000, following completion of the second runway and associated facilities.

The decline in the traditional industries of the west coast of Cumberland had led to high unemployment in the area. With the completion of the M6 through the region and the improvement of the A66 between Penrith and Workington, investment was attracted and new industries prospered as a direct consequence of better road communications. Close to the M6 interchanges at Penrith and industrial estates have been developed.

The economy of the Lake District is almost entirely dependent on tourism. The M6, with links into both south and north Lakeland, was of vital importance and extended the catchment area of day visitors to the extent that it is not uncommon for day trips to be made from as far away as the conurbations of the Midlands.

During the last 40 years of the millennium since the opening of the country's first motorway, the Preston By-pass Section of the M6, motorways became an integral part of the economy. Indeed the benefits that flowed from them, to individual areas and locations and to the economy as a whole, often became so assimilated that it is difficult to measure the 'motorway factor' in anything like empirical terms. People aged under 40, the majority (56 per cent) of the country's population, had no direct recollection of pre-motorway Britain. Inevitably motorways were taken for granted by many but, with their proliferation and increased traffic, became increasingly the focus of a strong environmental lobby by others.

In the case of one of the last motorways to be completed in Lancashire before the millennium, the M65, the economic transformation which it brought about in east Lancashire was so apparent that a great many people could, with ease, look back just a few years to when the economy and congestion of its towns held out little by way of optimism. Coming into use from 1981 onwards, it had an immediate effect in expediting the development of sites. The Lomeshaye Industrial Estate, connected with M65 and A56 by the Brierfield Link Road, was an early success.

Economic development is, however, a complex and dynamic process and was influenced by other factors as well as the 'motorway'. Some of the north-east Lancashire sites were designated as Enterprise Zones from 1984-94, offering a range of financial incentives for developers. The site at Shadsworth, which had experienced a notoriously slow rate of take-up for many years, largely due to inadequate road access and the fact that it was not an Enterprise Zone, had to await the final stage of M65, the Blackburn Southern By-pass, before developers started to look seriously at it as an investment location. As soon as this became a prospect and, even in anticipation of the outcome of a Public Inquiry held in 1991 at which the local business community, Local Authorities and Central Government all expressed strong support, demand for sites at Shadsworth increased markedly. Along with the nearby Walker Industrial Park, development accelerated further after the Blackburn Southern By-pass opened to traffic in 1997. With M65 completed from Preston to Colne, virtually all the land on the sites planned in conjunction with the motorway has been fully developed, providing thousands of jobs.

Regional issues were very much to the fore with the establishment of the Northwest Regional Development Agency. The NWDA's Draft Strategy of July 1999 was centred on a broad concept of sustainable development promoting economic growth and social inclusion whilst protecting the environment. Development was proposed for a portfolio of sites, which were already commitments or firm proposals, for inward investment. In Lancashire this included the proposed Cuerden Regional Business Park at the intersection of M6, M61 and M65, located between the existing Walton Summit Employment Area and Lancashire Enterprise's Business Park.

Elsewhere, in the region, the Draft Strategy included other well located sites at Rochdale, Warrington, Knowsley, Tameside, Runcorn, Liverpool, Wirral, Carlisle and Crewe. According to figures published by the former regional promotion agency INWARD, later part of the NWDA, 90 per cent of enquiries received for sites and premises specified locations close to a motorway. On this evidence alone it would appear that the 'motorway factor' will remain influential in industrial location and inward investment in the future.

19.2   Environmental

The dictionary definition of 'environment' is 'surrounding'. In commenting on the construction of a motorway, many so-called 'environmentalists' will refer only to the alleged adverse effects but logically, should confine their remarks to the immediate surroundings of the corridor through which the motorway passes. They fail to acknowledge the benefits which a motorway can bring to the 'environment', over a much wider area.

In the design of the motorways throughout the region, a great deal of attention has been given to both the horizontal and vertical profiles, in order to ensure that they blend into the surroundings. This was acknowledged by a Civic Trust Award for a section of the M6 through Westmorland.

The care taken in the design of bridges, and in the landscaping of an interchange in an urban area, was recognised by similar awards for Snow Hill Lane Bridge, M6, and the Worsley Court House roundabout at the northern end of the original Stretford-Eccles By-pass.

Tree and shrub planting has been undertaken on a massive scale. For example, in Lancashire alone, over one million trees had been planted within, and adjacent to, the boundaries of the motorways of the county, by the early 1970s.

It is contended, therefore, that the appearance of the motorways of the North West compares favourably with that of any other form of physical development.

It is unfortunately inevitable that a motorway will affect people living along the proposed route through an urban area. In order to keep disturbance to a minimum, routes were located, wherever possible, along-side the barriers created by existing transportation facilities, such as railway lines, and through areas of obsolete housing, or derelict former industrial land.

Within the Region, there were many such opportunities. For example, in the case of the M602 through Eccles and Salford, where the motorway is sited immediately alongside the Manchester-Liverpool Line, old railway sidings were utilised and, of the hundreds of houses which had to be demolished, the majority were of pre-1914 construction. Their replacement by modern housing, and the provision of new churches and other buildings were of considerable benefit to the community.

In the rural areas, the drainage systems of the motorways were often of benefit to agriculture, by improving the drainage of adjoining land. Excavated material unsuitable for construction was used to reshape adjoining land and improve its agricultural potential.

The designers and builders of the motorways in the North West led the way in the use of waste materials. The removal of vast quantities of burnt and unburnt colliery waste from the tips within the old mining areas, for use in the construction, enabled large areas of land to be reclaimed. Unsightly and offensive chemical waste, and pulverised fuel ash from power stations, were also used in the formation of embankments.

The greatest environmental benefit of the motorway network has, however, resulted from the transfer of large volumes of traffic from inadequate roads passing through the cities, towns and villages of the Region. It is understandable that, following the opening of a section of motorway, very little is heard from the 'silent majority' of those who have benefited, over a wide area, in terms of improved safety for all classes of road user, and relief from congestion, noise, and pollution.

Whereas it is accepted that some members of the public will be adversely affected by the construction of a motorway, the overall net benefit to the environment as a whole is considerable.

20 The Achievement

By the end of the 20th century, why did the North West Region have the greatest concentration of motorways in the UK?

Without doubt, the political pressure applied by the County Councils on successive Governments, over a long period, had a major impact in the development of the network. They were fully supported by the majority of the other Local Authorities, Members of Parliament, and industrial and commercial interests.

The early pre-war initiative taken within the four counties, with proposals for a north-south route through the Region, were followed by other motorways included in the various County Development and Structure Plans.

The most significant routes were those in the Road Plan for Lancashire 1949, which had drawn attention to the inadequate capacity of the main arterial routes through the county. It was pointed out that its industrial strength as one of the chief producing and exporting areas of the country, depended on the ability to move goods, quickly cheaply and easily from place to place.

There had been a reduction in the number of road casualties during the war years. By the late 1940s, however, the figure had risen to over 7,000 per annum on the roads of Lancashire. It had been demonstrated in the Road Plan that dual carriageway roads for 'vehicles only', and the elimination of single-level intersections, would produce a large saving in accidents – a prediction confirmed in practice soon after the first motorway was completed and brought into use.

The case for motorways had been established throughout the Region. This led to a series of campaigns mainly promoted by the County Councils and by groups of Local Authorities, such as those in 'SELNEC'.

The key figure in the North West was undoubtedly (Sir) James Drake. Using the media to the full, and with the backing of organisations such as the British Road Federation, he encouraged the Lancashire County Council to make almost constant representations to Ministers either directly, or by lobbying MPs. There were many in senior positions in the Ministry who were not averse to such approaches as they were equally keen to see progress being made, in order to meet the Government's objective of completing 1,000 miles of motorway by the early 1970s.

Campaigning had not, however, been confined to Lancashire. The Cheshire, Cumberland and Westmorland County Councils had pressed for the construction of the M6 through their counties, and also in Cheshire the importance of the M56 had been emphasised. In Manchester, the City Council had promoted its own Parliamentary Bill for the Mancunian Way.

The requirements for justifying a scheme by means of an economic assessment became more sophisticated. As activity in many of the traditional industries of the Region was adversely affected by changing markets and periods of recession, there was an emphasis on attracting new industry. It was, however, extremely difficult to allow for such a factor in forecasting traffic flows, for the purpose of an economic assessment. The 'political' significance of a scheme could, however, often override other considerations. In those circumstances, campaigning was even more important in a situation where the influence of the major Local Authorities began to decline.

One of the main reasons, however, for continuity in the programme of motorway construction in Lancashire was the support which the County Council gave to Drake by providing him with the staff resources for advance preparation. It was the practice to have several of the Road Plan schemes under design, well before they were accepted into the Ministry's programme. This approach was often welcomed by the Ministry, as it enabled a scheme to be brought forward at short notice to replace a project in another part of the country which, for various reasons, had to be withdrawn. The same enthusiasm was shown by the County Council in respect of those motorway schemes for which it was the 'Highway Authority'.

The provision of a comprehensive system of motorways in the North West during the second half of the 20th century was a remarkable achievement. This was essentially due to the dedication and profession-alism of the staff of the Highway Authorities and the firms of Consulting Engineers (Appendix 1), and the enormous efforts of the Contractors, often working under adverse conditions (Appendix 2).

It could not have been accomplished, however, without the full co-operation of many other organisations, for example, the Statutory Under-takers were actively involved in diverting their mains and services which were affected. The development of the network had a major impact on the railway infrastructure of the region. The design and construction of bridges carrying the motorways over railways was undertaken in a similar manner to that adopted for any other type of crossing. The need to ensure the operational safety of the railways was vital. The local Divisional Civil Engineers would, therefore, check any temporary works, and arrange for track possession and supervision on the site. In contrast, where a motorway was designed to pass under a railway, special measures were necessary, in order to minimise the effect on rail traffic. In such cases, the design, the award of the contract and the supervision of construction was carried out under the direction of the Chief Civil Engineer (London-Midland Region (BR)) and, subsequently, the Engineer holding an equivalent appointment.

Traffic growth continues unabated but it seems that, due to reductions in the level of expenditure for new road construction imposed by successive Governments, a number of motorway projects, which had been under consideration for many years, are unlikely to proceed in the foreseeable future. For example, the completion of the motorway 'box' around Preston; relief for the M62 by the eastward extension of the M65, the M58, and the M67; a Morecambe/Heysham Link from M6; the extension of the M56 westwards from A5117 to A550 near the Welsh border; the A556 (M) between M6 and M56; and the Stockport North-South By-pass. In addition, there is a strong case for widening the M6 to a dual four-lane standard between the Cheshire/Staffordshire boundary (Junction 16) and M56 (Junction 20); and upgrading certain lengths of 'all-purpose' road to motorway standard, such as the section of A74 from the northern end of M6 to the Scottish border; the A55 extension of the M53 into North Wales; the A550 from the M53 at Hooton to the A5117; and the Edenfield/Haslingden/Accrington Easterly By-passes connecting M65 and M66.

Has the impetus to continue with the development of the motorway network in the North West Region been lost?

Appendix 1

Highway Authorities and Consulting Engineers involved in the Development of the Motorway Network

Highway Authorities

1. TRUNK ROAD MOTORWAYS:
   (a) The Secretary of State for Transport (with former similar titles) represented by:
   - (i) The North Western Road Construction Unit:

Cheshire County Sub-Unit	M53, M56 (M63)M60
Lancashire County Sub-Unit	M55, M58, M61, M62 (M63)M60, M66, A666(M)ii

   - (ii) The North West Regional Office   M6 (M63/60)M60
   - (iii) The Highways Agency   M6, M60, M65

   (b) Agent Authorities

Cheshire County Council (ChCC)	M53, M6
Cumberland County Council (CuCC)	M6
Lancashire County Council (LCC)	M6, M61, M62, M65

2. LOCAL AUTHORITY MOTORWAYS:

Cheshire County Council	M531 (subsequently part of M53)
Lancashire County Council	M57, (M62/63) M60, A601(M), M602, A627(M), M65
Manchester City Council (MCC)	A57(M)
Greater Manchester Metropolitan County Council (GMC)	M602, A6144(M)
Trafford MBC (Trafford)	A6144(M)

NOTE: The Chief Civil Engineer (London-Midland Region (BR)) and, subsequently the Engineer holding an equivalent appointment, accepted the responsibility, on behalf of the Highway Authorities, for the design, the award of contracts, and the supervision of the construction of the bridges carrying railways over the motorways.

Consulting Engineers

CONSULTANT	CODE	SCHEME(S)
Babtie Shaw and Morton	BSM	M65
Sir William Halcrow & Partners	WH	M67
Howard Humphreys (inc. Harry Brompton & Partners)	HH	M56, (M63) M60, M65
Husband & Co	H&Co	M56
G Maunsell & Partners	GM	M53, A57(M),* M602 (Salford),* (M63)M60
Mott Hay and Anderson	MHA	(M62/63) M60
L G Mouchel & Partners	LGM	(M63) M60, M60
Parkman Consulting Engineers	PC	(M63/66) M60 (M62/63) M60
Pell Frischmann Consultants	PF	M6
Rendel Palmer & Tritton	RPT	M6
Scott, Wilson, Kirkpatrick & Partners	SWK	M6
Ward Ashcroft and Parkman	WAP	(M62/63) M60

* With the exception of A57(M) and M602 (Salford), where the firm was commissioned by the Manchester City Council and the Greater Manchester Metropolitan County Council respectively, all the Consulting Engineers were engaged on sections of those Trunk Road Motorways shown.

NOTE: Where the M number of a section of motorway has been changed, the former number(s) is indicated in brackets e.g. (M63)M60. This applies to all of the lists in Appendices 1 and 2.

Appendix 2

The Principal Main Contractors

CONTRACTOR	CODE	SCHEME(S)
AMEC/A McAlpine Joint Venture	AMEC/McA	M60
Balfour Beatty Major Projects		M60
Balfour Beatty Civil Engineering Ltd }	BB	M6
Balfour Beatty Construction Ltd		A6144 (M),(M63)M60
Percy Bilton Ltd.	PB	M56, M58
Buckton Contractors Ltd	BC	M65
A F Budge (Construction) Ltd	Bu	A601 (M), M65
Cementation Construction Ltd.	Cem	M65
Christiani Shand	CS	M6, M56
Cleveland Bridge & Engineering Ltd	CBE	M6
Costain (Civil Engineering) Ltd.	C	M60, M61, M62
G Dew & Co Ltd	Dew	(M62/63) M60
Dorman Long (Bridge Engineering) Ltd	DL	M6
R M Douglas Construction Ltd	Doug	M65
Dowsett Engineering Construction Ltd.	Dow	M58, M6, M65
Leonard Fairclough Ltd	LF	M56, A57 (M), M6 (M63) M60, M602
Fairclough Civil Engineering Ltd }		M53, M6 (M63) M60, M65 (M66) M60, 67
A E Farr Ltd.	AEF	(M62/63) M60
W & C French (Construction) Ltd	WCF	M6
Gee Walker & Slater Ltd	GWS	(M62/63) M60
Holland & Hannen and Cubitts (Civil Engineering) Ltd	HH&C	M56
John Laing Construction Ltd.	L	M6 (M63) M60
Peter Lind & Co Ltd.	PL	M56 (M63) M60
Marples Ridgway Ltd	MR	M56
Sir Alfred McAlpine & Son Ltd		M56, M65, M67
The Sir Alfred McAlpine & Son Ltd/ Leonard Fairclough Ltd Consortium }	McA	M53, M55, M57, M58, M6, M61, 62(M63) M60, M65, M66, A627(M),A666(M)
Alfred McAlpine Construction Ltd		(M63) M60, M65
Alfred McAlpine/AMEC Joint Venture		M65
R McGregor & Sons Ltd	RMcG	M56, M62 (M66) M60
Miller/Keir Joint Venture	M/K	M60
A Monk & Co Ltd	M	M53, M57, M6, M62, M67
Murdoch McKenzie Ltd	MM	M6
Norwest Construction Co Ltd }	NW	M57, M62
Norwest-Holst Ltd		M67
Sir Lindsay Parkinson & Co Ltd	P	M53, M6, M62, M66
RDL Contracting Ltd	RDL	M65
Reed & Mallik Ltd	R&M	M57, M62
Tarmac Ltd		M6
Tarmac Civil Engineering Ltd }	T	M6
Tarmac Construction Ltd		M6, M65

Appendix 3
The Senior Personnel of the Various Organisations

1. Staff of the Highway Authorities and Consulting Engineers responsible for the Preparation, Design and Supervision of Construction

Listed alphabetically, with organisation given in brackets followed by principal role(s).

NOTE:

(i) 'DTp' indicates the name of the responsible Government Department, irrespective of the title given to it at different periods during the development of the motorway network, e.g. Ministry of Transport, Department of the Environment or Highways Agency

(ii) Certain members of the Staff of the Lancashire County Council (LCC) and the Cheshire County Council (ChCC) were allocated to the respective Sub-Unit (SU) of the NWRCU, or seconded to its Headquarters, for varying periods, between 1967 and 1981. No attempt has been made to identify specifically the personnel concerned, with the exception of those appointed as Superintending Engineers.

(iii) Cumberland County Council (CuCC) did not participate in the NWRCU. It acted solely as an Agent Authority in a similar manner to the Lancashire and Cheshire County Councils, which undertook the design and supervision of construction of a substantial part of the network in that capacity.

(iv) The firms of Consulting Engineers are identified by the key letters after their name in Appendix 1, e.g. (BSM) indicates 'Babtie Shaw and Morton'.

Adamson Terry, (LCC), Deputy Resident Engineer
Airey David, (LGM), Resident Engineer
Aldred Peter, (LCC), Team Leader (Bridges)
Ambrose Keith, (ChCC), Team Leader (Bridges)
Andrews Cyril, (LCC), Resident Engineer
Angus Ron, (BSM), Partner
Ardern Fred, (LGM), Deputy Project Manager
Argyle Robin, (LCC), Team Leader (Bridges)
Armitage Bob, (ChCC), Team Leader (Roads)
Armitage John, (ChCC), Resident Engineer
Arrowsmith Edmund, (LCC), Soils & Materials Engineer
Ashcroft Peter, (LCC), Deputy Resident Engineer
Ashforth George, (ChCC), County Surveyor & Bridgemaster 1926-45
Atherton Bill, (LCC/NWRCU), Superintending Engineer (Bridges)
Atkinson Peter, (LCC), Soils & Materials Engineer
Ayres Dennis, (BR), District Engineer
Bailey Ian, (LGM), Resident Engineer
Baker Alan CB, (DTp), Director of Highway Engineering
Baldacchino David, (LGM), Highways Team Leader
Baldwin Sir Peter, (DTp), Permanent Secretary 1976-82
Barker Peter, (LCC), Team Leader (Drainage)
Barlow Dennis, (LCC), Resident Engineer
Barnes John, (LCC), Team Leader (Roads)
Barnett Alan, (GM), Senior Engineer
Barton Phil, (LGM), Design Manager (Telematics)
Barton Tony, (LGM), Quantity Surveyor Group Leader
Batty William, (BR), Chief Civil Engineer
Beevers Colin, (DTp), Regional Director
Bell Arnold, (ChCC), Resident Engineer
Benjafield Chris, (LGM), Team Leader (Highways)
Berry Norman, (LCC), Team Leader (Roads)
Best Keith OBE, (H & Co), Partner
Bingham Geoff, (GM), Partner
Bingham Peter, (ChCC), Team Leader (Bridges)
Blaikley Bruce, (GM), Deputy Resident Engineer

Bodgener Peter, (BR), Design Engineer (Bridges)
Booth Jim, (LCC), Deputy Resident Engineer
Booty David, (LGM), Director
Bott Paul, (ChCC/PC), Team Leader (Roads)
Bowden Geoff, (LGM), Structures Team Leader
Bowman John, (GM), Deputy Resident Engineer
Braithwaite Les, (LCC), Team Leader (Roads)
Bramham Ken, (ChCC/PC), Team Leader (Roads)
Bridle Ron, (ChCC/SU), Superintending Engineer
Brimelow Derek, (LGM), Project Manager
Bristow Ron, (GM), Project Engineer
Broughton Leslie, (CUCC), County Surveyor & Bridgemaster 1952-70
Bruton Jack, (NWRCU), Superintending Engineer
Buckland David, (LCC), Team Leader (Bridges)
Burgoyne Derek, (CUCC), Principal Assistant Engineer
Burns Andy, (LGM), Team Leader (Structures)
Burrows Nick, (LCC), Resident Engineer
Bushell George, (ChCC), Assistant County Surveyor (Bridges)
Cairns Harry, (CuCC), Soils and Materials Engineer
Calf John, (BR), Construction Manager
Callery Mike OBE, (ChCC/SU), Superintending Engineer
, (LCC), County Surveyor & Bridgemaster 1985-93
Cameron-Smith Arnold, (GM), Assistant Resident Engineer
Campbell M, (CUCC), Deputy Senior Resident Engineer
Cantrell Philip, (LGM), Partner
Carroll Frank, (LCC), Assistant County Surveyor (Lighting)
Child Paul, (LGM), Divisional Director
Chilton Rod, (PF), Project Manager
Chorley Mike, (BR), Resident Engineer
Chorlton Ian, (HH), Associate Director/ Project Manager
Clear John, (LCC), Resident Engineer
Clunas Michael, (HH), Associate Director/ Project Manager/ Resident Engineer
Coates David, (ChCC), Resident Engineer
Cockroft Norman, (LCC), Team Leader (Bridges)
Cocks Lynton, (LGM), Team Leader (Structures)

Cockshaw Sir Alan, (LCC), Team Leader/Resident Engineer
Cole Roger, (LCC), Team Leader (Bridges)
Coleman Stewart, (LCC), Team Leader (Roads)
Collins David, (LGM), Project Manager
Collins Simon, (LGM), Team Leader (Structures)
Cooke Peter, (MHA), Team Leader (Design)
Cookson Ben, (ChCC), Team Leader (Roads)
Cookson Richard, (ChCC), Team Leader (Roads), (PC),
　　Resident Engineer
Cope Eric, (LCC), Team Leader (Roads)
Coppins Brian, (ChCC), Team Leader (Traffic)
Corfield Peter, (LGM), Partner
Corner Arthur, (Trafford), Resident Engineer
Cox Don, (CUCC), Senior Resident Engineer
Cox Ken, (LCC), Assistant County Surveyor (Lighting)
Cox Ron, (ChCC), Team Leader (Roads)
Crawford Colin, (ChCC), Team Leader (Roads)
Cresswell John, (LCC), Team Leader (Roads)
Crossley Philip, (ChCC), Team Leader (Roads)
Crowe Martin, (PC), Team Leader (Bridges)
Cryer Mike, (ChCC), Team Leader (Roads)
Curzon Lou, (ChCC), Team Leader (Traffic)
Davidson Ian, (LGM), Deputy Resident Engineer
Davies Glyn, (ChCC), Land Surveyor
Davies John, (BR), Resident Engineer
Davis Martin, (LGM), Highways Team Leader
Davison John, (CUCC), County Surveyor & Bridgemaster
　　1970-85
Day Bernard, (LCC), Soils & Materials Engineer
Day Cecil, (ChCC), County Surveyor & Bridgemaster 1957-64
Dean Brian, (PF), Director
Dean 'Dixie' OBE, (LCC/ChCC/ CuCC), Resident Engineer
Dean Donald CBE, (NWRCU), Director
Dean John OBE, (LCC), County Surveyor & Bridgemaster
　　1967-68
Dewhirst Alan, (LCC), Resident Engineer
Dodd Lance, (SWK), Resident Engineer-in-Chief
Doyle Keith, (WAP), Senior Engineer
Drake Sir James, (LCC), County Surveyor & Bridgemaster
　　1945-72, (NWRCU), Director 1967-68
Drury Ken, (LCC), Quantity Surveyor
Duckworth Harry, (ChCC), County Surveyor & Bridgemaster
　　1964-65
Dudeney Don, (SWK), Resident Engineer (Bridges)
Dunlop Albert, (PC), Team Leader (Land)
Dunsmore Adam, (LCC/SU), Superintending Engineer
　　(Bridges)
Dunsmore Mac, (LCC), Team Leader (Bridges)
Eakin George, (WAP), Director
Eastwood Jeff, (MHA), Team Leader (Design)
Ebden Bill, (GM), Chief Design Engineer
Edge Ron, (ChCC), Soils & Materials Engineer
Edwards `Roly', (SWK), Geologist
Edwards Max, (LCC), Assistant County Surveyor (Motorways)
Eliott Ron, (PC), Lighting Engineer
Elliott Doug, (RPT), Project Director
Evans Archie, (SWK), Senior Engineer
Evans Di CBE, (LCC), Team Leader (Roads), (NWRCU),
　　Superintending Engineer
Evans Rees, (LGM), Deputy Resident Engineer
Farragher Ron, (WAP), Senior Engineer
Farrow David, (LGM), Deputy Resident Engineer
Fifoot Graham, (PC), Team Leader (Bridges)
Firth John, (LCC), Team Leader (Roads)
Fisher Anthony, (LGM), Project Manager
Fitzgerald Brian, (LCC), Resident Engineer
Forrest Gordon, (SWK), Resident Engineer (Roads)

Foulkes Paul, (RPT), Project Manager
Foxley Phil, (LGM), Team Leader (Highways)
Frescini Tony, (BR), Resident Engineer
Friston Tony, (ChCC), Assistant County Surveyor (Bridges)
Fuller Norman, (ChCC), Team Leader (Bridges)
Gartside Tom, (LCC), Resident Engineer
Gate Doug, (NWRCU), Director
Gee David, (LCC), Assistant Resident Engineer
Giles Stephen, (PC), Team Leader (Roads)
Ginns Harry, (DTp), Chief Highway Engineer
Glover Trevor, (HH), Deputy Resident Engineer
Gordon Ken, (CUCC), Section Engineer
Grace Henry, (SWK), Partner
Grady Kim, (HH), Team Leader Structures)
Gray J E, (ChCC), Team Leader (Traffic)
Gray John, (ChCC), Team Leader (Land)
Greatrix Ron, (LCC), Resident Engineer
Green David, (ChCC), Team Leader (Land)
Green Phil, (SWK), Soils & Materials Engineer/Partner
Green Roland, (CUCC), Principal Assistant Engineer
Greenwood Roy, (ChCC), Team Leader (Traffic)
Gregory Bill, (LCC), Team Leader (Roads)
Gregson John, (LCC), Deputy Resident Engineer
Greyling Nick, (SWK), Chief Resident Engineer
Griffin Bill, (LCC), Resident Engineer
Gulliver Ron, (LGM), Deputy Resident Engineer
Gyngell Paul, (BR), Resident Engineer
Haddock Steve, (LGM), Highways Team Leader
Haigh Jim, (LCC), Resident Engineer
Hall Arthur, (LCC), Team Leader (Bridges), (NWRCU), Supt
　　Engineer (Bridges & Construction)
Halls Brian, (SWK), Senior Engineer (Bridges)
Halls Peter, (SWK), Senior Engineer
Hammond Derek, (LGM), Highways Team Leader
Hardcastle David, (HH), Director (Transportation)
Harding David, (LCC), Assistant Resident Engineer
Hardy John, (HH), Resident Engineer
Harrington John, (LGM), Partner
Harris Sir William, (DTp), Director General (Highways)
Hartley Malcolm, (LCC), Resident Engineer
Harvey Ian, (CUCC), Principal Assistant Engineer
Haslam Brian, (BR), Bridge Engineer
Hayes Bob, (ChCC), Team Leader (Bridges)
Hayes Brian, (PC), Associate Director
Henderson Malcolm, (ChCC), Team Leader (Roads)
Henderson Ron, (SWK), Engineer/Quantity Surveyor
Henry John, (SWK), Partner
Henry Tony, (LCC), Resident Engineer
Herbstritt Dave, (PC), Team Leader (Bridges)
Hewitt Peter, (NWRCU), Scheme Manager
Hewson Frank, (LCC), Chief Resident Engineer
Heywood David, (LCC), Team Leader (Bridges)
Heyworth Des, (LCC), Team Leader (Drainage)
Hill Brian CBE, (LCC), Chief Executive/Clerk
Hobbs Raymond, (LGM), Team Leader (Structures)
Hodge Tom, (H&Co), Resident Engineer
Hodgson George, (LCC), Assistant County Surveyor (Bridges)
Hogg Leslie, (LCC), Team Leader (Roads)
Holden Alan, (LCC), Assistant Resident Engineer
Holden Peter, (LCC), Team Leader (Roads)
Holland David, (DTp), Chief Highway Engineer
Holliday Gordon, (LCC), Team Leader (Traffic)
Holman Don, (BSM), Associate Partner
Hood John, (LCC), Engineer/Quantity Surveyor
Hook David, (GM), Project Partner
Hotchkiss Jack, (LCC), Resident Engineer
Hough Roger, (LCC), Deputy Resident Engineer

Housley Peter, (LGM), Deputy Resident Engineer
Howcroft Alan OBE, (ChCC), Resident Engineer
Hunter Mike, (WAP), Senior Engineer
Ingram Jim, (LCC), County Surveyor &Bridgemaster 1972-74
Ingram Joe, (LCC), Team Leader (Bridges)
Inman Peter CBE, (LCC), Chief Executive/Clerk
Jackson Alan, (BR), Works Engineer
Jackson Arthur, (LCC), Engineer/Quantity Surveyor
Jackson Keith, (LGM), Director
Jenkins Trevor, (PC), Team Leader (Bridges)
Johnson Bill MBE, (LCC), Resident Engineer, Deputy County Surveyor
Johnson Eric, (ChCC), Team Leader (Roads)
Johnson Kay, (HH), Principal Engineer
Johnson Peter, (GM), Design Engineer (Structures)
Jones David, (ChCC), Lighting Engineer
Jones Howard, (LCC), Assistant County Surveyor (Bridges)
Jones Nigel, (WH), Resident Engineer
Jones Walter, (PC), Land Surveyor
Jordan Ian, (BSM), Senior Engineer (Design)
Kemp Bob, (ChCC), Team Leader (Bridges)
Kennedy Quin, (LCC), Team Leader (Bridges)
Kevill Dick, (LCC), Resident Engineer
King Alan, (BR), Divisional Civil Engineer
Kinley Bill, (LCC), Quantity Surveyor
Knapman Roger, (GM), Resident Engineer
Knight Bert, (LCC), Resident Engineer
Knight Viv OBE, (ChCC), County Surveyor &Bridgemaster 1973-74
Director of Highways & Transportation 1974-88
Knowles Alan, (ChCC), Team Leader (Bridges)
Knowles Peter, (SWK), Chief Resident Engineer
Land John, (PF), Resident Engineer
Large Tony, (ChCC), Soils & Materials Engineer
Lawton Frank, (LCC), Team Leader (Land)
Lea Walter, (ChCC), Assistant County Surveyor (Traffic)
Leather Dave, (LCC), Resident Engineer
Leather Ted, (ChCC), Lighting Engineer
Lee Bill, (ChCC), Resident Engineer
Lee Bob, (ChCC), Team Leader (Roads)
Lee David, (GM), Bridge Design/Partner
Lee Norman, (ChCC), Team Leader (Computer Design)
Lester Harry, (LCC), Deputy Resident Engineer
Lewendon Roger, (LGM), Resident Engineer
Lindsay Joe, (SWK), Associate Partner
Lingham Rory, (LGM), Deputy Project Manager
Little Gordon, (HH), Partner (Structures)
Livingstone Bob, (LCC), Supervisory Clerk of Works
Lloyd David, (CuCC), Supervisory Design Engineer (Motorways), Director of Engineering 1985-90
Lloyd George, (LCC), Team Leader (Bridges)
Lloyd Mike MBE, (ChCC), Resident Engineer, (PC), Director
Lloyd Ron, (ChCC), Land Surveyor
Lloyd-Owen Arthur, (BR), Divisional Civil Engineer
Lockwood Geoffrey, (CuCC), County Surveyor &Bridgemaster 1924-52
Lohn Mike, (LGM), Team Leader (Geotechnics)
Longworth Jim, (LCC), Head of Industrial Development and Promotion Unit
Lund John, (LCC/BSM), Senior Engineer (Design)
Lyle Ronnie, (LCC), Team Leader (Roads)
Lyon David, (SWK), Assistant Resident Engineer/Partner
Mac Gregor, (CuCC), Assistant County Surveyor (Bridges)
Macartney Alan, (H&Co), Partner
Mackrill Rex, (LCC), Soils & Materials Engineer
Maguire Jim, (LCC), Team Leader (Roads)
Mansley Harold, (ChCC), Team Leader (Roads)

Matthias Cliff, (LCC), Assistant Resident Engineer
Mc Dermott 'Mac', (SWK), Associate Partner
Mc Ilhatton Rene, (CuCC), Soils Engineer
Mc Intyre Ban, (ChCC), County Surveyor &Bridgemaster 1965-73
Mc Kay Colin, (CuCC), Principal Assistant Engineer
Mc Kenna Brian, (SWK), Senior Engineer (Bridges)
Mc Kie Alan, (LCC), Team Leader (Bridges)
Mc Nee Stewart, (SWK), Chief Resident Engineer
Measures James, (LGM), Director
Melling Doug, (LCC/BSM), Resident Engineer
Melville Ray, (LCC), Team Leader (Bridges)
Mercer Peter, (WH), Resident Engineer
Miller Alex, (LCC), Team Leader (Bridges), Deputy Resident Engineer
Miller Ian, (HH), Director
Milne Maurice CB, (DTp), Deputy Director General (Highways)
Moakes Willis, (LCC), Team Leader (Roads)
Moore Maurice, (LCC), Resident Engineer
Morris Alan, (LCC), Soils & Materials Engineer
Murray George, (LCC/SU), Superintending Engineer (Bridges)
Murray John, (LGM), Managing Director
Murtha John, (HH), Deputy Resident Engineer
Naylor Gary, (H&Co), Partner
Neilson Brian, (CuCC), Deputy Senior Resident Engineer, (ChCC), County Engineer
Nelson Colin, (GMC), Team Leader (Roads)
Nicholls Raymond, (ChCC), County Surveyor &Bridgemaster 1945-57
Nicholson Bruce, (LCC), Deputy Resident Engineer
Norris Robin, (ChCC), Team Leader (Traffic)
Noy Les, (LCC), Resident Engineer
O'Donnell Mike, (ChCC), Resident Engineer
Ogden David OBE, (ChCC/PC), Associate Director
Ogden Ted, (LCC), Assistant County Surveyor (Traffic)
Oliver Fred OBE, (LCC), Team Leader (Bridges)
Openshaw Tony, (LCC), Team Leader (Roads)
Ormerod Ken, (BR), Resident Engineer
Osborn Robin, (SWK), Team Leader (Bridges), Partner
Osborne Gordon, (MHA), Chief Resident Engineer
Osborne Peter, (GM), Roadworks Consultant
Ottway Terry, (WN), Deputy Resident Engineer
Paisley John, (DTp), Chief Highway Engineer
Parker Len, (SWK), Soils & Materials Engineer
Parkinson Charlie, (PC), Senior Engineer (Bridges)
Parkinson Clifford, (BR), District Engineer
Parody Derek, (PC), Section Engineer (Bridges)
Parry John, (ChCC), Team Leader (Roads)
Partington Ray, (LCC), Deputy Resident Engineer
Patrick Jim, (CuCC), Assistant County Engineer (Drainage)
Peat John, (LCC), Supervisory Clerk of Works
Pemba 'Tee', (SWK), Senior Engineer (Bridges)
Pennington John, (LCC/BSM), Associate Partner
Phillips Trevor, (LCC), Deputy Resident Engineer
Phillipson Jim, (LCC), Deputy Resident Engineer
Pickup Jim, (LCC), Deputy Resident Engineer
Pickup Roger, (LCC), Assistant County Surveyor (Motorways)
Pigott Alan, (SWK), Senior Engineer (Design)
Pilkington John, (LCC), Team Leader (Roads)
Pilling John, (RPT), Project Co-ordinator
Padmore Sir Thomas, (DTp), Permanent Secretary 1962-68
Potts Don, (ChCC), Team Leader (Bridges)
Powell Alan, (LCC), Soils & Materials Engineer
Price Norman, (LCC), Soils & Materials Engineer
Priestley Jim, (LCC), Assistant County Surveyor, (SU), Superintending Engineer (Roads)

Priestley John, (LCC), Resident Engineer
Pritchard Brian, (SWK), Team Leader (Bridges)
Probert Cecil, (LCC), Team Leader (Bridges)
Ratledge David, (GMC), Team Leader (Bridges)
Raistrick Brian, (ChCC), Team Leader (Traffic)
Redmill Trevor, (LGM), Team Leader (Structures)
Reece Trevor, (LCC), Resident Engineer
Rhodes Wayne, (LGM), Deputy Resident Engineer
Richmond Les, (LCC), Team Leader (Drainage)
Rigby Bert, (ChCC), Team Leader (Roads)
Riley Laurie, (ChCC), Lighting Engineer
Rimmer Brian, (BR), Works & Bridge Engineer
Roberts Eric, (CuCC), Principal Assistant Engineer
Roberts Hubert, (BR), Divisional Civil Engineer
Roberts Paul, (LGM), Group Leader (Quantity Surveyor)
Robertson Alex, (WH), Associate Partner
Robinson Brian, (ChCC), Resident Engineer
Robinson Ken, (BR), Bridge Engineer
Rogers Ian, (PC), Team Leader (Land)
Roscoe Bob, (LCC/BR), Resident Engineer
Rose Gordon, (ChCC), Team Leader (Roads)
Rothway David, (LCC), Assistant Resident Engineer
Salter Barry, (LCC), Team Leader (Roads)
Sanders Tony, (LGM), Group Leader (Quantity Surveyor)
Sanderson Richard, (LCC), Assistant Resident Engineer
Sargent Chris, (LGM), Resident Engineer
Satterthwaite Ted, (LCC), Team Leader (Bridges)
Saxon Norman, (LCC), Resident Engineer
Schofield Peter, (LCC), County Surveyor & Bridgemaster 1920-45
Schofield Richard, (LGM), Design Manager (Telematics)
Seel John, (LGM), Project Manager
Selfe Mike, (ChCC), Resident Engineer
Serpell Sir David, (DTp), Permanent Secretary 1968-72
Shackleton Julian, (RPT), Landscape Architect
Shackleton Keith, (LCC), Team Leader (Roads)
Sharman Andrew, (WH), Project Partner
Shepherd Ian, (LCC), Resident Engineer
Simm Peter, (ChCC), Resident Engineer
Simmonds Alan, (LCC), Team Leader (Roads)
Simpson Peter, (HH), Director
Sims 'Joe' OBE, (PF), Chief Executive
Sinclair Bob, (WH), Chief Engineer
Sinclair Hartley, (LCC), Superintending Engineer (Roads)
Skellern Peter, (LGM), Team Leader (Transportation)
Smales Alf, (LCC), Resident Engineer, (LCC), Assistant County Surveyor (Bridges)
Smedley Martin, (LGM), Geotechnics Team Leader
Smith Dave, (LCC), Soils & Materials Engineer
Smith Jack CB, (DTp), Chief Highway Engineer
Smith Jim, (LCC), Assistant County Surveyor (Bridges)
Smith Mike, (RPT), Resident Engineer
Smith Neville, (ChCC), Team Leader (Roads), (PC), Associate Director
Smith Peter, (WAP), Resident Engineer
Speak Jack, (LCC), Supervisory Clerk of Works
Spencer Jack, (LCC), Team Leader (Roads)
Spiller Mike, (LGM), Associate (Structures)
Spindel Julian MBE, (BR), Bridge Design Engineer
Staines Malcolm, (LCC), Team Leader (Drainage)
Stark Ken, (ChCC), Team Leader (Roads)
Starkie Ken, (ChCC), Team Leader (Roads)
Stone Colin, (ChCC), Team Leader (Bridges)
Sutcliffe Bob, (LCC), Deputy Resident Engineer
Sutcliffe Mike, (LCC/ChCC), Soils & Materials Engineer
Sutton John, (SWK), Associate Partner
Taberner Ron, (LCC), Team Leader (Roads)

Taffs Frank, (ChCC), Soils & Materials Engineer
Tait Adrian, (HH), Resident Engineer
Tart Geoff, (ChCC), Resident Engineer
Tatlow Peter, (LGM), Team Leader (Structures)
Tattersall David, (LCC), County Planning Officer
Taylor 'Chunky', (ChCC), Team Leader (Roads)
Taylor David, (RPT), Bridge Engineer
Taylor Ron, (WAP), Resident Engineer
Thomas 'Tommy', (LCC), Resident Engineer
Thomason Dave, (PC), Team Leader (Roads)
Thornton Malcolm, (ChCC), Team Leader (Roads)
Threlfall Bill, (LCC), Team Leader (Roads)
Tickner Brian, (LGM), Divisional Director
Tims Alan, (BR), Resident Engineer
Tims Albert, (BR), District Engineer
Tinsley Barry, (ChCC), Resident Engineer
Tobin Kevin, (LCC), Team Leader (Bridges)
Tonge Bob, (H&Co), Resident Engineer
Tooley Bill, (LCC), Deputy Resident Engineer
Townson Geoff, (LCC), Team Leader (Bridges)
Tucker Colin, (BR), Works Engineer
Turnbull Jeff CBE, (MHA), Director
Turton Frank, (BR), Bridge Engineer
Waddelove Gerard, (LCC), Team Leader (Bridges)
Wakfield Ernie, (CuCC), Senior Resident Engineer
Walker Philip, (HH), Partner (Roadworks)
Wallace John, (LCC), Team Leader (Bridges)
Wallwork John, (LCC), Team Leader (Bridges)
Walton George, (LCC), Supervisory Clerk of Works
Waterhouse Eric, (LCC), Assistant County Surveyor (Traffic)
Watson Martin, (ChCC), Team Leader (Roads)
Welch Martin, (BR), Bridge Engineer
Wellard 'Sam', (LCC), Assistant County Surveyor (Bridges)
West John, (LGM), Team Leader (Lighting)
Wharmby Enoch, (NWRCU), Superintending Engineer (Construction)
Wheeler Martin, (ChCC), Team Leader (Roads)
Whiteley John, (LCC), Resident Engineer, (LCC), Deputy County Surveyor
Whitney Claude, (CuCC), Assistant County Surveyor (Forward Planning)
Whittaker Eric, (LCC), Resident Engineer, (SU), Superintending Engineer
Whitworth Andrew, (GM), Resident Engineer
Whitworth Nicholas, (GM), Senior Assistant Resident Engineer
Wight Walter, (LCC), Deputy Resident Engineer
Wigmore Ken, (SWK), Chief Resident Engineer
Wilkinson Dave, (LCC), Resident Engineer
Wilkinson Giles, (HH), Associate (Earth Sciences)
Wilkinson Jim, (LCC), Team Leader (Drainage)
Wilkinson Leslie, (LCC), Team Leader (Roads)
Williams David, (ChCC), Team Leader (Roads)
Williams Don, (ChCC), Team Leader (Roads)
Williams Gareth, (LGM), Deputy Resident Engineer
Williams Michael, (H&Co), Partner
Williams Tony, (SWK), Senior Engineer (Design)
Wilson Tom, (CuCC), Deputy County Surveyor, (NWRCU), Director
Withington Andrew, (LGM), Project Manager
Wolstencroft Steve, (RPT), Communications Engineer
Woodhead Geoffrey, (BR), Bridge Engineer
Yeadon Harry, (LCC), Resident Engineer, (NWRCU), Superintending Engineer (Construction), (LCC), County Surveyor & Bridgemaster 1974-85
Young Cliff MBE, (LCC), Resident Engineer, (LCC), Assistant County Surveyor (Projects)

2. Staff of the Principal Main Contractors

Note:
 (i) The firms of contractors are identified by the key letters after their names in Appendix 2 e.g. (AMEC/McA) indicates 'AMEC/A McAlpine Joint Venture'.
 (ii) Due to the high level of mobility within the industry, no attempt has been made to identify the specific roles undertaken by the individuals named.

Abbott, Ivan	McA	Cooper, Alan	M	Greenwood, ?	P
Allwood, Peter	L	Cottam, Kevin	M/K	Grierson, Mick	M/K
Anderson, Peter	BB	Couchman, Maurice	M	Griffiths, Brian	T
Ashdown, Phil	McA	Coward, Harold	L	Grover, Fred	P
Ashley, Neil	C	Cox, John	T	Grundon, Graham	M/K
Ashman, Derek	LF	Creaby, Mick	McA	Haddock, Keith	Dow
Ashton, Harold	McA	Creane, Vince	T	Haider, G	HH&C
Atkinson, Tony	Bu	Crossley, Brian	McA	Haller, Richard	M/K
Austen, Fred	T	Crow, George	T	Hammond, Fred	T
Austin, Peter	R&M	Crozier, Andrew	P	Harper, Frank	McA
Bailey, John	LF	Currall, Stan	LF	Harrington, Michael	McA
Barcroft, Arnold	Dew	Cuttle, Mike	Doug.	Harrington, Tommy	McA
Barratt, Sam	McA	Davies, John	CS	Hatter, Fred	Dow
Bates, Graham	MR	Davies, Tony	McA	Hawkins, David	Dow
Bell, Peter	McA	Dawson, Tony	Dow	Hewitt, Arthur	LF
Bell, Peter	P	Dewis, Bill	L	Higgins, Bill	McA
Bennett, Mike	McA	Diamond, Des	McA	Higgins, Jack	Dow
Beswick, Graham	Bu	Dickens, Phil	R&M	Hogan, Bob	McA
Boggis, Harry	McA	Dobson, Geordie	M	Holland, Stan	McA
Bowden, Ray	BB	Donegan, Pat	L	Horne, David	P
Box, Gerry	L	Doughty, Nick	Dow	Horsley, Arthur	Dew
Box, Gerry	L	Doughty, Stuart	L	Ireland, Eric	T
Boyd, John	T	Driver, John	McA	Isley, Ian	T
Boyle, Campbell	T	Eades, Norman	M	Jackson, Chris	LF
Bradley, Mick	M	Eades, Norman	M	Jackson, Maurice	P
Braithwaite, Peter	L	Ecclestone, B	HH&C	Jagger, Steve	BB
Brant, Ray	T	Eckersall, Malcolm	LF	James, Delwyn	MR
Breakell, Roy	Cem	Edge, Oswald	McA	Jefferies, Peter	Cem
Breedon, Harry	RMcG	Edwards, Gareth	McA	Jellicoe, John	McA
Brennan, Kevin	Dow	Edwards, Tony	BB	Joel, Chris	McA
Broome, Martin	M/K	Egerton, Bill	McA	Johns, A	RMcG
Brown, Wilson	McA	Elbourne, Douglas	L	Johnson, Carl	LF
Buchanan, Neil	BB	Evans, Richard	McA	Johnstone, Don	LF
Buckley, Bob	McA	Everingham, Bob	McA	Jones, Bert	McA
Buckley, Paddy	McA	Farbon, Dave	McA	Jones, Bob	AMEC/McA
Bullas, Mike	L	Fay, Brian	RMcG/R&M	Kelly, K	PB
Burbidge, John	BB	Ford, George	R&M	King, Cliff	CBE
Butterworth ?	P	Forster, Brian	McA	King, Eddie	Cem
Byers, Arthur	McA	Francis, Bill (Sir)	T	Kirrane, Tom	T
Calam, John	L	Franks, Bob	BB	Kolon, Philip	T
Calvert, Barrat	T	Fraser, John	T	Koslowski, John	McA
Carsley, Bill	M	Fraser, Mac	McA	Lamerton, Alan	LF
Cartwright, Gordon	M	Gallagher, Kevin	AMEC/McA	Lavin, Jim	T
Casebourne, Mike	Cem	Garner, Ted	LF	Leach, Dave	M/K
Caton, Tony	LF	Genders, Harold	LF	Lee, Bill	T
Caufield, Joe	Dew	Georgel, Brian	T	Lee, Ellis	Dew
Caulfield, Dave	L	Gettins, Clive	McA	Lee, John	T
Chapman, Fred	T	Gibson, Keith	McA	Lees, George	T
Charles-Jones, Selwyn	L	Girling, Phil	AMEC/McA	Leigh, Ivan	AMEC/McA
Charters, Les	McA	Golding, Clive	AMEC/McA	Lewis, Alan	P
Church, Bruce	T	Gordon, Bill	T	Lewis, Peter	McA
Clarke, Jim	HH&C	Gorman, Joe	McA	Lillis, Bernard	R&M
Clements, Rex	T	Grant, Ian	CS	Lindsay-Smith, J	R&M
Cockshaw, Alan(Sir)	LF	Gray, Richard	M/K	Lock, Brian	L
Collinson, M	HH&C	Green, Brian	M	Loebinger, Peter	LF

Lord, Jim	McA	Pownall, George	McA	Smith, Bruce	M
Lord, Keith	M/K	Prentice, Doug	BB	Smith, David	CS
Lowe, David	LF	Price, T	PB	Smith, Jeff	BC
MacDonald, W	P	Pritchett, Fred	McA	Smith, Jim	CS
MacGowan, Alan	McA	Quayle, Bill	McA	Smith, Mike	McA
Mason, Aidan	McA	Quinn, Danny	McA	Smythe, Peter	LF
Matthews, L	HH&C	Radcliff, Bob	McA	Spence, Mike	L
McCarry, Mick	T	Redstone, Bill	T	Stanley, Brian	McA
McClennan, Ian	L	Reece, Don	McA	Staples, Brian	T
McCormick, Derrick	AMEC/McA	Reed, Colin	R&M	Staunton, John	McA
McEvoy, Jimmy	BB	Reeves, Oswald	Dew	Stephens, Peter	WCF
McKenna, Martin	McA	Reynolds, John	RMcG	Stevens, Howard	McA
McLoughlin, Stuart	CS	Rhodes, Jack	Dew	Stewart, Jimmy	BB
McMillan, Tom	T	Richards, Dick	MR	Stone, Mike	T
McNeil, M	T	Richardson, Dick	WCF	Sutherland, Maurice	McA
Meanly, Peter	C	Riley, Brian	Dow	Sweeny, John	Dow
Mee, Mick	McA	Roach, Frank	McA	Talbot, Frank	PB
Mills, Eddie	McA	Roach, Neil	WCF	Tarr, Bob	BB
Mitchell, Andy	McA	Roberts, Arthur	R&M	Thomas, Eric	McA
Moffatt, John	T	Robinson, Barry	McA	Thomson, John	Dow
Morley, Peter	CS	Robinson, Cliff	T	Threadkell, David	AMEC/McA
Murphy, Terry	BB	Rose, Andy	BB	Toolan, Jim	McA
Murray, Pat	RDL	Rose, Cliff	L	Townson, Ken	McA&CS
Nivison, Bob	M	Rouse, A N.	T	Trimble, Bob	T
Nuttall, John	T	Rowland, Steve	McA	Tweddle, Alan	M
Oag, Bob	Cem	Rushton, Stuart	T	Uglow, Dick	T
O'Brien, Malcolm	T	Russell, Nigel	BB	Varty, Alan	R&M
O'Connor, Charles	RMcG	Sawyer, A	P	Wainwright, John	T
O'Keefe, Dermot	P	Schofield, Ian	P	Williams, Chris	LF
Openshaw, Bill	R&M	Scott, Jimmy	BB	Walmsley, Bill	LF
Ormerod, Andy	BB	Scurr, John	McA	Walsh, Jack	T
O'Sullivan, Mike	C	Scurr, Tony	McA	Ward, G	PB
Padmore, Mike	C	Seaton, Bill	P	Whetman, George	L
Palmer, Rod	McA	Seston, Mike	L	Whitlock, Max	L
Parkinson, Fred	BC	Shanklin, John	McA	Wilde, Deryck	Dew
Parrish, Bob	LF	Sharpe, Steve	BB	Wilson, Trevor	McA
Peterson, Tom	PB	Shaw, Chris	MR	Winter, John	Dow
Philips, Norman	McA	Shaw, John	Doug.	Woods, Jack	Dew
Pickering, Stan	LF	Shemilt, John	PB	Wrennals, Billy	AMEC/McA
Piggott, Alan	CS	Shiel, Willie	T	Wright, Alex	RDL
Polding, Jim	LF	Shucksmith, Malcolm	LF	Wright, Geoff	McA
Popplewell, David	BB	Shuttleworth, Richard	AMEC/McA		
Porter, John	LF	Simpson, Graham	AMEC/McA		

Bibliography

Drake/Yeadon/ Evans, *Motorways*, Faber and Faber, 1969

Marshall, J.D. (ed.), *The History of Lancashire County Council 1889-1974*, Martin Robertson & Co. Ltd, 1977

Gray, Tony, *The Road to Success: Alfred McAlpine 1935-1985*, The Rainbow Publishing Group Ltd, 1987

Best, Keith, *Best Endeavours*, Keith Best, 1992

Crosby, Alan (ed.), *Leading the Way: A History of Lancashire's Roads*, Lancashire County Books, 1998

Index